Y0-BZY-120

THE SOCIAL CONSTRUCTION OF NATURE

THEORY, CULTURE & SOCIETY

Theory, Culture & Society caters for the resurgence of interest in culture within contemporary social science and the humanities. Building on the heritage of classical social theory, the book series examines ways in which this tradition has been reshaped by a new generation of theorists. It will also publish theoretically informed analyses of everyday life, popular culture, and new intellectual movements.

EDITOR: Mike Featherstone, *Nottingham Trent University*

SERIES EDITORIAL BOARD
Roy Boyne, *University of Teesside*
Mike Hepworth, *University of Aberdeen*
Scott Lash, *Lancaster University*
Roland Robertson, *University of Pittsburgh*
Bryan S. Turner, *Deakin University*

THE TCS CENTRE
The Theory, Culture & Society book series, the journals *Theory, Culture & Society* and *Body & Society*, and related conference, seminar and postgraduate programmes operate from the TCS Centre at Nottingham Trent University. For further details of the TCS Centre's activities please contact:

Centre Administrator
The TCS Centre, Room 175
Faculty of Humanities
Nottingham Trent University
Clifton Lane, Nottingham, NG11 8NS, UK e-mail: tcs@ntu.ac.uk

Recent volumes include:

Pierre Bourdieu and Cultural Theory
Critical Investigations
Bridget Fowler

Deleuze and Guattari
An Introduction to the Politics of Desire
Philip Goodchild

The Body and Society
Explorations in Social Theory
Second edition
Bryan S. Turner

Spatial Formations
Nigel Thrift

Cyberspace/Cyberbodies/Cyberpunk
Cultures of Technological Embodiment
edited by Mike Featherstone and Roger Burrows

For Weber
Essays on the Sociology of Fate
Bryan S. Turner

THE SOCIAL CONSTRUCTION
OF NATURE

A Sociology of Ecological Enlightenment

KLAUS EDER

Introduction and Parts I and II translated by Mark Ritter

SAGE Publications
London · Thousand Oaks · New Delhi

This edition revised and enlarged from a work originally
published as *Die Vergesellschaftung der Natur: Studien zur
sozialen Evolution der praktischen Vernunft* © Suhrkamp
Verlag, Frankfurt am Main, 1988

This translation © Sage Publications, 1996

Published in association with *Theory, Culture & Society*,
Nottingham Trent University

All rights reserved. No part of this publication may be
reproduced, stored in a retrieval system, transmitted or
utilized in any form or by any means, electronic, mechanical,
photocopying, recording or otherwise, without permission in
writing from the Publishers.

SAGE Publications Ltd
6 Bonhill Street
London EC2A 4PU

SAGE Publications Inc
2455 Teller Road
Thousand Oaks, California 91320

SAGE Publications India Pvt Ltd
32, M-Block Market
Greater Kailash - I
New Delhi 110 048

British Library Cataloguing in Publication data

A catalogue record for this book is
available from the British Library.

ISBN 0 8039 7848 0
ISBN 0 8039 7849 9 (pbk)

Library of Congress catalog card number 96-069547

Typeset by Type Study, Scarborough, North Yorkshire
Printed in Great Britain by The Cromwell Press Ltd,
Broughton Gifford, Melksham, Wiltshire

CONTENTS

PREFACE

Ever since the ecological crisis made it impossible to ignore the self-destructive relationship of advanced industrial societies to nature, we have been counting on the influence of *ecological reason*. There can scarcely be any dispute that it is reasonable to reduce the pollution of nature, but in the pages that follow doubts will be raised about the presumption that this ecological reason can actually correct the prevailing irrationality in dealing with nature. Ecological morality, which controls practical interaction with nature, remains oddly unimpressed by ecological reason. Those who preach ecological reason are amazed that it does not fall upon fertile ground. As a rule, they ascribe this to tangible economic interests. However, that does not go far enough, for it is not only the material interests of certain industries, but also the ideal interests of the populace – the often-invoked automobile club slogan 'free roads for free people', for instance – which resist this rationality. There is obviously a wide gap between ecological reason and ecological morality. We know what we should do, but we do not do it. Why does this happen?

Ecological reason seems to be only a subordinate aspect of our interaction with nature. When we speak of ecological reason we mean that the exploitation of nature has gone too far and that the pollution of nature must be limited. If we were to follow only this rationality, that would indeed make our exploitative interaction with nature more 'rational', but it would remain an exploitative way of interacting with nature. The exploitation discourse characteristic of industrialism, which has determined our relationship to nature until now, can be succeeded without interruption by the pollution discourse of environmentalism, which judges nature according to what it can endure. A specific mode of experiencing nature is characteristic of both discourses: nature is perceived and experienced as an object of human needs. Thus the kind of ecological reason that results from the pollution discourse need not, by any means lead, to an 'alternative' way of dealing with nature. Instead, it continues to reproduce our long-standing and culturally deep-rooted attitudes and modes of action in interaction with nature. Ecological reason does not seem able to break open the deep-rooted cultural prerequisites of our self-destructive relationship with nature.

Here we have identified the intention of this book: to clarify the causes for the impotence of ecological reason and to identify the conditions that have thus far obstructed environmental learning processes. It will be shown that modernity's characteristic pride in dominating nature has caused us to forget that we are living in a culture that more or less unconsciously 'forces' us into a self-destructive relationship with nature. Despite all our communication on ecological matters, we have remained culturally naïve 'Philistines' in our interaction with nature. This implies that we can only understand the impotence of ecological reason when we focus on the cultural habits that determine our relationship with nature. If we wish to make possible learning processes that can overcome this self-destructive relationship to nature, we must again become aware of the symbolic foundations of that relationship.

The analyses and interpretations that follow have the goal of correcting this deficit in cultural knowledge. The starting point of these reflections is the assumption that the culture which determines our behaviour and praxis in interaction with nature is shaped by the 'spirit of Protestantism'. The rationality of this Protestant spirit also determines ecological reason. What counts in this spirit is the use value of nature. Symbolic meanings beyond the use value of nature are disenchanted by the spirit. The iconoclasm of the Protestant spirit does not spare the images of nature we make for ourselves. Knowledge of the symbolic meanings of nature is relegated to poetry. An image of nature that does not reduce it to a mere means of satisfying material needs is preserved only in an aestheticizing counterculture. The image of nature that is preserved in the counterculture can become the target for projections of wishes, hopes and fears. Current ecological communication, however, continues to count on 'Protestant nature'. In the process it effaces the symbolic prerequisites of our relationship with nature. This reflection is virtually ruled out in the pollution discourse. In such a discourse, nature remains an 'object', an object which can be affected by acid rain, an object which can be karstified, an object whose genetic diversity is being destroyed, or an object whose equilibrium is being disrupted.

The cultural significance of the Protestant spirit for the modern relationship to nature becomes particularly clear when we attempt to understand the symbolic significance nature has had in other cultures and times. There we note, as the following investigations show, that the modern relationship to nature has reduced the symbolic significance of nature to a minimum. Nature has become a symbolic form without a significance of its own. Even garden plots, a refuge for the symbolic significance of nature, are being depreciated to the 'quick and easy'. Plants such as the thuja tree lose their earlier symbolic significance; they are nothing more than a hedge that requires no work, provides visual protection against others and creates the illusion of being evergreen. These remnants of symbolic signifiers of nature express a relationship to nature that strives to efface everything which cannot be measured by the yardstick of utility. Modern society has made great strides in the attempt to erase these broader symbolic meanings from its collective consciousness.

Today this utilitarian relationship to nature not only hampers the necessary changes and the associated learning processes for interacting with nature, but also is spreading to other areas. This utilitarian culture is striving to subordinate the most elementary and simultaneously the most 'social' level of interaction with nature, that is, the culture of food. Of course, it is doubtful whether this subjugation will be successful. The rules of food culture are even more difficult than other cultural practices to trace back to utilitarian considerations. For what may be eaten is determined by a logic that is irrational from the viewpoint of a utilitarian logic. Food has moral and aesthetic significance which extends far beyond its utilitarian function. Although the collective consciousness of these signifiers may continue to be neutralized by the triumph of utilitarian rationality, the mere form reminds us again and again of the signifier. The signified, food, cannot ultimately be separated from that which is to signify it.

This idea is already found in the works of a classic of sociology. Simmel puts it like this:

> The fact that we must eat is such a primitive and low-level fact in the development of our life values, that it is without question something every individual has in common with every other one. This is what makes gathering for a common meal possible, and the overcoming of the mere naturalism of eating develops on socialization mediated in this way. If eating were not such a low-level thing it would not have found the bridge over which it rises to the significance of the sacrificial meal, to the stylization and aestheticization of its ultimate forms. (Simmel 1957: 250)

Eating is obviously an activity whose significance extends far beyond the function of appropriating nature for the reproduction of physical nature. Eating as a form of appropriation of nature has a symbolic as well as a material significance. Even in eating, the appropriation of nature is not determined by the stomach alone, but also by the head. Eating is more than simply a mechanism for satisfying physiological needs; it also represents a cultural form. Analyses from social and cultural anthropology show that a commonly shared symbolic world is produced and reproduced in the medium of eating (Kuper 1977; Goody 1982; Douglas 1984; Fides 1991). Eating is not only a material, but also a symbolic, appropriation of nature. To put it succinctly, eating is an elementary form of the transition from nature to culture. Even our everyday speech indicates that eating and culture have something to do with one another. Expressions such as 'devouring books' or 'eating up novels' show this, as do compound concepts such as 'starved for knowledge' or 'thirsty for knowledge'. In the following text we are often forced to 'chew through' difficult material and 'digest' difficult texts (Erdheim 1982: 239). The analysis of the culture of food is obviously a privileged way to reconstruct culture, which we rehearse and reproduce in our interaction with nature.

Although after such an analysis we know how we reproduce the utilitarian culture of modernity in our daily praxis, it does not change anything about the culture. It does, however, show the limits of a utilitarian rationality in interacting with nature. And it shows that ecological reason, with a utilitarian foundation, does not suffice to produce a rational way of dealing with nature. That forces us to design alternative possibilities of an ecological reason and to experiment with the idea of an 'alternative' rationality in interacting with nature. It is tempting here to correct the Protestant spirit with restorational intentions, to plead for a 'Catholic spirit' in interacting with nature. Such an escape will be systematically avoided in this book. That also defines the theoretical intention of this book: to sketch out the foundations of a social critique of ecological reason by starting from a comparative analysis of the relationship to nature in different societies. Such a critique is the opposite of restoration. It may use elements of tradition, but it does not remain bound to them. This prevents any restorational intent.

The attempt to develop a concept of practical rationality in the reconstruction of the cultural foundations of man's relationship to nature runs like a leitmotif through the following considerations and analyses. Whether the attempt to make explicit the implicit cultural prerequisites of 'ecological communication' leads to a practical rationality beyond utilitarian reason remains an open question as long as we restrict ourselves to ideological critique. It becomes a political question as soon as we situate the discourse on nature in its practical context and transform a philosophical question into a sociological one. This eventually will help us to know more precisely why ecological reason is so difficult to realize in our society.

Acknowledgement

Thanks to Paul Statham for constructive discussions of Part III and for helping to put the text into good English.

INTRODUCTION

In the history of modernity, ecological reason is the youngest variant of practical reason. Just as the Protestant spirit has dominated practical reason to date, it also dominates ecological reason. The Protestant spirit of ecological reason aims at a rational form of adaptation to nature, an ecologically compatible form of dealing with nature. It turns against the unlimited exploitation of nature. It opposes irresponsible interaction with nature and pleads for the preservation of the 'natural environment' for current and future generations. It is concerned with the survival of nature. In short, the prevailing ecological reason is a form of practical reason that reproduces the Protestant spirit.

Since the beginning of modern society, the Protestant spirit of ecological reason has been seeking to reduce practical reason to utilitarian reason. It stands for a utilitarian form of practical rationality. Doubts regarding this form of practical reason have been growing, however, along with the ecological crisis of advanced industrial societies. This 'alternative' meaning of the ecologically rational is supposed to go beyond the utilitarian form of practical reason. In the following, this alternative relationship of society to nature can be paraphrased as the idea of a communicative form of practical rationality. What is at stake in this alternative relationship is the issue of a good or, rather, a better life in and with nature.

This alternative relationship will be explained below as a critique of the prevailing industrial understanding of nature. Such a critique of ecological reason presumes a form – which must still be clarified – of theoretical reason. This theoretical reason no longer seeks to instruct or to say which understanding of nature is correct and which is false. Its only remaining function is a negative one; its function is to enlighten people on the illusions of practical reason. Theoretical reason no longer consists in 'anticipating' the conditions for the possibility of practical reason, but rather in providing enlightenment on the illusions tied to it. Such a form of criticizing ecological reason forces a triple theoretical refraction. It compels us, first of all, to correct the culture-theoretical ignorance in the description of societal relationships to nature. Second, it forces a correction of the evolutionary theoretical perspective on the history of the relationship between society and nature. Third, to the extent the 'ecology of ecological reason' becomes a theme, it requires a concept of rationality which remains to be clarified. The three key concepts of a theoretical reflection on societal relationships to nature – culture, evolution and rationality – will first be briefly explained.

Sociological analysis, which treats the societal relationship to nature as a problem of practical reason, first requires a radicalization of the sociological perspective in terms of cultural theory. The point is to reconstruct the symbolic forms in which nature is represented, beyond the utilitarian relationship to nature which has become the cultural norm. These symbolic forms examine the 'natural' foundations of the social world: the seasonal rhythms or the cycle of life and death. This world cannot be guided by norms, such as the relations between I and Other. One cannot guide it, nor can one intervene in its almost frightening regularity. This uncontrollability forces us to characterize this world as that which is mysterious, unknown and incomprehensible, withdrawn from society and at the same time remaining within it.

Such a cultural theory sensitizes us to the symbolic foundations of communication which are prerequisites for all communication prior to any normative generalization of expectations. One could call these the aspects of a society that are taken for granted, the unanalysed aspects of a lifeworld – that which controls social relations between people even before any social order exists. Such cultural certitudes are also changed by communication; they are disenchanted and enchanted at the same time; they are simultaneously rationalized and mystified. This is the origin of the paradox that communication destroys cultural certitudes and yet relies on such certitudes in order to continue at all. Obviously these cultural certitudes are inexhaustible; there is no reservoir of them that could be consumed or exhausted in the course of history. Instead, this reservoir is replenished over and over again with new cultural certitudes over the course of social development. What has been characterized as the 'reenchantment of the world' (Moscovici 1976) is an indication that even modern culture continually produces such certitudes anew. Culture resembles a Hydra that regenerates more heads regardless of how many are chopped off.

Second, if enlightened by cultural theory, a sociological analysis of the societal relationship to nature changes our perspective on evolutionary theory. The notion that society seeks to survive in nature has dominated evolutionary thought in sociology. The social construction of nature opens up two differing and competing forms of social evolution in the history of human societies: a natural evolution and a cultural evolution. Far-reaching modifications of a theory of evolution are tied to this distinction. Natural evolution changes the form of social interaction with nature. Society uses its knowledge of nature to increase its 'productive forces'. This increases the complexity of society and, above all, the social division of labour. Cultural evolution, on the other hand, changes the rules of responsible action in society. It uses normative rules to promote its 'moral progress'. This leads to an intensification of social conflicts, which forces the differentiation of communicative forms of conflict resolution.

The relationship of natural and cultural evolution in the history of human societies has been decided (albeit with differing justifications) in the classical sociological theories of evolution from Marx to Luhmann in favour of a primacy of natural evolution. These theories describe social evolution as a continuous differentiation of society away from nature. The further this natural evolution advances, the more complex the relations of society to the environment become and the more precarious the equilibrium between nature and society becomes. This notion also sustains the current environmental discourse to a large extent. Such theories become problematic when they assign rankings to the stages of natural evolution designating the relative cultural (moral, aesthetic) perfection of society. Historical experience rather tends to hinder such assignments. Cultural evolution seems more to be a process which – at every stage of natural evolution – comes into effect, is impeded, partially succeeds and is again reversed. Cultural evolution is a process that is attempted again and again and only rarely succeeds.

At every stage of natural evolution, that is, in simple, traditional and modern societies, we find starting points of a cultural evolution, an evolution which is categorized in the self-concept of the respective society as 'perfection'. Modern society, which believed it had the key to this perfection, is compelled to conclude that there is a 'dialectic of enlightenment'. It additionally concludes that its cultural evolution threatens to destroy its own natural prerequisites and thus the conditions for the possibility of further natural evolution. And it concludes that its cultural evolution scarcely provides it with the means to break off this process of self-destruction. The doubts as to the possibility of a social evolution of society in the sense of a higher cultural development become all too understandable. A theory of social evolution must, therefore, incorporate the tension between natural and cultural evolution in the history of human societies as a theoretical problem and clarify the relationship of the two. That also implies breaking with those traditions of sociological theory formation that have equated social development with development of productive forces and/or social differentiation. Those traditions can be understood from the perspective of cultural theory as naturalistic theories of social evolution. The programme of a culturalist theory of social evolution opposes this. It centres its theory formation on the (empirical) question of what type of cultural evolution has taken place in various societies, where and to what degree.

Enlightened by evolutionary theory, sociological analysis of the societal relationship to nature also changes the notion of a practical reason in interaction with nature – this is the third implication of the sociological analysis of societal relationships with nature. The central question of this theory of social evolution is not whether societies fit into a classification scheme of natural evolution (which they do, more or less badly!). The central question is rather whether the appropriation of nature is tied to learning processes in the dimension of practical reason, and what type of reason in action it is tied to. It is not surprising that theoretical reason is increasingly irritated when it seeks to view social evolution from the perspective of rationality.

Such questions do not arise so long as the criterion of rationality is sought in 'pure reason'. From the perspective of 'pure reason', society appears to be a pure by-product of the evolution of the human mind. This evolution is measured on the scale of the cognitive capacity for adaptation to and control of the respective environment. And humankind, since reason is part of its psychic equipment, is superior here to other species. Reason, as Kant says, is a gift of nature that makes humankind the master of nature. Yet the 'human history of nature' shows that there is no theoretical reason beyond all practical reason. Every societal relationship to nature that incorporates theoretical reason on various levels of its evolution is at the same time the expression of practical reason. Theoretical reason merely elevates the ability of humankind to adapt to the environment. It does not constitute a societal relationship with nature.

Practical reason, on the contrary, makes it possible to act responsibly in the world – which has been made cognitively possible by theoretical reason. Thus an answer can be given to the central question for the critique of ecological reason, that is, whether and to what extent the social appropriation of nature is 'rational'. The problem of rationality is not that people's notions of nature must be correct. Rationality does not presume that people no longer hold magical ideas about the world. That would be a question of 'theoretical reason'. The problem of rationality is rather in what way people's praxis can be labelled rational – no matter how magical their notions may be. And that is a question of 'practical reason'. Practical reason is largely independent of the possibilities theoretical reason opens up. It is not a privilege of societies that can claim a higher theoretical reason for themselves. The rationality of a society is – this is the quintessence of these reflections – the result of a social evolution of practical reason.

This threefold theoretical refraction of the concepts of culture, evolution and rationality is the foundation for a theory of the social evolution of practical reason that does not assert unilinearity, but can instead make competing developmental paths visible. It suggests making a distinction according to whether a social evolution of practical reason relies on poiesis (or autopoiesis!) or on practice (or communicative self-creation!).[1] The difference between practice and poiesis, or the empirical proportion in which they are mixed, explains different forms of practical rationality and different paths of social evolution. With this programmatic approach, we are no longer continuing to write a 'universal history' of practical reason, but beginning instead to write a 'multiversal history' of practical reason. The question of the specific practical rationality of ecological reason can be adequately formulated only in the framework of such a multiversal history. The question can be formulated as to how much ecological reason is a continuation of practical reason, or whether it is a starting point for an 'alternative' practical reason.

---

1 This distinction refers to the conceptual choices marking the difference of the way in which Habermas and Luhmann conceive social reality. Cf. Luhmann (1984) and Habermas (1984, 1987).

This programmatic approach also changes the empirical perspective. The empirical enquiry is: where does one find the starting points in social evolution for a cultural evolution that embodies this 'alternative' reason? This question opens a broad field of investigation – for concrete analyses of evolutionary changes, for comparative studies, as well as for case studies. There is no methodological royal road for such analyses; we are left with the usual efforts of comparative analysis. There is no privileged historical time and no privileged geographical space for such analyses. Cultural evolution occurs in simple, traditional and modern societies. There is no society that excludes cultural evolution. There are only differences in the extent to which cultural evolution can be obstructed. And, contrary to the rationality claimed for it, modern culture seems more to belong to those societies in which the extent of self-obstruction of cultural evolution has become largest.

The following text is divided into three parts. Part I lays down the foundations in cultural theory for a critique of ecological reason. In the framework of a critique of the open and concealed naturalism of sociological theory formation, an attempt is made to describe the societal relationship to nature as a human history of nature, which breaks up the logic of natural evolution. The concept of a human history of nature prohibits making 'theoretical' reason the regulative principle of this human history of nature. Instead, it enquires into practical reason, into responsible dealing with that which has made the evolution of the human spirit possible. The reconstruction of a human history of nature shows that no interaction with nature is possible beyond the bounds of practical reason.

Part II enquires into the logic of cultural practices of the appropriation of nature. This is done with analyses of food taboos, sacrificial rituals and discourses about eating, that is to say, symbolic forms of the consumptive appropriation of nature. Food taboos determine what may be eaten and what is prohibited. This boundary between the edible and inedible does not just have economic functions; beyond that, it contains an implicit morality. Such cultural practices embody the break with nature *par excellence*, for they seek to control and civilize by symbolic forms the violence which is inherently present in all interaction with nature (including that with people, who are always also a part of nature). This civilization is explained in a contrast between two models of interaction with nature: the model of carnivorous culture and that of vegetarian culture. They contain antithetical options of social construction, with specific consequences for the reproduction of society in each case. The fact that the carnivorous model has (so far) been more successful determines the modern relationship to nature and the modern concept of ecological reason. Modernity, for its part, only reproduces the fundamental ambivalence with respect to nature which already characterized traditional societies. It is also the exponent of a new sensitivity to nature; it aestheticizes and moralizes nature. But it is also the exponent of the industrial model for exploiting and suppressing nature; it treats nature as an object without rights. That double relation prohibits the (negatively or positively viewed) notion of a unilinear and unambiguous process of rationalization in modernity. This ambiguity is precisely what distinguishes modern society from most others. Modern society, after all, holds open both the 'carnivorous' and the 'vegetarian' models of social evolution. Which of these paths modernity takes, whether a reenchantment of the world or the instrumental subjugation of nature, depends upon which type of ecological reason prevails in the ecological communication of society.

Part III deals with the consequences of the spirit of environmentalism on politics in modern society. This empirical perspective involves a fundamental switch in methodological perspective. What might appear at first glance as a rupture in the overall structure of the book is due to the 'reflexivity' of the spirit of environmentalism in contemporary modern culture. 'Reflexivity' means that cultural traditions of relating man to nature become the topic of political conflicts and make the intellectual discourse and its theoretical observation of reality a part of the political game. The methodological switch which follows from this reflexivity concerns the relationship of social concerns about nature with their theoretical observation. The perspective of a 'critique of ideology' which has guided the reconstruction of a social theory of nature in Part I is extended to a systematic discourse analysis of environmentalism. The social theory of nature is transformed into a discourse theory of nature which requires a methodology for analysis from within discourse. On such reflexive methodological ground the contemporary ecological discourse is discussed in terms of its logical structure and its political dynamics. The corresponding change in the institutional politics of nature is the subject of the last chapter, Chapter 7. It analyses the insertion of the discourse on nature, the ecological discourse, into a new institutional order, making the politics of nature the key for a new politics in advanced modern societies.

The spirit of environmentalism turns political. This is what justifies speaking of a new modernity, laying the ground for a politics of nature as a new politics. The transformation of environmentalism into ecological politics is the central mechanism by which modern society learns to overcome the limits of the cultural model of early modernity and to develop more adequate cultural grounds for a democratic polity beyond the confines of the modern nation state. The spirit of environmentalism thus has an unintended consequence: to reintroduce civil society into the modern state and foster a new stage in the development of modern societies.

PART I

A SOCIAL THEORY OF NATURE

1

THE THEORETICAL CONSTRUCTION OF NATURE: A CRITIQUE OF NATURALISTIC THEORIES OF EVOLUTION

Nature and society

The relationship between nature and society can be conceived of theoretically in two mutually exclusive ways: as a natural constitution of society or as a social construction of nature. These alternatives divide the theoretical discourse on the relationship between nature and society into two camps: a *naturalist* and a *culturalist* camp. The following reflections attempt to criticize the naturalistic interpretation of the relationship between nature and society and to find starting points for a culturalistic interpretation of this relationship.

In naturalistic theories of society, the relationship between nature and society is interpreted as one of domination. Such a domination relationship can be organized in various ways: one can give theoretical primacy to the technical side or to the organizational side of the construction of nature. This difference is represented by Marx and Durkheim.[1] Marx makes the social

---

1 These two social theorists cannot, of course, be nailed down to these positions. The difference between the elder and the younger Marx, as well as the difference between the elder and the younger Durkheim, make these classic theorists ambiguous. This very ambivalence of their theoretical approaches, however, continues to make them interesting. One can learn from them the options which confront any theory of society. These options can be systematized as follows:

development of productive forces central. Durkheim starts from the increasing social division of labour. Both theories share a naturalistic understanding of society. They measure the reproduction of society against a standard which is characteristic of the evolution of nature: the standard of adaptability, the standard of the control over the resources which make survival in nature possible. The social construction of nature is reduced to the social appropriation of nature, its evolution accelerated by cognitive learning processes. The development of productive forces, technical progress and the increasing division of labour are thus the expression of an evolution of society determined by the social construction of nature. The history of the social construction of nature appears to be a continuation of the history of nature.

The social construction of nature is necessarily an element of the social evolution of society. The classical theories of the social construction of nature have reversed this constitutional relationship. The older Marx makes the changing of the relations of production a by-product of the development of productive forces. The younger Durkheim explains the transformation of the normative order of society on the basis of an increasing division of labour. Yet the history of the social construction of nature is always the history of a cognitive, moral and aesthetic interaction with nature. The transition from nature to culture is not exhausted in a history of the subjugation of nature. The social construction of nature is always part of a human history of nature, which cannot be reduced to a mere history of domination.[2] The unique aspect of the human history of nature, being both part of and the result of a culture, eludes this theoretical perspective.

Against the naturalistic reductionism of the macro-sociological theories (as determined by the elder Marx and the younger Durkheim),[3] we shall

	Poietic reason	Practical reason
Nature	x	
Society	x	x

The fields marked 'X' are the objects of the prevailing social theories. Nature is assigned to the field of poietic reason and society to the field of poietic and practical reason. The process of the reproduction and evolution of the social relationship between nature and society as determined by practical reason remains excluded. The reflections sketched out below on a theory of the 'social evolution of nature' attempt to fill this gap.

2 The conceptualism has been adopted from Moscovici (1968). The theoretical starting point for the central position of the human history of nature is of course historical materialism, which undergoes an interesting reformulation in Moscovici's work. For a continuation of the critique of the Marxian concept of nature, see Moscovici (1979: 117ff.).

3 This might also explain why sociological theory formation still resorts to biological concepts to explain its systematic foundations. The talk of system formation, autopoiesis, complexity and differentiation originates from a view of the world which is itself founded in the difference between nature and society. Seen by itself that is an interesting view. It simply does not lead to a sociological theory and a theory of social evolution.

attempt below to reconstruct the specific cultural form of the social construction of nature. This programme is to be developed in two steps. In a first step, the thesis of a naturalism in social theory is explained using the examples of both the Marxist and the functionalist theoretical traditions. These theories describe the appropriation of nature as an adaptation to nature. The theoretical concept of a 'human history of nature', following Moscovici,[4] will be opposed to them (see the following section). In a second step, we attempt to develop the foundations of a theory of the human history of nature further. The naturalistic analysis of the relationship between nature and society is opposed by a culturalistic interpretation of this relationship, viewing nature as something that is constituted symbolically rather than objectively given. The consequences of this culturalistic conceptualization of nature are drawn in the final three sections of this chapter.

Three assumptions are tied to this theory of a human history of nature. A first is the assumption of a cognitive construction of nature. The forms of cognitive interaction with nature constitute in each case specific societal relationships to nature (pp. 21–24). A second is the assumption of a normative construction of nature. Nature is the medium of social exchange and distribution processes and does not go untouched by them (pp. 24–28). The third is the assumption of a symbolic construction of nature. This states that these differing relationships to nature are attempts to use socially produced nature as a semiotic system to symbolize unknown and uncomprehended things and thereby make them communicable (pp. 28–32).[5] Tied to these assumptions is a reformulation of the concept of nature in terms of cultural theory. The transition from nature to culture, the social construction of nature, culminates in the symbolic appropriation of nature.[6] With

---

4 The starting point in Moscovici (1968) makes possible a more suitable conceptualization of the relationship between nature and culture than is possible with older and more recent sociological theoretical approaches.

5 There is as yet no satisfying sociological theory of culture. See Malinowski (1994 [1944]) as a classical start towards one. For discussions of previous sociological approaches see Schneider & Bonjean (1980), Baumhauer (1982) and Drechsel (1984). For more recent discussions see the opposing positions of Wuthnow (1987) and Alexander (1989b), as well as the mediating position of Swidler (1986) and Eder (1992c). Boon has traced the history of the concept of culture. He also offers a good definition of culture: 'Culture pertains to operations which render complex human phenomena communicable' (Boon 1973: 7). For the history of theories of culture in a narrower sense, that is, related to systems of religious symbols, cf. Van Baal (1971).

6 Engels's notion of a 'dialectics of nature' (Engels 1951) is internally contradictory. On one hand, he proceeds from the notion of an eternal cycle of matter, while the decisive forces of development are labour and capital. On the other hand, the idea of a human history of the material world, that is, the development of nature, is formulated at the same time. This contradiction is ultimately resolved in favour of the notion of a self-sustaining natural environment. Environmental crises are then just minor disruptions in this process. On this point, see the classical formulations of Wittfogel (1932). A more recent version is found in Ribeiro (1971).

this theory of a human history of nature it becomes possible to determine the role of society in the constitution of nature more appropriately than do those theories which interpret the relationship of nature to society as a mere relationship of domination. It becomes possible to replace the 'affirmative' conceptualization of a societal relationship to nature in existing social theories with a 'critical' conceptualization of this relationship.

The critique of sociological naturalism

Marxian naturalism

In its disciplinary history, sociology was able to become established as a science precisely in opposition to the naturalizing view of social circumstances. Marxian theory conceived of itself as a critique of naturalism. The critique of political economy is the criticism of a naturalizing view of social circumstances. Marx, more than anyone else, opposed this naturalism with the notion of social circumstances that are not only made by people, but whose functioning can in principle become the subject of practical human action at any time. If one accuses even this theoretical approach of naturalizing fundamental assumptions, then social theory's critique of naturalism is being applied to itself. This critique points out that even the Marxian critique of naturalistic theories is not immune to naturalism. This Marxian naturalism is based on its concept of nature. What interested Marx in nature were property relations. Indifference to the material was characteristic of his notion of a societal relationship to nature. This might explain why there is so little demand for Marxian theory in current environmental debates.

The theory of historical materialism deserves a special importance in this connection. This theory, after all, continues Marx's programme of criticizing naturalism on the level of a theory of social development. It connects the presumed objective course of history, a naturalistic construction of social development, with normative assumptions as to how society could be restructured by the social agents. The Marxian concept of labour is symptomatic of this in its tying together of mutually exclusive elements: work as both natural and social activity, both poiesis and praxis. This concept of labour virtually provokes the dissociation of poiesis and praxis either in the direction of naturalism or in the direction of normativism. The naturalistic resolution of the theoretical strategy consists in reconstructing and explaining social relationships and the accumulating consciousness of them from the logic of the exchange value they possess. Historical materialism is based primarily on the notion of the historical process as a process in which the production of exchange value becomes increasingly dominant until it has found its purest social form in capitalism, which makes it decipherable as well. This argument squanders the opportunity to explain the appropriation of nature from the 'mystery of the value form of commodities', the use value of commodities. The social labour that has gone into the use value is more than mere instrumental activity. Labour referred to use value is culturally shaped appropriation of nature. Marx draws on this theoretical perspective only for archaic societies, for 'primitive communism', in which use value production is supposed to have dominated – and then the image of the good and unspoiled savage dominates.[7]

The use value perspective does, of course, remain a theoretical possibility in historical materialism. It becomes the condition which makes the critique of the history of exchange value possible. This also reveals that to the extent the use value of a commodity is displaced by its exchange value in history, the history of use value is displaced by the history of exchange value. The labour entering into the exchange value of commodities becomes the key to the origin and reproduction of social relationships. The apotheosis of this displaced history consists in making labour itself an exchange value. From that point on, labour is measured only by its contribution to the reproduction of an objective system whose meaning and use value systematically elude the participants. How to break open this systematic deception process remains a theoretical puzzle. Neither the mere mention of the deception nor the reference to a better prehistory can substitute for a theory that is capable of reconstructing the history of exchange value from the perspective of the history of use value or reconstructing the dominant relationship to nature from the perspective of an equal relationship.[8]

The normativistic dissolution of the naturalism underlying historical materialism consists in subsuming the concept of labour itself to the verdict of naturalistic objectivism. This can be seen in the fundamental theoretical dispositions in Habermas's attempt at a reconstruction of historical materialism (Habermas 1979). This reconstruction is both an attempt to replace the concept of labour, which is tied to nature, with the concept of interaction, which is tied to morality, and an attempt to conceive of development from the relations of production rather than the productive forces. This critique of the naturalism of historical materialism culminates in no longer interpreting history as the result of the evolution of social forms of productive labour, the outcome of the social construction of nature through labour; instead it is interpreted as a moral evolution, the outcome of social

---

7 References to processes of cultural evolution that do not submit to the verdict of 'primitivity' are found in Sahlins's analysis of the stone age economy (Sahlins 1972). The environmental crisis is stimulating voices pleading for cultural evolution on a lower level of natural evolution (where the question whether this is even possible will be left open here). Cf. Eder (1986b).

8 This latent naturalism has more or less dominated the various types of historical materialism. In Althusser's work it became obvious. By removing the subject from a theory of history on the grounds it was irrelevant, he can assert that social development follows a natural law. A different form – the most common – is naturalizing the relations of production. Relations of production become historical in this version through the movement of the forces of production (Friedman 1974; Legros 1977). The 'materialist theory of culture' (Hund 1978) also moves within this tradition.

self-organization through interaction.[9] Morality takes the place of nature; distribution replaces production.

Yet dismissing the concept of labour only tears apart the connection between use value and exchange value in a different way. The history of exchange value is tied into a history of different logics of distribution. The question of which exchange processes lead to just outcomes is placed in the centre of theoretical efforts. The history of exchange value remains the prevailing history. The normativistic critique of historical materialism indeed attempts to overcome the history of exchange value, but it does not arrive at the history of use value. Neither can it recreate the connection to the history of use value. The moralization of historical materialism corresponds to the naturalization of historical materialism. A theoretically totalized interior corresponds to the theoretically totalized exterior. There remains only the choice of advocating either nature or society. The normativistic dismissal of the concept of labour hence goes hand in hand with a new 'blind spot' in theory formation. It expels nature from theory, and along with it the history of exchange value, which determines not only production and distribution, but also the social construction of that which is produced and distributed.

The concept of use value, largely neglected in historical materialism, serves below as a conceptual point of connection for a critique of historical materialism beyond objectivism and normativism. The key to an anti-naturalistic concept of nature is the history of use value. Use value is based upon a different logic of action than exchange value: neither labour as instrumental appropriation of nature nor interaction as mechanism of the distribution of the products, but instead the transformation of nature into culture in the process of consumptive appropriation. The key to a possible 'alternative' history of the societal relationship to nature is founded in the use value of the products.

This perspective on history is closed off to historical materialism because it defines use values as anthropologically ordained, that is, as a system of natural needs, and Marx is consistent when he says that use value is external to political economy. This notion finds systematic expression (particularly in the *Grundrisse* from 1857 to 1858) in the way Marx determines the relationship between production (the social construction of nature) and consumption (the social construction of the products). Marx implicitly performs a subordination of consumption to production, as Sahlins (1976) in particular emphasizes. Because Marx makes consumption a mere natural act of satisfying natural needs, it is ultimately only production which

---

9 This applies to those theories of moral evolution that claim an autonomous logic of cultural evolution, but have not broken radically enough with the model of natural history. Cf. Habermas (1979) and Eder (1976). In that sense the reflections below are a sharpening of this approach by separating it from contexts of universal and natural history. The associated critique of Habermas of course also implies a revision of my earlier works. Finding the place of moral evolution in social theory is more complicated than prior analyses have led us to suspect.

constitutes the social nature of humanity, its non-nature. However, this non-nature is based on nothing other than the active appropriation of nature: production. Marx does occasionally offer a few phrases that could have pointed in a different direction. He remarks in *Capital* that what distinguishes the worst architect from the best bee is the fact that human beings can make an image of a product before producing. Consumptive appropriation is what determines the ideal image of the product/object. Production itself only supplies the material object for consumption. But Marx ultimately always remains faithful to the perspective of individually determined consumption.[10]

This naturalism is not without consequences for Marx's theory of ideology. This theory is based on the claim that it is the manifestation of reality which makes consciousness false. People do not deceive themselves as to reality; instead, reality deceives the people. The false appearance is the starting point for the imagination of individuals. Marx's theory of ideology ultimately starts from the idea that understanding follows from experience rather than organizes it. An empiricist conception of knowledge dominates here. As an individual the subject is at the mercy of the false world. The false world is not a social construction of the subjects, but rather a natural fact confronting the subjects. This theory compels us to reduce the intrinsic logic of symbolic worlds to the 'subject' as the only 'social' matter of fact. Marxian naturalism thus leads both to an instrumental interpretation of the appropriation of nature and to an empiricist understanding of the concept of knowledge, a concept which foreshortens the experience of nature to individual experience. The imagination of an object is reduced to its mere perception. As long as the ideas of people are nothing more than spontaneous perceptions of a false reality, they are also tied to the logic of this reality, the naturalistic logic of production. The experience of nature is further foreshortened to its cognitive-instrumental aspects.

The normativistic critique of Marxian naturalism, by contrast, solves the problem of a non-naturalistic social theory by removing society from its relationship to nature. Because nature is associated with the realm of labour, but labour is outside of the communicative action that is constitutive for social self-construction, it is possible to analyse society as being beyond and outside of nature. A consequence of this view of things – important

---

10 This Marxian image is cited by Sahlins (1976: 153). Marx put it this way in his manuscript from 1857/1858: 'Production brings forth the objects that meet the needs; distribution hands them out according to social laws; exchange redistributes according to individual needs what had already been distributed; the product finally leaves this social movement in consumption, directly becoming the object and servant of individual need and satisfying it in use'. And discussing the cycle from production to consumption and back: 'Production is determined by general natural laws; distribution by social chance, and it can therefore have a more or less encouraging effect on production; exchange lies between the two as a formal social movement, and the concluding act of consumption, which is conceived of not only as the ultimate goal, but also as the ultimate purpose, actually lies outside of the economy, except insofar as it acts back on the starting point, and introduces the entire process anew.' (Marx 1953a: 10f.)

particularly in political terms – is that the environmental problem, the central theme of public discourse in advanced industrial societies, eludes this theoretical view. The theoretically unfortunate consequence of the normativistic critique is that it simply turns the societal relationship to nature over to theoretical naturalism.

This 'transferred' naturalism also has consequences for normativistic critique. The transfer is connected to an insufficient theory of culture. Normativistic critique does indeed attempt to avoid the empiricism which is allied with naturalism by conceding a logic of its own to the normative dimension. It replaces the theory of ideology with the theory of a moral consciousness that permits one to apply standards of justice to the distribution of wealth in a society. Yet such moral rules constitute only a 'distributive praxis' and miss both 'productive praxis' and 'consumptive praxis'. Production and consumption are reduced to problems of strategic or instrumental action. People produce and consume in order to survive in nature. The social side of the relationship of nature and society is reduced to distribution. Production and consumption, however, are likewise expressions of the social construction of nature. Productive and consumptive action cannot be traced back to strategic or instrumental action, to the 'shopkeeper's spirit' in humanity. Just like any other kind of social action, they are constituted symbolically.

Naturalizing these fundamental forms of social action permits a peculiar division of labour between a 'reconstructed' historical materialism, which – in the form of a sociological analysis – radicalizes the normativistic programme of a self-development of class consciousness, and a 'cultural materialism', which – in the form of an economic analysis – radicalizes the naturalistic programme of historical materialism.[11] The inquiry into the structure and logic of the societal relationship to nature goes unanswered in this division of labour. Neither the naturalism of Marxian productivism nor the moralism of a reconstructed historical materialism suffice to answer this question. It goes unanswered because of the deficiency of both theories in terms of cultural theory. This deficiency compels one to interpret production and consumption as the result of power, compulsion and repression. Yet no power and no compulsion can constitute social production and consumption if the cultural predispositions are not present that guarantee the recognition of power and compulsion.

The critique of historical materialism that can lead us further, therefore, culminates in the thesis that when people behave in real life as producers and consumers they already presume a collectively valid order that produces the conditions for such behaviour. Production and consumption, if socially organized, always depend on a culturally shared world.[12]

---

11 For an attempt with a paradigmatic intention cf. Harris (1979).

12 Beginnings in that direction are found in sociology and social anthropology, for instance in Bourdieu (1980), Goody (1977), Douglas & Isherwood (1980) and Williams (1982). For recent theoretical discussion, see Miller, D. (1987), McCracken (1988) and Cheal (1990).

How can such a culturally shared world be localized in society? This question forces one to break open the productivism of Marxian theory and conceive the idea of a material basis more broadly. Marx did indeed formulate the programme for this. The material basis of a society reproduces itself, so he says, through production, distribution and consumption. All production and distribution is ultimately production and distribution of use values. Without consumption, a socially appropriated object is incomplete. However, Marx did not stick to this programme. The standpoint of production refers to labour, active interaction with the objective world. The standpoint of distribution refers to normative factors in the constitution of a material basis. The aspect of consumption ultimately contains an element that points beyond these normative aspects. Consumption is not a constant of nature; rather, it refers to symbolic elements that deal with notions of the good and the beautiful. Collectively valid symbolic determinations enter into consumption. Nature becomes more than an object of work or distribution; it also becomes a means of symbolizing the good and the beautiful (or their opposite). In consumption, nature is no longer an exchange value; it is above all a use value.

This is the starting point for a theory of cultural evolution which permits us to make a differentiation from a theory of natural evolution. If one wishes to prevent the reconstruction of historical materialism from ending in a productivist naturalism or a voluntarist normativism, then one must go back to the symbolic forms which permit people to make an image for themselves of what their needs are and of the objects corresponding to these needs. In other words, one must attempt to conceive theoretically of the symbolic logic of the consumptive appropriation of socially produced and distributed nature. The social construction of nature only comes to an end in the social construction of its consumptive appropriation. And this is not determined individually but socially. It is the key to the cultural evolution of society.

Theory development in sociology, however, has contributed little to the treatment of this problem left open by Marx. It has exhausted itself in identifying with or distancing itself from Marx. In the end it only reproduces the Marxian problems and drags them along, unsolved, in another form. Functionalism in social science has become the most prominent victim of this uncritical linking up with Marxian naturalism.

Naturalism in systems theory

Functionalism in the social sciences did not solve the Marxian problem but only intensified it. Modern systems theory has become the apotheosis of sociological naturalism.[13] This naturalism is already laid out in the core

---

13 The history of functionalism in the social sciences reaches from the early formula of Malinowski, which was still explicitly naturalistic, all the way to the change in the direction of systems theory, undertaken by Luhmann (1984). Parsons is only a transitional figure in this context. For the debate in social anthropology, see Hill (1977b).

theoretical assumption of classical social science functionalism: in the theory of social differentiation. The theory of social differentiation distinguishes three elementary structure formation processes: segmentary differentiation, stratificatory differentiation and functional differentiation.[14] These mechanisms of differentiation differ in the ability of a social system to protect its own reproduction. This ability itself is determined as power over the (internal or external) environment of society (as higher complexity, for instance). The production of networks of obligation between segmentary units gives institutional form to a mechanical equality. Having power is tied to personal qualities: appearance, strength, wisdom – in short, personal prestige. Stratificatory differentiation reproduces power relationships between groups on the basis of social criteria of affiliation. This system of vertically-ordered social affiliation culminates in a supreme, usually personified authority (god-king, emperor). Power can be concentrated at the apex of the hierarchy and thus be employed in a more focused fashion. Functional differentiation, finally, makes it possible to specify power relationships functionally and to give institutional form to flexible interdependencies between the fully differentiated sources of power.

This theory of social differentiation measures the change in social structure formation by the criterion of the power resources which a social system has available to it (whether in the 'complexity' of the system or in the system's capability for 'autopoietic reproduction'). It thus continues the Marxian programme of an autonomous development of society beyond the control of subjects. Social development appears to be the continuation of natural evolution. Differentiation theory thus leads to a naturalistic evolution theory. In that way it operates parallel to Marxian theory. It treats nature as mere environment, and the relationship between nature and society as a mere difference of complexity.[15]

The cultural dimension surreptitiously becomes a mere resource for differentiation theory. Culture becomes a means to the end of reproducing the social system. In Parsons's version, it even achieves an especially important significance. It becomes the 'determining' resource in the process of increasing social complexity. In Luhmann's version, culture as the self-description of society ultimately becomes a mechanism of the autopoiesis of the social system. But limits to this instrumentalization of culture are set within culture itself. The inherent logic of symbolic structures does not

---

14 On the theory of differentiation see the contributions in Luhmann (1985b). Additionally, the classical contributions by Smelser should be noted. As a summary see Smelser (1985). For a critique see Eder (1992a). The Marxian distinctions can be reformulated with relatively little difficulty in Parsons's AGIL schema (1971). One sees here that the language has changed, but not the way of looking at the problems. In that sense, the fundamental theoretical dispositions made by Marx also apply to Parsons and functionalism in social science.

15 This thesis that differentiation theory is a theory of the natural and not of the cultural evolution of society is indeed implicitly contained in many micro-sociological critiques of functionalism. They have not, however, been able to offer a countermodel except the proposal to become 'more concrete' and investigate 'individual cases'.

produce only a difference between cultural form and differentiation form. It goes further: it is a prerequisite of the possibility of social differentiation.

Simple societies are limited to the reproduction of social differentiation on natural qualities of people. People conceive of the differences between people in the same way as they separate nature. The differences between people are an analogue of the differences in nature. Of course, the complexity of this model by analogy is limited.[16] 'Homo naturalis' is a conceptual model which symbolizes the natural differences between people (age, gender) with the aid of differences in nature. Nature is 'repeated' once again in society. That makes cultural evolution possible on this level of complexity. A more complex model of social differentiation is tied to the idea of a hierarchical order as is constitutive for *traditional societies*. This presumes a novel image of nature. Nature and society alike are seen as part of an order of creation, a hierarchical order of nature. Just as nature is subordinate to society, so are people subordinated among themselves. 'Homo hierarchicus' (Dumont 1967) is a conceptual model that makes it possible to expand differences in natural endowment into differences in the social background. The difference between nature and society has grown larger in the sense that nature and society are no longer merely parallel systems of differences, but rather the social hierarchy is now the extension of the differences in nature 'upwards' and thus in the direction of higher purity.[17] Quite different paths of 'high cultural' evolution are tied to this.

Modern society is characterized by tying social differentiation to the notion of an egalitarian order which permits more complex social structure formations than is possible with the notion of a hierarchy. People are conceived of as being different only with respect to abilities (of which an individual person can have many). This appeal to individual abilities ('achievement') presumes a relationship of society to nature which is characterized by distance in a double sense. Nature is no longer the extension of a social hierarchy downwards, which hierarchizes even the parallelism of differences. Nature is rather an object, a 'mechanical clock', that can be manipulated and moved according to the will of people. Society sets up the standard values according to which the system of nature functions. Society is now connected to nature only through the effects brought about in the system of nature. The differences between people now consist in the abilities of people to impose their will on nature. Neither 'natural' categories such as age and gender nor 'ascriptive' categories such as status background are suited at this level of differentiation away from nature to reproduce the necessary degree of differentiation. It is 'subjective' categories which open up new types of paths for cultural evolution. The state

---

16 The talk of a 'model by analogy' goes back to the theoretical description of simple cultural systems in Godelier (1973, 1991).

17 On the hierarchical model cf. especially the studies by Dumont (1967). This cultural pattern is tied to a specific degree of differentiation of society away from nature. It protects and legitimates a specific form of social differentiation.

of society is produced through the linkage of the individually accountable abilities (however this may be symbolically controlled). This new form of social relationships remains neutral with respect to ascriptive characteristics: age, gender and social status are no longer legitimate social differentiating features. 'Homo aequalis' (Dumont 1977), as the quintessence of the subject doubly estranged from nature, makes possible social differentiation as a 'voluntaristic' linkage of different individual abilities.

A reformulation of the forms of social differentiation in terms of cultural theory reveals the secret logic of the theory of social differentiation: it provides a secondary naturalization of social differences among people. Social differences are explained with the aid of an evolutionary theory which determines these differences as 'input' in an independent process of selection.[18] In more recent functionalism, this naturalism becomes conceptually visible in the increasing borrowings from biological explanatory models. Society, like nature, is viewed as an autopoietic system that maintains itself by the regulation of contingency.[19] The 'culture' of a society is then reduced to the questioning of this process of social differentiation, a theoretical notion that can scarcely deny its proximity to the old Marxian theory of ideology. The naturalism of fundamental theoretical assumptions wreaks its revenge in the treatment of the phenomenon of culture. Culture remains the superstructure over a naturalized society that functions by analogy to the principles of biological systems.[20] The 'cultural ignorance' of functionalism in the social sciences ultimately consists in not seeing the non-instrumental aspects of the social construction of nature and thus losing sight of the constitutive function of culture in the social evolution of society.[21]

Beyond sociological naturalism

The really surprising element is the fact that social science functionalism shares cultural ignorance with historical materialism. Historical materialism

---

18 On the Darwinist borrowings in the theory of evolution cf. Luhmann (1978). Similarly, although coming from different methodological premises, Giesen (1980). Raising the suspicion of naturalism urges itself upon us *nolens volens*.

19 The distinction of segmentary, stratificatory and functional differentiation has by now become part of the classical stock of assumptions in the social sciences, although this is precisely where the critique of unilinear notions of development should best start.

20 Even the reinterpretation of the concept of an 'autopoiesis' of social systems by Luhmann (1984) in the light of communications theory does not solve the problem of grasping the difference between natural and cultural evolution theoretically. The specifically social logic of symbolically mediated communication remains in the dark.

21 The concept of autopoiesis (Luhmann 1984) attempts to decouple the theory of social systems from environmental dictates as much as possible. This makes it permissible not to view nature any longer as environment but only as one aspect of social self-creation. Of course, then nature is reduced to the descriptions society produces of it. The issue of why nature is described this way and not some other way remains open. The descriptions of nature are assessed only as to whether they are functional for the autopoiesis of society or not. Then the question whether the discourse on nature produces too much resonance or not also makes sense (Luhmann 1989).

as well as differentiation theory are correct in one respect: there is a human history of nature which can be reduced to a natural history of society. This is the natural history of society which culminates in European modernity. This society is based on a culture that rewards a productivist interaction with nature.

These theories use categories here that 'fit' this special evolution. These are, above all, the concept of natural selection and the concept of struggle with nature.[22] Engels in particular, fascinated by the objectivizing and demystifying function of biological evolution theory (it was initially a symbol of enlightenment directed against the church, a demystification of religion), built the idea of a natural selection into his theory. The class-struggle metaphor still breathes the spirit of this demystification. The selection-theoretical model derived from it has enjoyed increased attention again in the recent development of sociological theory (Giesen & Lau 1981; Schmid 1982; Burns & Dietz 1992). It is used to be able to provide the basis for an objectifying and 'value-free' distance from society as the object. The struggle metaphor is abstracted into the idea of linking selection rules of the environment to selection rules of the system that belongs to this environment. The social Darwinist figure of argument – with which historical materialism worked, as did the early evolutionists (who should be seen as precursors of functionalism) – has indeed largely disappeared from sociological discourse. Yet the idea of a struggle with nature continues to be the unquestioned foundation of sociological theorization.[23] This consensus reaches from theories of cultural materialism, through Parsons and Weber, all the way to normativist theoretical approaches.

These two categories are themselves key concepts of the productivist project in European modernity. That means they lose explanatory power to the extent they are projected onto other societies and other cultural traditions (such as 'primitive' societies, for instance). The lower the stage of development, the harder the struggle with nature, so goes the common notion. Not until modernity, with the capitalist (or socialist) development of productive forces, was the struggle with nature won. The ignorance of the aforementioned theories in terms of cultural theory does not consist only in the mere use of these concepts, but rather in their failure to situate these concepts historically and culturally. What is lacking is reflection on the partial historical and cultural validity of these theoretical concepts. This lack

---

22 Compared to this naturalistic theoretical programme, a theoretical programme related to the actor is insufficiently complex. It is not good enough to view culture instead as the result of a nature of human beings, that is to say, their range of competence, which allows them to form symbols and shape the world in their own image. This confrontation only reproduces the old dispute between materialism and idealism, between empiricism and apriorism. In that sense this theoretical dispute is fruitless. Mental systems are 'inward' by nature and as such are not part of the environment of the social system. Luhmann (1984, 1985a) has insisted on this with (justified) vigour.

23 That should not tempt us to fall into a bad idealism. There is also some truth to Brecht's saying, 'First comes gluttony; then morality follows.' We do have to 'consume' nature.

of reflection substantiates the reproach of an ignorance of cultural theory, and it justifies that attempt at a correction of these concepts according to cultural theory. The correction of these concepts by cultural sociology pursues the objective of making it possible to criticize the affirmative attitude towards 'technical progress' that is connected to the evolution of the modern relationship to nature. In social science functionalism, the degree of social 'resonance' with technical progress becomes a fetter which must be cast off (Luhmann 1989). Historical materialism has come to take technological progress for granted to such an extent that its only remaining concern was to strip off the social fetters on technological progress. It is no surprise that these theories can say nothing more in the face of ecological problems than that technological progress must not put shackles on itself.[24] The affirmative attitude towards the productivist model of the modern relationship to nature remains; it is only fed back into and corrected by its own effects.

The attempt below will be to apply three corrections from cultural sociology to this naturalistic paradigm.[25] The basis of these corrections is a critique of the metaphor of natural selection and the metaphor of the struggle with nature. This critique makes clear the desideratum of a concept of nature which conceives of nature as socially constituted and culturally defined. To the extent that the critiques are elaborated, it is possible to define the relationship to nature of the social practice connected with these concepts, that is, production, distribution and consumption. These forms of social reproduction can be appropriately analysed only if one eliminates the cultural ignorance of productivism (which reduces production to instrumental action) and of economism (which reduces distribution to strategic action), as well as of consumerism (which views consumption as the mere satisfaction of physiological needs).[26] We will thus not be concerned with exchanging fundamental concepts of social theory. We are concerned instead with reinterpreting them, piece by piece, in terms of cultural theory. Cultural sociology of nature is seen as a way to expunge the latent naturalism from social theory.[27] This 'new deal' in cultural sociology is intended to make it possible to view social evolution as part of a human history of nature and thus to obtain connecting points for a theory of the cultural evolution of

---

24 This formula becomes plausible when one sees that the decisive impulses in the debates on sociological theory come from the sociological concern with culture; the works of Bourdieu (1980, 1984b) are exemplary in this regard.

25 The concept of natural selection is central to a system-theoretical functionalism (Luhmann 1978) as well as to an action-theoretical rationalism (Giesen & Lau 1981; Schmid 1982).

26 The metaphor of the struggle with nature has been used for the defending and the questioning of the relationship between society and nature since the Industrial Revolution, especially for socialistic thought.

27 The critique of the metaphor of the struggle with nature has virtually become the motto of the environmentalist critique of ideology. Cf. Eder (1986b).

society. Only such a theory makes it possible to grasp social evolution in a non-naturalistic manner.

The cognitive construction of nature

The natural division of society

A first correction of the theory of natural evolution from cultural sociology concerns the cognitive definition of nature. This cognitivistic correction first changes the theoretical status of the concept of natural selection. Nature does not separate people and turn them against one another. Rather, people separate themselves according to culturally-determined forms of interaction with nature. That which appears to be natural selection is the social separation of abilities, a natural division of people.[28] Society enables the natural division of people by differentiating abilities and skills. It separates the hunter from the gatherer, the gatherer from the farmer, the farmer from the craftsman and the craftsman from the engineer. In that way, the cognitive differentiation of knowledge becomes an initial mechanism of the cultural construction of a societal relationship to nature.

Moscovici has explained the idea of a natural division in his *Human History of Nature* (1968). This division results from the transformation of knowledge about nature. It is specifically not the division of labour; it is the division (and then the specialization) of activities that determine interaction with nature. The elementary natural division is that between hunting and gathering. This division can scarcely be separated from the elementary division of society, namely the sexual one. The first natural division as a rule follows the differentiation of man and woman – though here, too, there are already exceptions (Moscovici 1972). The invention of agriculture cuts across this clarity. It is the starting point for a natural division which is radically decoupled from the biological division of society: the division between farmer and craftsman. Moscovici calls the result of this natural division the organic state of nature. The organic state of nature is characterized by the invention of a type of interaction with nature which is distinguished from the activity of the farmer by its shaping and forming character: nature is transformed into something different in the hands of the craftsman. The production of metal objects makes a second nature of nature. The farmer, by contrast, takes care that nature can continue to reproduce itself; he acts in such a way that nature remains identical to itself. That is why these two different types of activity, even in traditional societies, were labelled by different concepts.[29]

---

28 The concept of a natural division is of course close to concepts of differentiation theory; it differs, however, in that it already presumes cultural demarcations, that is, a theory of the social production of cultural differences (Moscovici 1968).

29 For the Greeks, the work of the farmer is called *prattein* (so it is 'praxis'), while the work of an artisan is called *poiein* (in the sense of 'making') (Vernant 1971). See also Chapter 2, fn 17.

The craftsman's work is in turn the starting point for an additional natural division. The knowledge acquired in craft work is systematized logically; the observable effects of this work become the object of explanation attempts. A new type of interaction with nature arises, supported first by architects and finally by engineers. They interact with nature by calculating it. The architect plans on the drawing board with the aid of assumptions on statics and material properties. The engineer recombines nature and calculates the energetic effects that result from it for people. By expanding this activity, society enters a new state of nature. Moscovici calls it the mechanical state of nature. In the mechanical state of nature, nature is not only transformed; it is recombined. The steam engine is the symbol of this new relationship with nature. Nature can be formed and transformed by the constructive will of those who employ it.

Where this mechanical state of nature first became social reality, in European industrialization, an additional division of abilities has been set into motion. The increasing domination of knowledge of nature by science becomes the starting point for a further step in the natural division of society. Knowledge of nature becomes dependent on theoretically produced knowledge. Nature is 'synthesized' by theoretical knowledge (Moscovici 1968: 95ff.). Its properties are 'developed'. What Moscovici calls the cybernetic state of nature comes into being. The theoretical scientist (physicist, biologist or chemist), who produces nature according to theoretically designed models, is distinguished from the engineer. The logic of possible natural divisions closes on itself because the last division becomes the object of the cognitive construction of the state of nature. Reflexivity closes the cycle of natural divisions.

This conceptualization of a human history of nature breaks with the theory of the natural evolution of society in one decisive respect: it does not explain the connection of nature and society as a connection in which nature is seen as an objective constraint and society as an attempt to break up this objective constraint and take its place. The Darwinist interpretation of social development does precisely this. The correction by cultural theory consists in emphasizing the constructive aspect in the evolution of the relationship of nature and society and showing that nature is socially produced. Thus, it is not a general theory of the natural evolution of society which is being formulated, but instead a theory of the social evolution of nature. The goal is to show that nature is the result of human praxis (which, in principle, could be different). Thus the possibility of a critique of social states of nature is opened up and a first link is created for the attempt to reconnect the natural evolution of society to a human history of nature.

The material appropriation of nature

The forms of the material appropriation of nature vary with the differing forms of the cognitive construction of nature. The material appropriation of nature is insufficiently understood if it is conceived of only as exploitation of nature – a correlate of the thesis of a cognitive construction of nature. Such a perspective offers itself only if the relationship to nature is understood in an objectivistic way. Then nature is the non-human: that which, in contrast to people, can be legitimately exploited. This perspective is the expression of a culturally-specific interaction with nature. Therefore it cannot be theoretically generalized, and it has become problematic today. The evolutionary process which drove the idea of an exploitation of nature to its culmination, that is, the evolution of modernity, makes us sensitive today to the 'ecological limits' of this exploitation of nature. That makes the special historical form of this relationship between nature and society once again conscious. Modernity represents a culture which has reduced the material appropriation of nature to the exploitation of nature and thus provoked the ecological crisis.

Environmental crises are certainly no monopoly of modern industrial societies.[30] The same applies to the knowledge arising in this experience, which today we would label 'ecological' knowledge. Environmental crises in particular involve a form of interaction with nature which organizes the activity of human beings as an interactive context fed back into nature. The knowledge of the 'pollutability' of nature broadens the exploitation discourse into a pollution discourse, which has made ecological corrective actions possible in the human history of nature over and over again. Such 'ecological communication' (Luhmann 1989) shows that nature is not an object in the way that the phrase 'exploitation of nature' insinuates.

The category of the exploitation of nature is insufficient to grasp theoretically the appropriation of nature, which is produced by the 'natural' division of human abilities and skills. The phrase 'exploitation of nature' describes a special case of the relationship to nature: exploitation of nature means organizing the natural division of people as a power relationship. Rather than the farmer, it is the specific social form of natural division that forces farmers in the modern world into environmentally disastrous 'instrumental action' which is to blame for the environmental crisis. A sociological concept of productive force thus does not reduce production to an instrumental form of conflict with nature of the type connected with the notion of instrumental action.[31] It understands the societal relationship to nature instead as a culturally constituted and reproduced social relationship. This sociologization no longer makes the modern relationship to nature the

---

30 On the significance of environmental factors in the development, crisis and decline of high cultures cf. especially the literature on ancient Mexico, where the environmental differences provide ideal comparative material. See, for instance, Sanders & Price (1962).

31 This implies that the 'mistakes' of historical materialism are not based on its primacy of the forces of production, but rather in a conceptualization of the forces of production that is inadequate in terms of cultural theory. What should be criticized is the non-reflexive concept of nature. Specifically, this critique obliges us to abandon the limitations of a sociology which neutralizes the nature issue but reduces nature to a technical problem (cf. Rammert 1983). This was not changed until the emergence of an environmentally motivated critique of technology (Japp 1987).

measure of other cultural forms of this relationship, but sees it rather as one specific evolution among many other possibilities.

If one can characterize the exploitation metaphor as a historically specific description, then the question can also be raised as to whether the instrumental relationship to nature is not only inadequate to grasp the complexity of the relationships between society and nature, but perhaps might itself be the expression of a pathological form of this relationship. The idea of a cognitive construction of nature is still insufficient to clarify this question. Such an assertion must distinguish normative criteria. This presumes showing that, beyond cognitive definitions of nature, normative definitions of nature also intervene in the human history of nature. The theoretical assumption is this: a normative evolution of nature also takes place in the human history of nature.

The normative construction of nature

The use value of nature

A second starting point for a fruitful correction by cultural theory of the sociological concept of nature is the normative construction of nature. Every state of nature must also be socially reproduced. The human history of nature is not exhausted in the cognitive social construction of nature. It is advanced in the normative social construction of nature. This second correction by cultural theory of a sociological concept of nature demonstrates the limits of a normative reconstruction of historical materialism, as well as those of the normative reinterpretation of systems functionalism.[32] After all, it implies the assumption that the relationship of nature and society cannot be viewed as a morally neutralized area. Rather, with respect to the problem of nature, sociological normativism shares the concept of a morally neutralized economy with theoretical economics. This conception views nature as an object which can be exchanged and appropriated at will. Thus the exchange value of nature becomes the regulative principle of the appropriation of nature. Having been made exploitable by production, nature turns into an exploitable and ultimately exploited nature by way of the market.[33]

---

32 The normativistic critique of historical materialism and of functionalism in the social sciences (Habermas 1979, 1984) dismisses the problem of nature by seeking the mechanism of social evolution only in interaction conflicts and assigning nature to the 'systemic factors'.

33 On the logic of exchange, see the model by Sahlins (1963) and its complement for modern societies in Blau (1977). The fact that this model reaches from kinship to capitalistic markets makes it a fruitful instrument for theoretical analysis. If one wishes to make the model historically specific, then one must specify more precisely what is being exchanged. Exchange logic itself is founded on normative premises, which in turn have non-normative prerequisites. This requires semiotic assumptions that break the usual bounds of analyses in cultural sociology. One must specify what symbolic meaning the thing one is exchanging has. This broadens the sociological analysis from 'functional' analysis to a 'structural' analysis. As early starting points for the debate cf. Bauman (1973), and as an example with potential for further research, Sahlins (1976, 1981).

The conception of a 'natural' economy leads to the reduction of nature to a factor of production, an economic resource, which is constitutive for economic theory. If one interprets interaction with nature only in economic terms, the interaction with nature remains external to it. The economic employment of natural resources becomes a second nature, a social nature. The naturalization of society as market process – analogous to the struggle of all against all – produces the fiction of a natural economy. This critique goes beyond even the normativist correction of historical materialism and of systems functionalism.[34] It leads to the assertion that, to the extent that it is socially appropriated by cognitive abilities, nature also forces a normative definition of itself upon us. Nature acquires a 'political' content (Dreitzel 1976). The social definition of the normative, and thus political, content of nature can thus become an additional link for constructing a theory of cultural evolution.

The phenomenon of a normative construction of nature can be illustrated in the critique of the phrase 'struggle with nature'. This phrase apprehends the normative construction of nature in a culturally specific way. In European industrialism, the struggle metaphor became the central topos for reproducing the modern relationship to nature. It found its most unbroken expression in the socialist tradition. There the struggle with nature was first linked to the expectation of a victory over nature (and to the apparently concrete prospect of such a victory, thanks to technology). But the idea of a struggle with nature is itself a historically specific form of a relationship between nature and society. The fact that nature threatens society is an experience known to all societies. Reacting to this threat with struggle is characteristic of modern society.

In European modernity, the competing interpretation was defeated. The modern relationship to nature tends to follow more the model of interaction than that of struggle. The interpretation of nature as a hostile object has displaced the interpretation of nature as an 'alter ego' of mankind. That increasingly reduced the acceptance of this other interpretation. The defeated interpretation of nature as something with which people not only 'struggle' but with which they also 'interact' has been ridiculed.[35] If one confronts the notion of an interactive relationship to nature with the notion of struggle, the moral implications of the societal relationship to nature become clear. One can see that the notion of a struggle with nature presumes

---

34 That also means that more is involved than simply merging the concept of labour once again with the concept of interaction. See, for instance, Honneth (1982).

35 On the transformation of cultural certainties which announce something like this cf. Lepenies (1977, 1978). Ecology, a result of this transformation, is the opposite of the struggle with nature. Phrases like 'the planet is our partner' signal an interactive relationship with nature. To what extent this is romantic, regressive or the opposite, cannot be discussed here. Cf. my works on contemporary social movements, especially Eder (1986b).

a moral notion that denies the consequences of one's own actions. The phrase 'struggle with nature' is part of an ethic of principles (as opposed to a utilitarian ethic). Nature is seen as an enemy (no matter how that may be conditioned by historical experience with natural disasters) which must be subdued. This principalistic mode of action is no longer capable today of controlling the risks that have accumulated in the wake of modern appropriation of nature. 'Risk society' (Beck 1992) is the result of a modernization that has been unable to complete the break with a relationship to nature based on an ethic of principles.

Two experiences have weakened this idea of a struggle. The first is the experience that the victory over nature goes hand in hand with the destruction of the natural foundations of life. The modern crisis in the relationship of nature and society, the ecological crisis, has become the starting point of a redefinition of this relationship. The struggle with nature, with the goal of dominating nature, is broken by the struggle over nature with the goal of being able to preserve nature as an environment of society. The domination of the knowledge of nature by science and the accompanying reflection on the relationship of nature and society are the second reason for the breakup of the struggle metaphor. Both factors contribute to an ethics of responsibility in the relationship to nature. This contrast between an ethic of principles and an ethic of consequences in the relationship to nature makes it clear that thinking of this relationship as a morally neutralized area is misleading. Interaction with nature has a moral dimension. The economy of this interaction does not escape from morality. The economic appropriation of nature is tied into a moral economy. That expands the concept of appropriation of nature by a moral dimension beyond its cognitive aspect.

Moral economy

There is no natural economy. The idea of nature as an exchange value is likewise a fiction. Nature does not yield to the rules of the market without problems. Instead, the normative content of nature slips beneath the laws of the market. One must oppose the idea of a nature whose normative element is reduced to its exchange value with the idea of a nature whose exchange value is already normatively defined. There is no exchange value beyond normative precepts of society. There is no economy beyond a moral economy. The exchange value of nature is a normative construction of society. It is nothing other than a historically-specific and evolutionary normative determination of the use value of nature. The normative definition of nature cannot be separated from the production and reproduction of a normative order of society. The mechanism that makes the social appropriation of nature on the level of distribution possible is the mechanism of the moral construction of nature. The appropriation of nature in the distribution process does not reduce the interaction with nature to 'strategic action'.[36] The interaction with nature on this level is always regulated action as well.[37]

The 'normative' appropriation of nature is part of the moral economy of society.[38] Moral economy means seeing not only the logic of the market but also the logic of its overall normative conditions as a medium of the appropriation of nature. Nature does not escape economic praxis; it is always marketed, among other things. Yet at the same time, the normative definition of nature impresses its stamp on the market. Even the market does not escape that which it markets. Nature is commercialized and at the same time baulks at this process. If we do not care to attribute this difficulty to a personalized nature (and thereby mystify nature), then there remains only the possibility of explaining it from this normative social construction of nature. The concept of moral economy thus aims at viewing the economic sphere as a normatively constituted context. Modern society nevertheless has largely dissolved these normative elements of nature – that has at least become a common assertion – and has reduced the moral economy to the status of a quasi-natural economy. The normative element of nature is reduced to its use. That has become the cultural foundation of capitalist interaction with nature. Capitalistic commercialization is tied to a utilitarian concept of nature. This concept of nature instrumentalizes nature and makes it a means to social ends.

This specifically modern understanding of nature reaches all the way into economic theory itself. Its ignorance of cultural theory causes the economy to appear as a process in which nature is appropriated according to the laws of commercialization. Economic theory acts as if the economy were located beyond a normatively defined nature. However, it thereby makes nature a part of the ideology of society. It makes that which as a normative definition of nature and as moral economy is the prerequisite of capitalist utilization, empirically invisible. The modern relationship to nature is only a special evolutionary (and problematic) case of a relationship to nature. The economic perspective certainly seeks to make this unrecognizable. Yet to the extent that this economic view can be reconstructed as a culturally specific and systematically distorted one, the self-evidence of the utilitarian concept of nature begins to crumble. What remains is the insight that even modern society is not characterized solely by the remnants of moral economy and of a normative relationship to nature. Instead, like every other society, it possesses a moral economy and, like every other society, it is dependent on a normative definition of nature. The specific normative

---

36 The concept of 'strategic' action also presumes normative definition processes – in contrast to the concept of 'instrumental' action, which presumes cognitive definition processes.

37 The question of the possible changes and their direction will be excluded here. It refers to the problem of a theory of the developmental logic of cultural evolution and a theory of evolutionary learning processes that would support it.

38 The concept of moral economy (Thompson 1971) aims to consider economic processes as part of a more comprehensive cultural process. In that way it aims to relativize the logic of the economic sphere by a historically-specific cultural logic.

construction of nature becomes clear to the very extent to which the logic of the normative appropriation of nature is questioned.

The reconstruction of the normative social construction of nature is the condition which makes possible a critique of the 'natural' economy that determines the modern relationship to nature. A critic of natural economy relates the logic of the normative social construction of nature to its concrete conditions. It shows that this social construction of nature is part of a moral economy, the normative elements of which are themselves controversial. Even nature – and this is the decisive theoretical argument – does not escape from the field of social conflicts. As the critique of political economy has already shown, the economy is the expression of a social praxis, whose market appearance should not hide from us that it is also the object of moral conflicts.[39]

This aspect becomes virulent to the extent that the form of the appropriation of nature becomes the object of moral conflicts. That is articulated in conflicts over what should be considered 'natural' and 'artificial' as well as those over whether the natural or the artificial is 'better'. What is at stake in these conflicts is more than just the normative or political content of nature. The current conflicts over the societal relationship to nature show that an additional level of the cultural construction of nature beyond the cognitive and normative definitions is beginning to become an issue. What is at issue is the symbolic meaning of a nature that has entered into or still is entering into the use value of nature. This is seen in the attempts at a 'romantic' redefinition of nature, in attempts at a 'pleasurable' relationship to nature. The symbolic meaning of nature becomes particularly controversial in the ecological discourse, implicitly and explicitly.[40]

The symbolic construction of nature

The enjoyment of nature

The problem of the symbolic appropriation of socially produced nature becomes a third starting point for a correction based on cultural sociology of the paradigm of a naturalistic theory of evolution. This necessitates asserting a level of the cultural definition of nature beyond the cognitive and

---

39 The association with the concept of political economy is intended. Cf. also the works of Baudrillard, who enlarges the practically structured economy beyond a moral economy to a symbolic economy. This is an attempt to generalize political economy as well as the critique of it.

40 The association with 'ecological communication' produced by the concept of an 'ecological discourse' is likewise intentional. Cf. the rather descriptive use of the term 'ecological discourse' in Kitschelt (1984) and the explicitly theoretical use of the term 'ecological communication' in Luhmann (1989).

normative descriptions of nature, namely the level of a symbolic construction of nature. The way in which nature is produced and distributed after being made available by production leaves open the rules according to which nature is consumed. Beyond cognitive and normative definitions, nature has a meaning that is produced and reproduced in the consumption process. This meaning is not contained in the object of 'nature' itself. It is given to nature in the process of consumptive appropriation. The symbolic representation of nature and the associated communicative practices (ritual as well as discursive!) are not simply the result of affective and emotionally alleviating functions. They are instead the expression of a societal relationship to nature manifesting itself in consumption. Beyond (cognitive) poiesis and (normative) praxis, the symbolic meaning of nature is explicated in a discourse on nature that focuses on joy and sorrow, hope and fear in the interaction with nature. This discourse examines collectively valid symbolic forms of the societal relationship to nature. This 'doxa', like every 'doxa', has 'heterodox' ideas of nature (Bourdieu 1984b). That makes this discourse on nature ambiguous. The heterodox discourse reaches back to cultural patterns that have so far played only a minor role in the evolution of the relationship of nature to society. Thus the current discourse on nature makes it possible to communicate ideas that have been excluded in the history of modernity as romantic, exotic and premodern.[41]

The 'orthodox' discourse on nature sees it as something that is only consumed for utilitarian reasons. The 'heterodox' discourse, in contrast, makes an issue of nature's condition, its crises and its wounds. The modern heterodox discourse makes an issue of aspects of the societal relationship to nature that were always part of the societal relationship to nature in traditional societies. In these societies, nature was something one approached with respect, something one did not touch or which was appropriated only in a ritually regulated manner. The heterodox discourse on nature therefore draws attention to the fact that nature can have meanings that transcend the morally based critique of the modern societal relationship to nature. This idea transcending moral critique reaches from human interaction with animals all the way to the idea of an alter ego (of a personalized and active nature) reflected in nature. The symbolic representation of nature reveals schemata of experience and perception of the world that shatter the schema of a mere objectivity of nature. The exposure of such symbolic meanings broadens the sociological analysis of nature by a genuinely cultural dimension.

It is obvious to look for and identify such symbolic representations in traditional or foreign societies, but they are also found in modern societies. The multivalence of the modern discourse on nature is seen precisely in the fact that nature possesses a symbolic function even in the modern society,

---

41 For a genuinely sociological analysis of the romantic concept of nature and its carriers, namely romantic and neoromantic movements, see Weiß (1986).

that it too is a means of conceiving of the modern world. The environmental discourse is the current example of a heterodox discourse, in which alternative rules for the consumptive appropriation of nature are defined and forms of a symbolic representation of nature are produced. That is nothing other than a renewed attempt to conceive of an alternative culture and thus of an alternative modern social order.

One can regret this focus on the symbolic foundations of modern society in the environmental discourse on nature and interpret it as the expression of faulty control of the social system that relies too much on its environment, that is, mental systems. Then the discourse on nature becomes the result of an 'excessive' resonance in society to problems of its interaction with nature (Luhmann 1989). The 'political content of nature' (Dreitzel 1976) is seen as an evolutionary labyrinth that stands in the way of the 'autopoiesis' of the social system. Yet such an interpretation remains a merely normative statement. It is itself part of the politicization of nature under different normative circumstances. An objectifying sociological analysis, by contrast, starts from the fact that societal relationships to nature are based on historically recognized and transmitted cultural patterns which determine communication on nature (Dreitzel 1981; Thomas 1983). The cultural patterns can be seen not only in the specificity of the European relationship to nature. They are also seen in national traditions that vary within the European traditions (Claessens & Claessens 1979; Eder 1993a).

How much the environmental discourse contributes to the 're-enchantment of the world'[42] is dependent upon the social conflicts over the symbolic meaning of nature. A genuinely sociological analysis of the symbolic dimensions of nature views the environmental discourse[43] – independent of the current boundary conditions that gave it a central socio-political meaning – as the result of symbolic conflicts in society. That which is considered environmentally relevant or environmentally meaningful is controversial and in the last instance it depends on fundamental cultural convictions. Whatever these convictions might look like in detail, they extricate the human history of nature from the natural evolution of society. And they open the possibility of undertaking the experiment of an 'alternative' cultural evolution of society.

Nature as culture

Thus the social construction of nature is determined as a threefold process. It is first a cognitive and moral construction of nature. Cognitive descriptions of nature produce a world-view that channels the empirical experience of

---

42 Theoretically and sociologically well grounded accounts of this fashionable concept are found in Weiß (1986) and Moscovici (1976).

43 For a 'history of ecology' cf. among others Merchant (1980) and Brüggemeier & Rommelspacher (1987), Pepper (1984), Worster (1987), Bramwell (1989) and Deléage (1991). For a systematic reconstruction of this history see also Eder (1994).

nature. Moral symbolizations of nature, on the other hand, produce a consciousness of how one should interact with nature. Both forms of the social construction of nature depend on a symbolization of nature. These symbols are not derived from nature. Nature is only the 'signifier'. The 'signified' in the descriptions of nature is society itself. Society sets down the elementary rules for perceiving and experiencing the world in the symbolization of nature. Such symbolizations are used to adjust the elementary schemata for perceiving and experiencing the world.[44]

Durkheim conceptualized such symbolic connections as 'elementary structures of sociality' and localized them in religious symbols. Durkheim sought the shared world that makes society possible in the 'elementary forms of religious life' (1968). This obviously does not apply to simple societies. Natural symbols constitute forms of commonality beyond cognitive or moral rules. This commonality results from concrete ties into a historically and spatially specified symbolic context which all those who wish to communicate with other members of society must acknowledge. Here one glimpses a shared, self-evident symbolic world, the a priori in nature, as Douglas (1975) puts it.[45] This world brings about communication even when the logic of argumentation or the logic of discursive speech are no longer effective. In the extreme case, someone who does not accept this self-evident symbolic world will be considered a deviant who is excluded from society. Whoever questions this commonality that protects the 'natural' identity of society, whoever no longer shares this common world, places him or herself on the margin or outside of society. He or she is declared 'insane' by society.

This level of social self-construction permits the ultimately decisive breach with the naturalistic tradition in sociological theory. The breach between naturalism and symbolism becomes an issue in the evolution of Durkheim's work itself. This breach was not followed up in the development of sociological thought. Instead, the theory of society itself naturalized its categories. It formulated the concepts it produces to describe society on the pattern of the description of nature. Instead of understanding that the theoretical description of society must break up all natural categories, because natural categories are only the signifier, but not the signified, it derives society from 'objective' (and/or 'subjective') environment – from 'nature'.[46] To the extent it can be made obvious that nature is a cultural product, this notion becomes obsolete. A sociological theory of nature thus

---

44 The function of such natural symbols (Douglas 1973) is that with their help the normative and cognitive designs of the world can be communicated. The communicative function of natural symbols consists in making communication in society possible. In this connection, cf. especially Leach (1976).

45 See Douglas (1975: 275ff.).

46 Nature then acquires a peculiarly central significance for a theory of society – whether as subject, which is naturalized as the psychological environment of society, or as object, which is naturalized as the ecological environment of society.

becomes a key for a turn in sociological theory formation in the direction of cultural theory.

The theoretical description of a self-evident symbolic order that contains the minimum of commonality, the minimum of common culture, implies at the same time that even natural symbols, although they are elementary foundations of communicative processes in society, cannot be decoupled from the logic of discursive communication. There is always the possibility of focusing on the nondiscursive foundations of discursive social self-construction, thus making them the topic of discourses. Society can, however, ideologize these foundations. It can stylize nature into either the ideal model of society or the enemy of society. Both are ideological rationalizations of the relationship to nature. Such foundations are, in a word, indicators of the state of society, not the state of nature. Both Marxist and functionalist sociology have cooperated in this ideologization and hence in a specific variant of the social production of nature.

The blind spot of sociological theory, nature, is of course also becoming a topic of interest for external reasons. As nature turns into the environment of society, made controversial by society itself, it becomes in equal measure a medium for the reproduction of the culture of a society. Modern society is therefore increasingly compelled to find a description of nature that can also be part of the self-description of society. A critique of the modern relationship of nature to society is, in that sense, part of a process in which this self-description is renovated. It aims at clarifying the options that were available to historical societies and are available to modern societies. One must show the conditions under which self-evident certitudes are called into question or the realm of self-evident certitude is expanded. One can do this with a historical and comparative approach to symbolic systems that can be found in different societies with different levels of development of natural history. Such a historical/sociological approach is attempted in Chapter 2.

2

THE EVOLUTION OF THE SOCIETAL RELATIONSHIP TO NATURE AS A LEARNING PROCESS? AN ECOLOGICAL CRITIQUE OF PRACTICAL REASON

An evolution of reason

The idea that *societies can learn* immediately arouses the suspicion of a reification of the concept of learning not without reason. If one attempts to analyse the development of social systems as the result of social learning processes, does that not simply amount to a stylization of society into a macro-subject? Is society not simply taking over the role of the subject in this case? Is this not just a revival of the (metaphysical) idea of a collective subject? The fact that *practical reason* is in action here is an even more provocative assumption. There is some substantiation for the suspicion that this is just a revival of old Hegelian cognitive structures.[1] There is nothing objectionable in this in itself. All the theoretical approaches that determine sociological thought today find precursors in the early modern era of Europe. Economic behaviouralist theory traces its lineage back to the Scottish philosophers and systems theory goes back to the French encyclopedists.[2] So when one enquires into the connection of social learning processes and social evolution, it is impossible to avoid Hegel.

Assumptions about social learning processes prove particularly irritating when doubters of reason can cite better arguments on their side than ever before. Doubt as to the moral progress of humanity has always had good grounds. Today the strongest bastion of faith in progress – namely, the superiority of humankind over nature, its increasing dominance and control of nature – has begun to falter. The current ecological crisis is not just a contingent event that befalls the world from time to time. It is no longer just misfortune. Instead, it calls the superiority model into question, and this

---

1 These Hegelian cognitive structures are competing above all with the evolutionary ideas that were taken from science, especially biology. The individualistic verdict of a collective subject 'society' formulates a methodological objection to such cognitive structures.

2 Regarding these philosophical precursors, cf. the borrowings of the New Political Economy from Adam Smith, particularly in Lindenberg (1983, 1986) and the borrowings of Luhmann from the cognitive styles of the French encyclopedists, especially in Luhmann (1980, 1981).

expands the ecological crisis into a crisis of society itself.[3] That is why it becomes a theoretical challenge to reconstruct social learning processes. The reasons just cited provoke an enquiry as to how far such a concept can carry us, in view of old and new experiences of irrationality. This is the motivation for turning again to the attempt, initiated by Marx's theory of practical reason; continuing from that, the programme of a theory of the social evolution of reason will be explained.

Localizing the a priori of practical reason in society rather than in the human spirit is the starting point of the Marxian critique of Hegel. Marx sought the social a priori of practical reason in two different historical processes: the history of the domination of nature and the history of social and political struggles. He viewed these two historical processes as complementary ways of realizing practical reason in history. This distinction underlies the fundamental problem of Marx's evolutionary theory, the hindrance of productive forces by the relations of production.[4] This fundamental problem can first be formulated more abstractly. In the history of the domination of nature, a type of practical reason evolves which finds no counterpart in the history of social and political struggles. The practical reason that is embodied in social labour is hindered and obstructed by social circumstances. Social development becomes a natural process, in which practical reason remains latent. The potential of the practical reason embodied in the history of the conflict with nature remains unexhausted. Only social and political struggles, that is, social praxis, can set this potential for practical rationality free and give a different direction to the social evolution of practical reason.

This theoretical idea does avoid the (romantic) implication of seeing the realization of practical reason in the mere liberation of nature. It also avoids a variant of this notion: conceiving of nature as a repressed subject that could be brought back to itself by its representatives, people. It leaves the idea of a practical reason in the societal relationship to nature unclear. An adequate concept of practical reason in the societal relationship to nature, after all, cannot be obtained from either the idea of a struggle with nature (by the society struggling with nature) or the idea of an identification with nature (by the society snuggling up to nature). This Marxian conception does not provide any theoretically convincing point from which the assumption of a practical reason in the relationship of society to nature could start up. We must therefore rethink, with sociological means, the role practical reason plays in the societal relationship to nature. The proposal is to localize in the interaction with nature the objective preconditions for a social praxis that sets down the specific path for the social evolution of practical reason. The

---

3 For a theoretically ambitious sociological analysis of the ecological crisis, see Beck (1992).
4 This contradiction is one of the classical assumptions of Historical Materialism. On this point see Chapter 1 in this volume.

history of social conflicts can then be read as an attempt to correct or reproduce these objective preconditions.

This reformulation enables us to make practical reason, which Marx sees embodied in the societal relationship to nature, the starting point for a critique of the Marxian notion of social evolution. The critique asserts that Marx reduces the practical reason embodied in the societal relationship to nature to a utilitarian reason. For Marx the 'liberating' effect of social struggles leads only to a liberation of utilitarian reason which makes it possible for mankind to assume dominion over nature. That this does not in fact liberate humanity, but ties it instead into new relations of domination, is one of the negative historical experiences we have had with this type of reason. The utilitarian reason being created in the modern interaction with nature is a restricted form of practical reason. If one can show that the Marxian description of the social evolution of practical reason concerns a special evolutionary case – and that is a matter of one's theoretical distance from this interaction with nature and thus an issue of theoretical reason – the problems with Marxian theory become easier to understand. They are based on the fact that Marx made modern society, and the practical reason evolving in it, into the (next-to) last stage of a universal social development and thereby made them absolutes.

In order to grasp the idea of a social evolution of practical reason theoretically, therefore, we must go beyond Marx. The hypostasis of the type of practical reason realized in the modern era must be corrected. This correction must not be restricted to the interaction of people with one another, the history of social and political struggles. It must start with the interaction with nature. It must be made clear that utilitarian reason, which has reached an as yet unequalled stage of development in modernity, ends up as practical unreason in the interaction with nature. Only by making sure of a practical reason in the interaction with nature can the prerequisites for a social praxis that will 'liberate' practical reason be determined. The proposal, starting at Marx and at the same time going beyond him, is that utilitarian reason be viewed as a systematically restricted form of communicative reason and that the social evolution of practical reason be oriented to the idea of a communicative reason. The key to an alternative social evolution of practical reason is therefore the idea of a communicative interaction with nature,[5] in which a potential for practical reason accumulates which need not necessarily lead to practical unreason.

A theory of the social evolution of practical reason is developed below in three steps. In a first step, a reconstruction of the cognitive learning processes of societies is conducted on the basis of the forms of knowledge present in a society. Then it is shown how these learning processes are initiated and reproduced in different social states of nature. The practical

---

5 This Romantic tradition in the understanding of nature is found in the Marxist tradition in the works of Bloch (1959) and Marcuse (1964).

rationality that is worked out on the evolutionary level of the modern social construction of nature, the 'cybernetic state of nature', is reduced to the concept of ecological reason. In a second step, there is an enquiry into the question of the moral learning processes that decide on the normative orientations of practical rationality in the interaction with nature. In that way, the reconstruction of the social construction of nature is supplemented with an aspect that places the social evolution of societal relationships to nature in the context of a social evolution of practical reason. Moral learning processes decide on the practical utilization of the potentialities opened up by cognitive learning processes. They guide the orientation of the practical reason which is realized in a societal relationship to nature. The present reflections aim at analysing the alternatives for the moral orientation of the 'cybernetic state of nature'. This brings up the topic of an ecological morality transcending ecological reason. In a third step, finally, the connection between ecological morality and ecological reason is treated as the central evolutionary problem of practical reason in modern society. The 'ideal–typical' distinction of two competing paths for the social evolution of practical reason finally serves to sketch out the contours of a social critique of ecological reason.

Practical rationality and nature

Forms of knowledge and cognitive learning

Cognitive learning processes are the key to the forms in which a society regulates its relationship to the natural environment. In these social learning processes, forms of knowledge of nature arise which in each case indicate different levels or stages in these cognitive learning processes.[6] Every society has an everyday knowledge that is part of everyday activities in its interaction with nature; these reach from cooking, to handicrafts, to the rules for direct interaction with the surrounding nature. Beyond this everyday knowledge there is a knowledge that demands a socialization into specialized abilities. This institutionally produced knowledge can be labelled professional knowledge. Finally, every society has a theoretical knowledge, which is often called 'useless' or 'unpractical' in everyday activity.[7]

---

6 The fundamental features of this model have been adopted from Moscovici and appropriately adapted. See Moscovici (1968).

7 The distinction of forms of knowledge here has, first of all, only a classificatory function. It arranges knowledge according to the abilities an individual must have in order to reproduce it. The levels can be distinguished in systematic terms according to the level in the ontogenesis of mental systems on which this knowledge is socialized and reproduced; everyday practical knowledge corresponds to the concrete-operational stage, rule-based professional knowledge to the formal-operational stage and theoretical knowledge to true formal thought. This assignment must not be interpreted in terms of a constitutive theory. The levels of knowledge are not 'constituted' by individual cognitive abilities. They simply require individual cognitive abilities at different stages of development.

The everyday knowledge type qualifies one to master everyday routine activities. It is a knowledge that results automatically from concrete experience in everyday life. In modern societies, this everyday knowledge is extended to the (pseudo-professions) of do-it-yourself work. Whether cooking or gathering berries, the requirements on people demand nothing more than those abilities which they possess as soon as they have given up playful interaction with the world of objects for goal-oriented interaction in their mental ontogenesis.[8] This everyday knowledge is part of those self-evident certitudes that are transmitted 'naturally' in every socialization process.

Alongside this practical everyday knowledge, every society also has the professional knowledge type, which differs in one central respect from everyday knowledge. This knowledge must be acquired in special learning processes, which are controlled more or less by ritual; one example would be the professional rules in medieval guilds. The knowledge transmitted is often secret, which distinguishes it from everyday knowledge. The construction of a bow and arrow is just as much a part of this professional knowledge as are metal fabrication and machine design.[9] While this knowledge presumes more than everyday knowledge, it still does not require the clarification of the theoretical foundations of the interrelations recognized from experience or trial and error.

Finally, theoretical knowledge is distinguished from professional knowledge. This type of knowledge is not limited to modern societies. It is also present, as Horton has shown, in traditional African cognitive systems, so it is not limited to Western science.[10] The difference separating traditional from modern theoretical thought is not one of cognitive abilities, but rather that between a 'closed universe' and an 'open universe'; that is to say, it is a difference between theories tied to the social context and theories that are designed to be context-free. The difference thus pertains to the degree of social differentiation, but not the logical structure of the thought.

The specific characteristic of modern theoretical thought is the scientific testing of experience. This science received a special characteristic in the early modern era. Mechanistic philosophy, the atomistic speculations and the design drawings of 'theoretical' engineers are examples of the first forms of modern theoretical knowledge. In premodern societies, this theoretical thought does not speak the language of science. It speaks a language that stems from another world-view. Part of this is the knowledge that has

---

8 On everyday knowledge and the things it takes for granted see Douglas (1975), as well as the ethnomethodological literature.

9 The abilities of Stone Age people as craftsmen require a cognitive knowledge that cannot be explained merely from experience. It presumes knowledge of physical interrelations that is condensed into the form of techniques that must be learned. Cf. Rust (1974).

10 Arguments for the universality of theoretical knowledge are found in Lévi-Strauss (1962) and also in Horton's comparison of traditional African and modern systems of thought (1967). For a systematic case study of 'primitive' science, see Ortiz (1971), who analysed the concepts of time and space among the Pueblos. Also important in this context is Needham's (1972) analysis of the rational structure of Chinese science.

accumulated between the separation of humanity from nature and the modern era and constitutes the 'science' of the alchemist, the medicine man, the master builder, the astronomer and the geometrist.[11] Somewhat confusingly, this theoretical thought has been called traditional thought. It is not traditional thought, but rather theoretical thought in a traditional language.[12] In premodern societies, all mathematics and physics are anchored in traditional conceptual schemata (numerology, cosmology, natural philosophy).

Common to both modern and traditional thought is that both proceed hypothetically. In both cases, theories are tested for their empirical correctness. Both modes of thought produce a knowledge that cannot simply be 'used', but can instead predict how nature will behave. The very kind of thinking that was declared a characteristic of modern thought also occurs in traditional societies. It occurs in cosmogonic and cosmological conceptions of the origin and order of nature. Corresponding to those conceptions are types of calculability of natural phenomena with the aid of counting and measuring. It also occurs in the 'savage thought' whose 'scientific mode of thought' was analysed by Lévi-Strauss. Like any other type of theoretical thought, this thinking in a 'mythological language' permits the construction of categorical classes and the construction of quantitative and numerical relationships of invariance. One example is the Paleolithic stone engravings, which Marshack has interpreted as archaic science.[13]

In the 'human history of nature', therefore, we find numerous starting points for initiating and advancing cognitive learning processes. The concept of labour is not sufficient to encompass theoretically the practices that advance these cognitive learning processes. Moscovici has pointed out that the concept of labour[14] leads to an obscuring of the differences between

---

11 On this traditional science in general cf. Mason (1962), and on the special and interesting case of Chinese science, Needham (1972). The innovations provided by traditional science to the evolution of science include, as Goody shows, writing (Mesopotamia), the alphabet (Greece) and printing (European Middle Ages). Cf. Goody (1977: 36ff., 74ff., 112ff.).

12 For a systematic comparison between traditional and modern science, see especially Horton (1967). Goody (1977: 46f.) emphasizes the dependence of this difference on contextual conditions (particularly the existence of writing). Cf. also the articles in Kippenberg & Luchesi (1978). The classic on problems in this field is Evans-Pritchard (1937).

13 On the latter point, cf. Marshack (1972), who analysed the notational and counting systems of Mesolithic cultures. Cf. König (1973) and Goody (1977: 74ff.) as well.

14 The concept of labour has been evaluated in a particularly controversial manner in the discussion relating to Marx. Cf. Marcuse (1968b) as a critique and then particularly Habermas (1968a) who plays this concept off against interaction. Cf. Offe (1983) for an attempted rehabilitation. This concept is insufficient for the reconstruction of the relationship of nature and society. For expansions and the conception of a sociological history of nature cf. Moscovici (1968). For an application of such a perspective to the case of the origin of modern science, see Böhme, van den Daele & Krohn (1977). The interrelationship between structures of theoretical thought and inventive activities is crucial to the assertion of a logic of social construction. For a programmatic statement on this, see Moscovici (1968: 52ff.). A case study of the thesis of the social production of cognitive knowledge is found in Knorr-Cetina (1981).

productive activity, which produces goods and objects, and creative (inventive) activity, which produces knowledge. Productive activities determine a society's wealth (or poverty). Inventive activities determine a society's knowledge (or lack of it).

In the history of active human interaction with nature, inventive activities are the key to the cognitive learning processes that take place in a society. A reconstruction of such cognitive learning processes faces a difficulty that has to do with the delimitation of the scope of inventive activities. We must not reduce this history to a 'history of science', because the history of inventive activities is always also a part of the history of everyday knowledge. It is likewise part of a history of the specialized knowledge of 'professions'. It is ultimately also a part of the history of the theoretical knowledge of nature embedded in religious world-views. Therefore, we cannot search for the history of inventive activities in a universal and isolated history of science. The category of science presumes schemata of division that we use today in order to describe the modern form of inventive activities (and insufficiently at that!). If there is no clearly differentiated science in simple societies, that does not imply that there would have been no inventive activity there that could have led to theoretical knowledge as the highest stage of cognitive learning processes.

Only in the ideal do inventive activities lead necessarily to theoretical knowledge. In reality, inventive abilities lead first of all to everyday knowledge and professional knowledge.[15] Cognitive learning processes thus take place in all societies, simple as well as complex ones. How much theoretical knowledge is involved varies between the societies. That is not the key to the evolutionary meaning of cognitive learning processes in social systems. The evolutionary function of cognitive learning processes (independent of whether they lead to elaborated theoretical systems of knowledge) consists in creating increasingly complex empirical contexts for social practice. This practically mediated interrelationship of social learning processes and social evolution will be explicated below with a systematic intention. Subsequently, the meaning of modern cognitive learning processes for practical reason can be explained more precisely.

Cognitive learning processes and social evolution

The initial evolutionary conditions for cognitive learning processes can be distinguished systematically according to the functional differentiation of different forms of knowledge. The more complex a society, the more the forms of knowledge differentiate away from one another. Inventive activities on the levels of everyday knowledge, professional knowledge and theoretical knowledge become increasingly separated as the complexity of

---

15 This is formulated as a follow-up to Moscovici's central thesis of natural division. See Moscovici (1968: 128ff.).

the society increases. This differentiation has been called 'natural division' by Moscovici and cited as the criterion for distinguishing social states of nature in the human history of nature.[16] The extent of the natural division determines how the inventive activities will develop, and what knowledge will be produced.

Natural division separates what is connected in the activities of hunting and gathering. The famous phrase in which Marx located in the future the characteristics of past interaction with nature, applies here with a slight alteration: consuming in the morning, fishing and doing handicrafts in the afternoon and criticizing in the evening. The activities of the hunters and gatherers express a relationship between mankind and nature that can be labelled 'synthetic'. This is still praxis in the comprehensive sense of the word. The work of the farmer and the craftsman is distinguished from that of the hunters and gatherers by separation. The work of the new groups is specialized in the use of power in addition to their own – in the case of the farmer by using (domestic) animals or, in the case of the craftsman, by using technology. The engineer and the scientist, in turn, presuppose the separation of their work from that of the craftsman. The engineer's work is specialized in calculating the interrelationships between interventions in nature and in rationalizing productive activities. The engineer specializes in inventive activity. This differentiation of inventive activities is the most extensive natural division so far. It appears as the most complex form which the 'human history of nature' has so far known.[17]

In the beginning of the human history of nature inventive activities are tied into the everyday work of gathering and hunting. The inventive activities that characterize this elementary state of nature are oriented to the purpose of optimally employing the motive abilities of the hand, the legs and the fingers and amplifying them with tools. Tools are conceived of as

---

16 The distinction of reproductive, productive and inventive activities permits us to drive the discussion of the relationship to nature beyond the restrictions of the concept of labour. Thus, the chapters on food taboos and sacrificial rituals in this volume are examples of an interaction with nature which is culturally determined even before any labour exists. The concept of labour, on the other hand, does not reach the level of theoretical reason. Labour is merely an 'extension' of theoretical reason, which is its prerequisite. The differentiation of these levels implies the separation of reproductive, productive and theoretical activity. This separation dismisses theoretical reason from its everyday and productive contexts. This has often been felt to be problematic. The current complaints on the loss of life experience in science and on the lack of a practical reference point for theory are thus a call for de-differentiation.

17 In this respect, cf. the difference between *prattein*, the Greek word for farming, and *poiein*, the word for the craftsman's work. Cf. Vernant (1971: II, 16ff.). The two concepts symbolize different activities, *praxis* and *techne*. As the polis expanded, they became the key to the hierarchical order of Greek society. Equality (relative to the aristocracy!) was restricted to citizens living in the city, that is, craftsmen. In comparison to that, the engineer's work is operative activity, which transcends both *praxis* and *techne*. On this point, see Moscovici (1968: 173ff.).

extensions of the hand.[18] This 'primitive' technology is found in every society, but only in simple societies was it able to determine the social organization. That also has to do with the fact that simple societies were not aware of shortages before they were displaced by more complex societies (Sahlins 1972). Stone Age societies had considerable time for activities other than hunting. They were not determined by labour. They were not compelled to develop inventive activities beyond a certain level. The fact that cognitive learning processes are taking place without the condition of 'shortage of time' explains their slow pace in these societies.

That does not mean, however, that there were no cognitive learning processes. On the contrary, the diversity of theoretical knowledge about nature shows the inventive spirit of these societies. The 'primitive' relationship to nature does have formally systematized types of knowledge. In these societies, a theoretical knowledge develops which reflects on empirical knowledge, and has been called 'savage' thought by Lévi-Strauss (1962). This systematized thought is not a cognitively inferior mode of thinking. Even the hunter or gatherer can be a philosopher. Savage thought is the expression of a social learning process in which there was no objective (or ecological) constraint to think instrumentally.

Two inventions advanced the first natural division: pottery and agriculture. Pottery is a more complex sequence of actions that combines different actions and also uses chemical alterations that are triggered by the combined actions. This is an activity that tends to be reproduced outside of everyday routines. A professional organization of these activities was rewarded. The craftsman separated from the hunter, who made his tools himself. Corresponding to this craft activity was a partial differentiation of inventive knowledge, not without consequences for theoretical thought and the construction of theoretical systems of knowledge. Agrarian activity had similar effects. It no longer relied on observing and perceiving actions (as with hunters and gatherers) but rather on specialized knowledge for deliberately changing the natural environment. By domesticating plants and animals, the farmer actively intervened in the cycle of nature. The craftsman transformed nature with the help of nature when he performed the transformation of dirt into pottery with the aid of fire. By virtue of his abilities as craftsman, he turned nature into artifice.[19]

This form of the malleability and calculability of nature, experienced by the farmer and the craftsman in the successes of plant and animal domestication or pottery making, triggered an expansion and proliferation of theoretical knowledge. These activities led to an empirical science of motion, velocity and time. The optimization of manual dexterity by artisanal

---

18 That is among the classical interpretations of 'original' technology. Cf. Gehlen (1960). Lévi-Strauss speaks of *bricolage* in this connection, a concept that points to the restriction to reproductive contexts. Tinkering is done at home (Lévi-Strauss 1962).

19 See Gouldner & Peterson (1962). For further developments of this topic cf. Heise, Levski & Wardwell (1976).

knowledge required the exact determination of the motion, velocity and duration that control the activities of the hand. This created the preconditions for the idea of an objectively controlled universe. Hence, even in non-state agrarian societies, systematic knowledge and calculations of the motions of the stars existed. This astronomical knowledge was systematized and elaborated in the early high cultures (the best known example being Babylonian astronomy).[20] It culminated in the mathematical arts (arithmetic and geometry).

Farmers had parallel experiences. Their activity also freed itself from daily activity. They had to control the conditions under which plants are sown and harvested; they had to set the dates for planting and harvesting; and take corrective measures, such as irrigation. They were forced to optimize the use of their labour through knowledge of conditions and consequences because, unlike nomads, they could no longer simply abandon the land when it became exhausted. This spatial restriction and the sedentary character associated with farming created the objective conditions for the idea of a centre in the universe.

The differentiation between farmers and craftsmen thus accelerated cognitive learning processes. Types of knowledge were tied to the differentiated agricultural and artisanal activities and thereby removed from having to be reproduced in everyday life. This more complex relationship to nature was connected with a new reflective knowledge. The natural philosopher came into being as farmers and craftsmen became differentiated as social categories. The natural philosopher strives to identify the natural substances that constitute nature and its properties. The relative differentiation between inventive activities was the objective precondition for the origin of ecological systems of knowledge, which were conceived and developed by specialist theoretical thinkers.

This situation found a form of great consequence for evolution in ancient Greece. The thought of the craftsman and the natural philosopher are isomorphic. The isomorphism in the search for the properties and substances of matter operated for the craftsman via the technical imitation of the hand's dexterity, and for the natural philosopher via logical abstraction. That cognitive learning processes were so far advanced on the level of the first natural division of society distinguished ancient Greece from other cultures on the same level. Presumably the incorporation of the artisanal

---

20 The following quotation makes this clear: 'The development of pottery, it may be conjectured, also facilitated the occurrence of vital changes in man's conception of both external nature and himself. For it provided a dramatically evident exercise of man's control over nature and was a symbolically suitable expression of a culminating growth of man's powers. This is all the more likely because pots emerged in association with the cultivation of plants and cereals, and were used to store, transport, and cook them. Strange as it may sound, then, pot-making may have contributed importantly to the slow growth of human beings' conception of themselves as artifactors, by making them increasingly aware of and confident in their own instrumental powers.' See Gouldner & Peterson (1962: 326).

culture into a slave-holding economy was the reason for the premature end of these cognitive learning processes. For this economy levelled off the classical social difference between agrarian and artisanal culture. The social preconditions of this culture – that is, the fact that only a craftsman, but not a farmer, could be a full citizen – were destroyed. The artisanal culture was lost as an innovative culture with the establishment of the slave-holding economy.

In other social learning processes the craftsman became the starting point for a second natural division: the differentiation of the engineer from the craftsman. Already appearing in antiquity, this differentiation became a characteristic of the Renaissance. The technology invented by the engineer made other properties of nature available for use. No longer substances, but forces, no longer *facultates*, but relations and transformations of forces, were sought in nature. The engineer learned how to make these forces useful. He or she now had a relative rather than an absolute position with respect to the object. The concept of motion, which describes the actions of an engineer, is the result of an operative combination that was able to take advantage of new linguistic freedoms. The translation of force into speed and conversely of speed into force, the static calculation of dimensions that are necessary to put together a form (an architectural one, for instance), the principle of action and reaction and the like are physical actions that work with fully reversible operations within a context-free language.

The engineer's knowledge is mathematical knowledge, which presumes two things: first, the analytical separation of magnitudes (variables), the combination of which yields the desired effect (work), and second, the combination of these magnitudes in large-scale mathematical calculations. This makes the inventive activity of the engineer into the objective precondition for a changed 'philosophical' interaction with nature: mechanistic philosophy. The consequences of this development have been seen since the sixteenth century in Europe. This is how philosophical thought departed from a final to a causal explanation, from the cosmological to the object-rational principle.[21]

These changes advanced the development of natural philosophy towards a mechanistic philosophy. The precursors of this philosophy were already present in the fifteenth and sixteenth centuries. The search for analogies in that which is upright or that which is passionate and so on tended to break apart the principle of the metaphysical/cosmological order. The introduction of three-dimensional space changed the frontal perspective on the world. This was prepared with the observation of geometric figures. Examples might be the reduction of motions to circles or spheres or the reduction of planetary paths to a celestial harmony. The 'new philosopher'

---

21 On astronomy in traditional societies, cf. Mason (1962: 15ff.). The significance of natural regularities is a part of the foundations of traditional systems for explaining the world. Examples of this are found in Forde (1970) and Kirk (1970).

who replaced the natural philosopher strove to make the forces of nature measurable and calculable. This relativization of natural sizes, and thus the role of the acting person, was investigated in the theoretical constructions of nature. This occurred first in astronomy, which explored the objective laws controlling motions from varying perspectives and described the perceived phenomena as composite phenomena. Mechanics came to occupy the centre of philosophy. Behind the force which produces a motion in space, mechanistic philosophers discovered the principle of energy. They conceptually constructed the force behind the phenomena over time as the energy hidden in the forces. This revolution of the seventeenth century was not a scientific, but a philosophical one.[22] It marked the establishment of mechanistic philosophy and the understanding of the world with which it is associated. Thus the inventive activities of the engineer exponentially accelerated the pace of cognitive learning processes in the modern era.

The mechanistic philosopher represented a decentred attitude toward the world, which had its structural foundation in the inventive activity of the engineer. But inventive activity became even more specialized at the beginning of the nineteenth century, because the problem arose of how to apply mechanistic philosophy to the world of objects. The scientific revolution of the nineteenth century marked the beginning of this development. The scientist became the rival of the engineer. The engineer substituted machines for the physical and mathematical aspects of labour. Now the scientist strengthened the machine by adapting nature to the use of machines: through chemical inventions (materials science), physical inventions (electricity, nuclear fission) and biological inventions (genetic manipulation and the like).

The reversal from philosophy to science occurred in stages: from the *scientia* of the Renaissance to Descartes' *sciences*, to the sciences of the nineteenth century.[23] The philosophical revolution of the seventeenth century became possible through the mathematical analysis of experience and the assumed measurability of natural phenomena. Newton's intention was to bring mathematical principles to natural philosophy. Then, with the aid of geometry and mathematics, Descartes developed a new philosophy.

---

22 A discussion of the changes in the knowledge of nature in the conceptual dimensions of object/motion/space is found in Nitschke (1967: 34–136). On the theoretical conflicts in this period see especially Maier (1955: 273ff.), who reconstructed the conflict between teleological and causal explanations in detail. On the origin of the new mechanistic philosophy see Moscovici (1968: 308ff.). The origin of modern science from the spirit of mechanization is analysed by Maier (1938) and Dijksterhuis (1956). See also Giedion (1948). For newer, sociologically oriented approaches see Lepenies (1978), and Böhme, van den Daele, Hohlfield, et al. (1978) and Böhme, van den Daele & Krohn (1977). An excellent epistemological reconstruction is found in Lorenzen (1960).

23 On the logic for reclassifying modern knowledge cf. Foucault (1966: 229ff.), and on the differentiation of natural history away from history cf. Lepenies (1977, 1978). The newly arising type of the basic scientist escapes this classification of knowledge. This figure stands apart, is often interdisciplinary by orientation and therefore predestined for theoretical innovations.

The crucial break with mechanistic philosophy finally consisted in reflecting mathematical principles back on to the world rather than on to philosophy. To be sure, Dalton still called his science a 'chemical philosophy' and Lamarck called his a 'zoological philosophy', but these philosophers replaced logical exercise with mathematics, sensory observation with experimental methods, and performed the measurement of effects with the assistance of instruments.

Engineering knowledge was reorganized in this process. In the seventeenth century, similarity only applied to that which fell under the same classification, whereas previously similarities were constructed by way of analogy (between, for instance, upright plants and the upright gait of human beings). In the nineteenth century the systematic division by the sciences commenced, that is, a scientific classification of the world of objects (and with it, a separation of the human sciences from nature). This made the concept of universal 'science' possible. In modern society, where this transition occurs, a new mode of experience determines the tempo and extent of cognitive learning processes.

Since the nineteenth century this transition into a new state of nature has been in full swing. Theoretical knowledge has not only been decontextualized (as in mechanistic philosophy) but also relativized. A new type of observer, the epistemologist, has taken over the role of the 'mechanistic' philosopher. The concept of force, which for Newton was the cause of the observed laws, gravitational attraction to be specific, has become relativized; force is now related to space and time. The idea of space and time as 'containers' for force (and motion) has been dissolved and reorganized in a conception that dissolves the ultimate absolutes. Nature has come to be understood as a system of transformations, into which actions are integrated as physical events. The scientist differs from the mechanistic philosopher by radicalizing the constructivism of the theoretical language and hence the context-independence of the description of natural phenomena.[24]

---

24 This process is described by Piaget as follows: 'In the Aristotelian universe, man contemplates a motionless world from the outside and the entire effort of decentering demanded of him consists in viewing himself spatially as a part in the whole; the other parts of the whole are then available by direct contemplation. In the universe of Copernicus, Galileo and Newton, the observer is in motion and his actions are an integral component of the kinetic and mechanical system, which he can survey through an operative decentering process which consists in placing the motions into a reciprocal relation with one another. From this viewpoint there is no longer any direct contemplation of motion. The observer understands himself by deduction and calculation, that is, by an operative construction. Since he is also in possession of an absolute space and an absolute time he believes he is able to reach a wide range of reality that is no longer relative. In relativistic mechanics, by contrast, even his spatial and temporal assessments are relative, with everything which that implies. That is, these are integrating components of a system of objective transformations with which they remain connected. The meters and clocks constructed by the subject are no longer external to the lengths or the times to be measured; rather, they are changed by the transformations, so that one can no longer simply determine them, but must instead reconstruct them deductively. Measured and measurer have become mutually dependent . . . and from their reciprocity one can deduce the invariance of the laws to be worked out.' (Piaget 1950c, 97ff.).

The philosophical consequences of this new state of nature are well illustrated by atomic theory.[25] Since Greek antiquity (and presumably even earlier) people have attempted to find out the ultimate building blocks of matter. The breakthrough in modern atomic theory consisted in giving significance to measurable relations in chemical reactions. In 1808, John Dalton found an interpretation of the empirically observable relations in chemical reactions which made the breakthrough to the modern theory of nature possible. He postulated that all matter consisted of atoms, that all atoms of one chemical element were the same and that chemical elements were accordingly differentiated by the mass of their atoms. He postulated furthermore that atoms are indestructible. Chemical reactions can then be explained as transfers of atoms; chemical compounds result from the fact that a determined number of atoms come together into a complex, that is, a molecule.

That has led to the abandonment of the strict determinism of classical mechanics, as the attempts to derive thermodynamics from it show. It has been replaced by probabilistic reflections. Chance events produce equilibria. This understanding of natural events in opposition to classical mechanics is the foundation of modern knowledge of nature. There are regularities of self-organization. The early modern engineer-dependent atomic theory has been dissolved: knowledge of nature turns into the theoretical construction of nature from the interplay of chance and regularities of self-organization for elements behaving arbitrarily. There is no longer any objective nature to which one can relate knowledge. The objectivity of nature can only be produced by theoretical means. We can only see from our effects whether these cognitive constructions are meaningful or not. With this, most extensive natural division so far, theoretical knowledge acquires a novel self-reflexive structure. Nature is conceived of as a complex which is fed back into theoretical knowledge. The human being is no longer master of nature, but only part of it. Theoretical knowledge becomes the 'spirit' that is developed in an environment and simultaneously has an effect on the environment. It describes itself as 'ecology of the spirit' (Bateson 1972). Moscovici called the state of nature based on this structure the cybernetic state of nature.

In this state of nature of contemporary societies, the question of reason comes up more intensively. For in contrast to societies of earlier evolutionary stages, modern societies have become even more dependent on nature. They have tied their survival as societies (and not just the survival of people or groups of people) to nature. In these societies the problem of ecological reason arises for the first time. The issue is: what is the social praxis that can deal with this new experience in evolution?

---

25 For a systematic presentation of the world-view of modern physics, cf. Weizsäcker (1971).

The evolution of the relationship of nature and culture

Practical rationality and ecological reason

The human history of nature cannot be based on a theory of the inherent logic of 'theoretical reason' as is done by classical histories of technology or histories of natural thought. Beyond 'theoretical reason', it is rather a history of attempts to initiate cognitive learning processes. The human history of nature comprises the inventory of cognitive learning processes which have been tried again and again and have more or less succeeded. All of these learning processes have had evolutionary effects through their temporal succession and spatial interaction. They have elevated the complexity of the experience of the world so much that there has been an evolutionary premium on natural division. Depending on the degree of differentiation of inventive activities, the pace but not the logic of cognitive learning processes changes, as does the extent of the knowledge produced by them.

Table 2.1 *A schema of natural divisions*

	Everyday rules	Systematized rules	Theoretical rules
Elementary natural division	Routines of interaction with the natural environment	Techniques for stone working and processing organic nature	Intuitive forms of theoretical knowledge
First natural division	Household labour	Systematic cultivation of craftsmen's competence	Dogmatic forms of theoretical knowledge
Second natural division	Wage labour	Engineering skill as key to inventive competence	Philosophical forms of theoretical knowledge
Third natural division	Do-it-yourself	Scientific professional competence	Decentred forms of theoretical knowledge

Table 2.1 attempts to present the double reference of a theory of the human history of nature in tabular form, that is, the reference to growing complexity in the vertical direction and to cognitive learning processes in the horizontal direction. Here degrees of complexity are conceptualized as stages of natural division, and stages of cognitive learning processes as the transformation of everyday rules into systematized rules and ultimately into theoretical rules.

With this theory we are in a position to distinguish states of nature that establish varying initial conditions for cognitive learning processes in the course of evolution. Yet one problem remains unsolved: the problem of whether in this evolution in the human history of nature there is a criterion for distinguishing evolutionary steps which can indicate a development of practical reason in the human history of nature beyond the criterion of the complexity of the state of nature as determined by the degree of natural division of human activities in the interaction with nature. The question is: Is a practical rationality evolving in the human history of nature that permits one to distinguish societies according to their practical reason in interacting with nature?

This question transcends the question of cognitive learning processes. It enquires into what impels cognitive learning processes of societies. It enquires into the forms of social praxis that can initiate cognitive learning processes, give them a certain direction, restrict them or even block them. One could trace the history of the interaction with nature back to an inherent dynamism of theoretical curiosity. One could trace it back to a compulsion to increase the wealth of the society. Both factors always play a part in cognitive learning processes. They represent the two poles of practical perspectives that determine the conditions for utilizing knowledge of nature. Which of these mechanisms dominates at the various levels of natural division remains contingent within a theory of the human history of nature. The distinction of states of nature on the scale of natural division leaves it open which of these two mechanisms of social learning processes governs the relationship of society to nature. It is not necessary, then, to look for additional theoretical perspectives that increase the explanatory power of a theory of the human history of nature.

The result of these reflections based on Moscovici (1968) indicates that this history must not be seen as a unilinear, universal cognitive learning process, but instead as the totality of cognitive learning processes that must be situated spatially and temporally. The functional differentiation of inventive activities (the 'natural division'), however, is the only possibility provided in this theory for stating the unity of this human history. This theory describes the human history of nature as a sequence of states of nature which owe their sequential reproduction to the selective stabilization of natural categories, the selective stabilization of functionally differentiated inventive activities. The human history of nature is thus assumed to embody an evolutionary process which owes its unity to the growth and extent of knowledge about nature.

The distinction of elementary, organic, mechanical and cybernetic states of nature is adequately conceived with the criteria 'degree of natural division' and 'complexity of the state of nature'. Yet this distinction provides no criterion for the practical rationality that is made possible in these states of nature. This sequence shows only that the issue of a practical reason or unreason in interacting with nature comes up more intensely the more natural division increases. The more we know about nature, the more relevant becomes the practical reason that establishes how we are to deal with this knowledge.

The following three assumptions about a development taking place in history point in this direction:

1   The relationship of humanity to nature is being disenchanted. No longer nature as such, but rather a man-made nature appears as a threatening world that determines the ordinary life of people.

2   The area of nature that is accessible to human action is expanding. An increasingly mutual dependence of humanity and nature is arising.
3   The knowledge of nature is monopolized in the scientific system. People are becoming increasingly dependent on the specialists who reproduce social knowledge of nature.

The classical assumptions of evolutionary theory[26] lose their 'progressivist' implication in this interpretation of the human history of nature. These evolutionary assumptions leave open the question of whether the sequence of states of nature assumed to lie in the theory of a human history of nature is 'progress' or not. 'Progress' is a concept that refers to the advancement of learning processes. Yet the degree of this advancement is relatively insignificant to the evolutionary course of a human history of nature. It is indifferent with regard to the cognitive abilities that accumulate in societies. A theory of social evolution takes learning processes as a mere fact that happens. Thus a peculiar ambivalence is built into Moscovici's theory. It both breaks with the productivist perspective of Marx and remains tied to it. That motivates a more radical breach with Marx (or with the theorists following him). In the differentiation of inventive activities, a social evolution of practical reason takes place beyond the functional differentiation of inventive activities, an idea that is the core assumption of the reflections below. The theory of the functional differentiation of activities can be conceived as a special form of a theory of the social evolution of practical reason, a theory which reduces the praxis of interacting with nature to poiesis.

Poiesis has to do with what is considered 'useful' and necessary in a society for survival. Poiesis contains a model of human activity that is bound to utilitarian reason. Praxis, on the other hand, assumes inventive activities that imply a knowledge which need not necessarily be 'useful'. The concept of practical reason results from the fact that the inventive activities which constitute and reproduce a state of nature are always communicative processes at the same time, that they are the expression of a 'collective reason'.[27] A theory of practical reason in interacting with nature must be able to distinguish in the empiricism of history between evolutionary processes in which this practical reason has been allowed to act and those

---

26 For the classical descriptions of evolutionary trends in the evolution of knowledge, cf. Piaget (1950a, b and c, 1970). The theory presented here corrects earlier adaptations for a theory of social evolution, such as Eder (1976).
27 The concept of an evolution of collective reason was developed by Toulmin (1972). He makes the systematic attempt to bring the theoretical transformation together with the changes in the intellectual disciplines and professions. That is one of the most interesting attempts to interpret the evolution of ideas sociologically. With other intentions, but similar in form, cf. Bachelard (1938).

evolutionary processes which attempt to substitute the 'poietic' (or 'productivist') model of a utilitarian culture for the practical model of
communicative culture.[28]

The practical context in which cognitive knowledge is applied cannot fail
to irritate a theoretical reason which, as in classical evolutionary theories,
strives to justify itself as the result of progress.[29] Theoretical reason can
escape this irritation only when it understands itself to be part of this
application context. Such an attitude transforms it into a disillusioning
reason. An interpretation of evolutionary processes oriented towards this
interest does not seek to identify the goal of evolutionary processes; instead,
it shows to what extent the possibility of rationality and irrationality is
opened up in these processes. This attitude particularly recommends itself to
modern society, which has turned theoretical knowledge itself into an
ideology (Habermas 1968c), turning theoretical knowledge into a mechanism for the ideological reproduction of society. A critical theoretical reason
must always make sure of this social function, and that means it must infuse
theoretical reason with a sociologically enlightened reflexivity.

Such a disillusioning can start with the very type of reason which the
modern cybernetic state of nature claims for itself. One can reduce this
reason to the concept of ecological reason. Modern society has advanced its
cognitive learning processes on the basis of the third natural division to such
an extent that it has been able to construct the most complex relationship to
nature that has ever existed. In so doing it has also laid claim to the right to
dominate nature. This has misled it into interpreting the modern societal
relationship to nature as the result of a natural evolution. It was possible to
reduce the history of the societal relationship to nature to something close to
nature, that is, adaptation, struggle for survival, selection and so on.
Practical reason in interacting with nature appeared to this theoretical
perspective as a long obsolete viewpoint, one no longer appropriate given
the state of modern knowledge.

But this description of the human history of nature in modern society
suppresses the possibility of practical unreason in interacting with nature.
That is the starting point of a disillusioning analysis of the modern societal
relationship to nature. To the extent the societal relationship to nature is
considered to be beyond practical reason it is possible to lose sight of the

---

28 An interesting interpretation of the connections between thought/types of knowledge and
social structure from the perspective of differentiation theory is found in Luhmann (1981), and
a reinterpretation from the perspective of a theory of autopoiesis in Luhmann (1990).

29 The critique of theoretical reason no longer describes only a theoretical, but also a
methodological consciousness. This consciousness places the evolution of knowledge under
restrictive overall conditions. All knowledge must now be justifiable with respect to its
production conditions, not just in relation to experience. This is the beginning of a novel history
of nature. Thus Kant is not the end of the evolution of the theoretical spirit, but the start of a
new type of evolution into which sociological analysis itself can be integrated as a component.
As an example of the radicalization of this intention see Toulmin (1972).

possibility of practical unreason as well. And this removes each historically-specific relationship to nature from the critique of practical reason. The result is the triumph of utilitarian reason in modern Europe, which has rendered practical reason impotent in the face of irrational applications of practical reason.[30]

The causes of this special social evolution of practical reason are connected with a special social mode for applying inventive knowledge, which characterized the end of the second natural division and has become a handicap for the practical rationality of a state of nature on the level of the third natural division. The differentiation of engineering work away from craft work led to a devaluation of the latter. The nineteenth century 'worker' came into existence.[31] The craftsmen's work was mechanized. Increasingly, they lost those abilities which distinguished them from the machines invented by engineers. As it concerns the transformations in work, the history of proletarianization is the history of the industrial transformation and devaluation of craft work. Labour became *ponos*, a burden that must be carried. Nature became a hostile opponent, to whom this burden was attributed. The contours of the specific type of practical reason that determine the modern relationship to nature became clear here.[32] Practical reason in interacting with nature experienced a fateful reduction to a productivist reason. It became utilitarian reason, which bases the practical interaction with nature merely on its use.

We now realize that utilitarian reason, which goes hand in hand with the cybernetic state of nature of modern society, is connected with the origin of a practical unreason in interacting with nature. And it would appear as if the currently proliferating discourse on ecological reason does not correct this unreason, but merely adds a euphemistic form of expression to it. To be sure, with the transition from the mechanical to the cybernetic state of nature in modern society, the human history of nature can point to an impressive history of cognitive decentring, which has advanced our knowledge of the world of objects. On the other hand, the control of the human history of nature is increasingly becoming a problem. It is obviously more

---

30 The radicalization of the Kantian critique is, as already suggested above, the sociological critique of theoretical knowledge. On this point see Bourdieu (1984a), who subjects *homo academicus* to such an epistemological analysis by sociological means. The programme of this book also calls itself explicitly a social critique of theoretical reason. Implicitly, of course, this assumes a social constitution theory of theoretical reason. The problems in a primacy of practical over theoretical will not be explicitly addressed here. That primacy results here from the argumentation itself.

31 This process of the dislocation and proletarianization of small-scale crafts has been discussed by Marx using the example of the mechanization of publishing. The 'worker' is a category that first came into existence in this process of destruction of crafts. On this subject area, cf. Stürmer (1979). On protoindustrialization, see Medick (1977).

32 That has consequences for the discussion of the concept of labour. Thus, it is dubious whether labour is a key category of social analysis, as Offe (1983) contends. In his reduction of labour to wage labour, after all, he suppresses the components in 'labour' created by the social construction of nature. The skilled worker is the late revaluation of this role.

and more difficult to control the consequences of the mechanical state of nature and the cybernetic one now coming into view.

The theory of a human history of nature thus compels us to turn our attention to society and the social conditions of practical reason in interacting with nature.[33] It cannot, however, simply refer to this society affirmatively. That would only block our view of the unreason embodied here. The theory cannot simply elevate the practical rationality that has entered into the interaction with nature to the criterion for a social evolution of practical reason.

What practical rationality potential is unleashed in a social state of nature has to do with the moral learning processes that take place in the process of the social construction of that nature. Moral learning processes are a corrective mechanism for that practical unreason which has been formed in a societal relationship to nature. Thus not only the objective conditions of practical rationality evolve in the social evolution of practical reason; so do moral demands on practical rationality.[34] Only if we are able to grasp this double structure of a theory of the social evolution of practical reason in theoretical terms will it be possible to identify the contradiction between the practical rationality created in a social state of nature and the moral demands of a society on itself. And only then will we be capable of conducting a social critique of the practical rationality of a social state of nature, a disillusioning of its pretensions to rationality.

Practical rationality and ecological morality

In the social evolution of practical reason in modern society, moral learning processes have so far only been allowed to work on selective occasions, as the critique of modern ideology shows. That which is thought out in these moral learning processes is not embodied in evolutionary terms. There is no guarantee of practical reason. Frequently, the opposite impression is created, namely, that a practical unreason is connected with these moral learning processes. Thus, the social evolution of practical reason is certainly not guaranteed by moral learning processes. That is why a theory of the social evolution of practical reason must not proceed from ethical systems as indicators of practical reason in a society. It should not proceed either from

---

33 This look back has profound methodological consequences. It forces us into a new variant of theoretical reason. In the old variant, theoretical reason consists in the a priori critique of practical reason. In the new one it is the social critique of practical reason. Reason a priori tears apart the connection between nature and society. It searches for the foundations of practical reason in a transcendental nature. The social critique of practical reason makes this connection visible once again. It shows that in interacting with nature, society is forced to examine the conditions for applying its knowledge, and thus to pose the question of the underlying society's practical rationality.

34 The human history of society, in contrast to the human history of nature, a distinction made by Moscovici (1968: 482ff.), does not concern the division of abilities, but rather the distribution of chances for communicative participation.

other social embodiments of practical reason: the institutions and the everyday life experience in which we can observe the effects of moralization efforts in a society. A theory of social evolution must relate to that type of social praxis in which moralization is an issue, in which moralization efforts are under way. That implies, however, identifying the social exponents of moralization efforts: specifically, social, political and cultural movements.

The social evolution of practical reason in modernity has so far been a highly selective evolutionary process. Contrary to the optimistic image of classical theories of evolution, this evolution turns out to be an exclusion process of moral learning processes from society. This is a path of the social evolution of practical reason which has attempted almost compulsively to restrict the validity of moral principles (for instance, through ideas of the chosen people, the straight and narrow path of salvation, the one holy church, the uniqueness of one's own tribe and so on). This selective particularization of morality has been driven to an extreme with the positing of modernity as the telos of moral evolution.[35]

The assertion that a moral evolution of the human race is taking place which culminates in modernity can therefore be characterized historically as an evolutionary myth which is still quite effective. It recounts a story of practical reason which reaches modern society via the stages of a primitive and a traditional form of social self-construction. But the mere description of these stages makes it clear that this model of social development is indebted to the idea of an increasing elevation of complexity and the underlying logic of the functional differentiation of society. The empirical assumption of this myth is: the more complex the society, the more practical rationality exists in it.

This imputation, however, conceals that complexity does not guarantee the social evolution of practical reason at all. We can only distinguish paths of the social evolution of practical reason which differ from one another in that social praxis uses the morality of a society in different ways. In that way we can also point out failed paths and get initial evidence to make statements about which paths are the more practically reasonable. The claim that modern society has unleashed practical reason is empirically unwarranted. It is a part of the ideology of modern society. Historical experience of modern society contradicts this assertion.

Modern social history is characterized by social divisions that have increased the pace of social evolution exponentially. The elementary social division is that which divided the gatherer from the hunter, a social division which still goes hand in hand with 'natural division' (Moscovici 1972). The 'first social division' made society hierarchical; the 'second' one turned it into a class society. This determined the evolution of practical reason into

---

35 This critique is also directed against the fashionable critique of modernism, because it demands a self-reflexive modernity, not a 'post-modern' culture.

modernity. The 'third social division' into culturally defined and incommensurable life-worlds is the condition for the social evolution of practical
reason out of modernity. This specifies a mechanism of social evolution, and
its acceleration, which is also the basis for the social evolution of practical
rationality. The theoretical discourse on the social evolution of modernity
has, of course, tended to conceal the social conditions for this rationality. It
formulated that evolution in a priori terms and thus misunderstood it. A
theoretical reason that tries to make sure of practical reason in history can
therefore not limit itself to an a priori critique of practical reason (and thus to
an immanent critique of its theoretical representations). If the social
evolution of modernity is more than just an increase of evolutionary pace,
then we cannot avoid a social critique of practical reason. The core of this
social critique is this: if a society claims a higher form of morality for itself,
then it is also asserting a power claim against other societies. If it goes so far
as to try to monopolize a universal morality for itself, then it is attempting to
assert a better position in comparison to other societies.[36]

A social critique of practical reason first of all implies something negative:
relativizing the claim to see a universal evolutionary process in the evolution
of practical reason towards modernity. It then compels us to view the social
evolution of modern society as the expression of a specific social evolution of
practical reason. The 'progressivist' element of classical evolutionary theory
finds only an ideological embodiment in this evolution.[37] Classical theory
makes assumptions on moral learning processes which are correct, but applies
them incorrectly. It draws this false application from the self-description of
modern society and takes it seriously in terms of theory. It falls victim to this
self-description and thereby loses the critical potential inherent in a theory
that confronts the possible moral learning processes of a society with its
institutionalized practical reason. The classical theory of moral evolution
assumes moral learning processes that can take place in every society. This
nullifies the privilege of a moral learning process which modern society
granted itself: the claim to embody higher standards than all other societies.

The classical assumptions concerning progress in social evolution are
therefore nothing other than hypotheses on moral learning processes in

---

36 This social function of morality is easily overlooked in the sociological discussion of
morality. The consequence of this for the analysis of modern societies is that the 'dialectics of
enlightenment' are turned into a unilinear history of the progress of reason. Another escape
would be to forego a strong postulate of universalism. For such an attempt cf. Nunner-Winkler
(1986). But then this has no effect on sociological theory.
37 Ginsberg summarizes these trends as follows: 'In the first morality is dominantly
customary and there is little or no reflection on the grounds of action, though if challenged
traditional explanations will be forthcoming. In the second there is growing reflection by story
tellers, poets and moralists and later by philosophers who seek to disentangle the rules of action
and the ideals of conduct by the method of critical analysis. In the third phase dialectical
analysis begins to be combined with empirical study of the conditions and consequences of
action and the study of ideals is brought into connection with the study of conditions under
which they can be brought to fruition.' (Ginsberg 1956: 311).

society. That can be shown by the following three assumptions on moral learning:

1   As humanity is objectively individualized, that is, dislocated from concrete interaction contexts, the notion arises that correctness of behaviour is something that is independent of extreme sanction and that it supports itself. The subjective individualization forced in this way emphasizes internal motives over external conformity.
2   As the group of persons who can be the target of moral judgements widens, a compulsion to generalize moral rules arises. The defining factor for this in simple societies is kinship, in traditional societies it is the ruling group, and in modern society it is membership in 'bourgeois' society.
3   As social circumstances become increasing complex, moral judgements are formulated more and more abstractly. This abstraction is also found in daily life, in the legal system and in philosophical ethics (for instance, in the Stoic principle '*deus est mortali juvare mortalem*', in the Brahman principle that all people participate in the eternal consciousness, as well as in modern humanitarianism, which propagates equality and equal freedom for people).

Individualization, generalization and rationalization are the result of moral learning processes that are found in both simple and complex societies. The close connection that was created in the classical theories between theories of moral learning processes and theories of social evolution therefore shatters as the practical application conditions of moral learning processes are scrutinized. That is precisely what a theory of the social evolution of practical reason does: it points out the social conditions for the origin and application of social learning processes and makes possible a social critique of social learning processes.

In moral learning processes societies set down the standards they apply to themselves. In this perspective, modern society is one of those societies that have set the standards high, but it is not the only one to have done so. That relativizes the evolutionary significance of modern society in a theory of the social evolution of practical reason. The growing complexity of society, which has reached an evolutionary high point in modern society, intensifies the contradiction between moral ideas and that which a social praxis actually implements. A theory of the social evolution of practical reason can expose this contradiction and thus determine the potential rationality of a specific social evolution.

On the path of the social evolution of practical reason typical of modernity we note an increasing contradiction between that which moral learning processes offer as practical rationality and that which is actually kept. The reconstruction of moral learning processes in modern society offers us a critical standard with which we can measure social evolution: we can determine the specific form of social evolution as something which either encourages moral learning processes or hampers them. The rationality of a morality is used as a means to the end of the social evolution of reason in a way that has yet to be clarified. Whether in this social evolution of practical reason the application of the moral viewpoints present in a society also implies an implementation of these viewpoints or the opposite happens remains the problem to be explained which a theory of the social evolution of practical reason defers but does not solve.

First of all we can only note one thing as specific of the social evolution of practical reason in modern society: this path of social evolution has turned over only ideological functions to morality and has at the same time led to criticism of this evolution process wherever this ideological function is comprehended. At the same time it has started moral learning processes, as a protest against the social development into and through modernity. It has called the existing conditions – economic, legal and cultural – into question and started alternative processes of a social evolution of practical reason.[38] In modernity, the criticism of society, that is its social application of practical reason, becomes a part of this social evolution. The connection between moral learning processes and the social evolution of practical reason can thus be re-established.[39]

That also increases the dynamism of modern society, which accounts for the difference from premodern societies. In the latter, the social evolution of practical reason was determined either by the economy of social relationships or by the organization of bureaucratic systems.[40] With the establishment of modern society, the dynamism of society shifts to social conflicts over the cultural orientation of societal development. Modern society is that one which increasingly bases its own development on political and social conflicts, that is, on social praxis.[41] Thus practical rationality becomes a reflexively employed mechanism for the reproduction of modern society.

Modern society has unleashed praxis as the mechanism for the social evolution of practical reason. That is why it is increasingly being forced to correct its natural evolution according to the standard of practical rationality. This has consequences for the social conflicts in a society, for its

---

38 Such improbable learning processes include the prophetic and Protestant oppositional movements to the dominating high religious culture, as well as the development of a scientific culture in ancient Greece and in the Renaissance. Cf. Vernant (1962), Burke (1974).

39 This can be shown from the form of social movements that embody such practical critique. Cf. Eder (1985).

40 We sometimes speak of societies that are based on kinship relationships. That is not necessarily an accurate characterization, because kinship also matters in other societies. The crucial point is that kinship relationships are only the symbolic medium for creating economic relationships. Something analogous applies to the 'exchange of women' in simple societies. We continue to speak of state societies. The rules of belonging to the state are the symbolic medium for creating an institutional order (which tends to be contingent in simple societies.) For the common usage, see Eder (1976).

41 On this, cf. the works of Touraine (1973, 1978) who speaks in this context of the level of 'historicity' as a level beyond institutional order.

political and social praxis, but above all it has consequences for its natural foundations. It makes nature, or more precisely nature as produced and made available in cognitive learning processes, the touchstone of practical reason. In the question of nature, modern society collides with the practical reason it ascribes to itself. The uncontrollable domination of nature coming to the fore in modernity has intensified the contradictions between the embodiment of practical rationality and idea of practical reason produced in moral learning processes.

The nature question decides whether in modern society it is possible to take a path of social evolution of practical reason which will allow us to block off practical unreason in interacting with nature. The nature issue is predestined to start a renewed ideologization of modern practical reason. For the social state of nature that has been achieved in modernity offers a concept of practical rationality that can do without morality. The 'cybernetic state of nature' looming on the horizon is based on a concept of practical rationality that reduces morality to the reproducibility of this state of nature. The morality of utilitarian reason, having become dominant in modernity, finds an objective, quasi-natural foundation here, which permits it to continue the social evolution of practical reason as an evolution of utilitarian reason without interruption. This new state of nature euphemizes this utilitarian rationality as ecological reason. Ecological reason thus becomes the critical point in the conflicts over the practical rationality of current social developments.

The issue is whether this ecological reason will become part of a form of practical reason that can avoid the pitfalls of utilitarian rationality. What is at stake is whether ecological reason can be connected with an appropriate 'ecological' ethics. If this were to succeed, then an ecological ethics could no longer be reduced to a utilitarian ethics. Then the seducibility of morality by knowledge, that characteristic of modern utilitarian reason, could no longer continue to be the characteristic of the social evolution of practical reason in modernity. The question of whether, despite all the knowledge now available to us, we are producing an ecological reason today from which ecological morality is absent therefore compels a renewed critique of ideology: a critique of ecological reason.

PART II

FROM NATURE TO CULTURE

3

CULINARY MORALITY: A COMPARATIVE ANALYSIS OF FOOD TABOOS

Eating is an eminently social business, as Simmel (1957) emphasized. Eating rules are social rules *par excellence* (Walens 1981: 67ff.). The shared meal brings people together at one table. That compels them to be social. Beyond that, eating regulations control the forms of social behaviour. This makes eating a key to the 'civilizational process' of humanity (Elias 1978, 1982; Mennell 1987). In order to be able to explain this social and civilizing function of eating rules, one must understand the cultural logic on which those rules are based.[1] The cultural logic of eating rules will be displayed below in a special case of eating rules, food taboos. Food taboos are culturally deep-seated and emotionally highly-charged food prohibitions. They express a collective moral feeling or moral sentiment which exists prior to any moral consciousness.[2] We refer to the collectively shared disgust at

---

1 The following reflections can be understood as an attempt at a reformulation of the repertoire of sociological theories in the light of cultural theory. For recent debate in this sphere cf. especially Archer (1988), Swidler (1986), Wuthnow (1987) and Alexander (1990). Central importance in this debate belongs to the stimuli of structuralist cultural and social anthropology (Drechsel 1984; Willis 1984).

2 One can call this the morality of a society, if one distinguishes morality from ethics (the cognitive institutional form of morality) and law (the normative institutional form of morality). But beyond that, this collective moral sentiment holds a deeper significance. It represents a symbolic relationship to nature. It establishes how we behave towards the surrounding nature and our own nature. The symbolic foundations of social order, the unconscious foundations of morality, are incorporated in food taboos. This distinction has been lost in cognitivistic moral theory. Nevertheless, there are impressive examples for a cognitivistic conception of morality (cf. the articles in Edelstein & Nunner-Winkler 1986). For a reintegration of this line of debate into sociological debates, however, a sociological theory of culture is a systematic prerequisite.

eating the meat of certain animals as food taboos. This group does not eat pork, the other refuses dog meat and still others do not eat beef. Why, the question goes, are certain animals excluded from culinary consumption?

It is obvious that fundamental moral problems of a society are regulated with food taboos. The thesis from which we shall work below is that one can understand food taboos as elements of a culinary morality in which the 'unconscious' prerequisites of the moral 'consciousness' prevailing in a society can be found. Food taboos are, in short, moral norms prior to any morality. Food taboos are predestined to represent a collective moral 'unconscious', for they are norms at the interface between nature and culture. Because of this quality, they have also been called totemistic norms. Taboos related to the killing or eating of animals are part of the totemism complex. Ever since the systematic critique of the functionalistic explanation of totemistic ideas by Lévi-Strauss (1964c), these phenomena have occupied the centre of the conflict over an appropriate theoretical treatment of the relationship of nature, culture and society.[3]

The classical theories of totemism explained this form of symbolizing the world only as the expression of a primitive mentality, as a form of primitive thought and primitive morality. They themselves, however, as Lévi-Strauss demonstrated, are nothing more than an expression of totemistic symbol formation. 'Totemism' is an invention of modern theorists who are analysing symbolic forms they do not understand. In that sense they resemble magic theories. That is the quintessence of the critique of totemism theories by Lévi-Strauss. This critique does not turn totemism into a false theory. Totemism is, on the contrary, a correct theory of itself: that is, a theory of those who invent totemism.

In this way, fundamental issues of the self-understanding of modern knowledge on society come into play by way of the symbolic order of eating. Hence it is virtually imperative to make the symbolic order underlying food taboos the starting point for a discussion focusing not only on the problem of a morality presumed for all cognitive and normative structuring of the world, but also on the reflexive structure of modern thinking about the social sphere. The analysis of food taboos below is thus always conducted as a simultaneous systematic critique of the theories explaining these food taboos. The attempt to answer the question as to the significance and function of food taboos will proceed in three steps. The first step consists in performing a systematic reconstruction of various attempts to explain these food taboos. The goal of these reflections is to test what answers have been provided to the simple question of why there are food taboos in the first place. The second step consists in analysing food taboos in various societies from a comparative perspective. To this end, the food taboos of the Jivaro

---

3 The discussion of totemism can be extended in this way in a specifically sociological gesture. The starting point of this discussion is marked by the critique of the totemism concept in Lévi-Strauss (1964c). Totemism is – to summarize Lévi-Strauss – not a primitive type of thought, but rather a universal form of thinking.

Indians in Brazil, the food taboos in classical Judaism and the food taboos in modern western European culture are analysed. In a third step, finally we enquire into the morality implicit in these taboo systems.

Theoretical approaches to the explanation of food taboos

What are animals good for?

Three different theoretical strategies of explaining food taboos have been developed:

1   a theory which explains food taboos as the result of economically rational norms of behaviour;
2   a theory which explains food taboos from their function for the production of social solidarity; and
3   a theory which explains food taboos as the expression of cognitive anomalies.

These three theories can be boiled down to the following three pithy formulas:[4]

1   animals are good to eat;
2   animals are good to prohibit; and
3   animals are good to think.

In the first theoretical variant, assumptions about 'preference structures' are supposed to capture the individual and/or collective use of food taboos. Here the theoretical explanation operates with rationalistic assumptions. In the second variant, assumptions about 'mechanisms of social integration' are supposed to capture the function of food taboos. This implies a functionalistic explanation. In the third variant, 'patterns of cultural interpretation' establish the meaning of food taboos. One can call this a structuralist explanatory approach. These three explanatory approaches will be discussed using the example of food taboos.

Approaches to rationalistic explanations   In classical functionalist anthropology, material bases were presumed to lie behind all taboos. Ultimately it is the needs of the stomach which are satisfied by marking taboo.[5] An animal

---

4   The distinction 'good to think' and 'good to prohibit' picks up from Tambiah (1969). What is added is a naturalistic version that is found dispersed in works that are close to social anthropological functionalism or the more recent cultural materialism. On the latter, cf. particularly Harris (1977).

5   Malinowski, the founder of classical functionalistic social anthropology puts it like this: 'The path that leads from the jungle to the stomach and on to the mind of the savage is short: the world presents itself to him as a confused image, in which only the useful animal and plant species, primarily the edible ones, stand out.' (Malinowski 1948: 27). This argumentation shows the initial kinship between naturalistic and functionalistic explanation attempts.

is permitted if it is 'good to eat'; an animal is forbidden if it is 'bad to eat'. Dietary prohibitions ultimately originate from the desire for an efficient appropriation of nature. This need to control nature presumes a common participation in nature by humans and animals. That restricts boundless exploitation; thus it implies economically motivated prohibitions on eating animals. Food taboos become the expression of an economic rationality.

The cultural materialism that has come into fashion in recent years (Harris, 1968, 1979) contains a radicalization of this argument; in conflict with 'dialectical, formalistic and other obscurantist' theoretical traditions, this school explains the origin of norms, including food taboos, from the use which a renunciation of meat would have for the survival of a society. Such aspects concern, for instance, avoiding depletion of game from excessively intensive hunting and desertification from excessive grazing. What is primarily at stake, therefore, is the avoidance of costs which would be implied by raising animals for eating. Accordingly, ecologically motivated utilitarian considerations are presumed to be behind food taboos.

Approaches to functionalistic explanations The rationalistic theories begin to have difficulties when they are supposed to explain the totality of prohibited animals, rather than just individual animals. Why, for instance, is it prohibited to eat a turtle, although that food provides only a minimal contribution to protein supply and is ecologically irrelevant? An answer that can avoid these difficulties is found in the classical functionalistic theories. They do not look for the reasons behind the existence of food taboos in individual and/or collective preference structures, but explain them instead by the compulsion to maintain a social order itself. The turtle is not tabooed because it tastes bad or offers little protein relative to other animals, but because it is good to prohibit. It is a communications medium for normative regulations that assure the maintenance of a social order in space and time.

This explanatory strategy is particularly characteristic of the functionalistic school of 'British Social Anthropology' from Radcliffe-Brown to Evans-Pritchard. The description of animals as inedible has the function of fostering solidarity in society and making social integration possible. This is the background to the thesis that animals are good to prohibit. According to this theory, social integration is guaranteed by creating mutual dependencies and reciprocity relationships, which are manifested in the standardization of 'legal obligations', specifically kinship roles and the associated duties and prohibitions. Functional needs of a social order predicate the commandments or prohibitions which are then in turn legitimated within the social order. This theory proceeds from the assumption that social integration depends on normative regulations that establish what belongs to the society and what does not. This theory asserts, therefore, that systems must be distinguished from an environment and that norms perform this function in the case of social systems. Taboo norms are then only a special variant of the mechanisms that have the function of making a social system distinguishable from its environment (social or nonsocial!). This functionalistic explanatory logic avoids the snares of economic rationalism, which must always presume a psychological disposition – more precisely, a disposition towards rational behaviour – variable within cultural limits. However, it does not avoid the snares of a reification of the social sphere. After all, systems do not just exist; they are symbolic constructions, the logic of which cannot be adequately comprehended within the logic of the differentiation between system and environment.

That can be seen from this very phenomenon of food taboos. The symbolic significance of food taboos cannot be grasped with a theoretical construction which only explains that food taboos are good for the differentiation of system and environment. This theoretical construction would have to explain instead why it is precisely certain taboos (and not arbitrary ones) which are used for this function of system formation. In order to answer this question, one would have to delve into the process which results in systems. Systems are only the 'by-product' of a permanent process of symbolic construction of social reality. That forbids the use of system formation as the key to an analysis of symbolic forms.[6]

Before social systems arise they are conceived. The turtle is not tabooed because it tastes bad or offers little protein relative to other animals, nor because it serves the maintenance of the social order, but because it has a significance.[7] This implies, however, engaging with the perspective of the actors themselves and attempting to understand why the animal kingdom is divided into edible and inedible. The answer that animals are good to eat presumes an answer to the question of why particular animals are suited to the thinking of a social order and to the representation of a social structure. This presumes an alternative form of analysis: a structural analysis.

Approaches to structuralist explanations   The foregoing considerations suggest seeking the explanation of food taboos in the cognitive construction of these food taboos themselves. They permit the step to a third variant

---

6 This critique applies especially to the radicalization of social scientific functionalism by systems theory. Of course, the argument that system genesis is the blind spot of explanations based on systems theory seems, at least at first sight, to have been invalidated by the theory of autopoietic systems. On this theoretical development cf. Luhmann (1984). That social evolution can be reduced to the automatic unfolding of the objectivizations of the social sphere is disputed below. The autopoiesis of social systems is always at least one step behind the actual poiesis of the social sphere. Objectivizations do not precede social praxis, they can only follow it.

7 A beautiful example for this is the reproduction ritual for flies and mosquitoes in northern Australia. Why is such a reproduction ritual held, even though the mosquitoes are a plague? Spencer & Gillen already gave the answer in 1904: 'However, it must be remembered that flies and mosquitoes, though in themselves intensely objectionable, are very intimately associate with what the native above all things desires to see at certain times of the year, and that is a heavy rainfall.' (quoted in Lévi-Strauss 1964c: 64). That is, mosquitoes are not useful objects, but signs for something else: mosquitoes stand for rain.

explanation: animals are not simply good to eat and to prohibit but especially good to think up a (cognitive) order in the world. Animals are good to think because they are physiologically varied. One can divide them, classify them and bring an order into the animal kingdom. This makes available the model of an order that one can use for conceiving a social order. This theoretical perspective can be labelled 'structural'.[8]

Nature is used in order to conceive of a social order. The natural differences serve for conceiving the social differences. The fundamental structuralist assumption is that an order is projected into nature which then can become the model of a social order.[9] The natural order is not projected onto the social order. The natural order is only the medium for constructing a social order. Structural analysis thus does not lead to a naturalization of the social sphere but, on the contrary, to a socialization of nature. This theoretical assumption is joined by a methodological assumption. The idea underlying structuralism (Durkheim & Mauss 1963; Lévi-Strauss 1962) is that one can determine the meaning of each individual element only when one knows the structures of a cognitive order of the world. Analysing food taboos structurally then means determining the place a tabooed animal occupies in a classification system of the animal world. If this methodological rule is satisfied, then the theoretical assumption comes into effect: deciphering the social logic on which this classification of nature is based.

Such classification systems can be constructed in very different ways. The mechanisms of their construction are binary schemata which divide nature into classes in a series of cumulative differentiations. Some schemata such as the difference between animal and human seem to be culturally universal; there are other binary schemata that depend on the state of empirical knowledge and on interests. Binary schemata order the world. Those empirical phenomena which resist binary schematization therefore become problematic. Anything that displays unclear contours in the logic of drawing classification boundaries stands out. Where an animal belongs at once to two classes or does not fit into any class, it becomes the representative of possible disorder. Douglas (1966) attempted to find some such cases which are anomalous in terms of classification. Indistinctness that pertains to the difference between human and animal is particularly precarious. It is normal for animals to run from people and shy away from human contact; it is anomalous if they do not do this, if, that is, animal and human realms overlap. This applies to some domesticated animals (cats and dogs perhaps), which are viewed as being part wild animal and part human.

Other indistinctness in classification can arise when consistency rules with respect to brooding behaviour, sleep behaviour, eating behaviour and anatomical peculiarities are part of the classification logic. Carnivorous

8 For the best introduction to this way of thinking see Leach (1976). The classic texts are found in Lévi-Strauss (1962, 1967). Oppitz (1975) provides an overview.
9 For the structuralist concept of a model cf. Lévi-Strauss (1963: 277ff., 324ff.).

animals, for instance, are supposed to have fur and claws in contrast to herbivores, which have hooves and a soft skin. Those herbivorous animals that have fur or claws then appear to be problematic. Egg-laying animals live in the air, and are thus birds as a rule. Animals living on the ground have four feet and walk or climb. Those species that have four legs and lay eggs (such as turtles) then appear problematic, as do those land animals that fly like birds or live in the water, or those land animals that have more than four feet or no feet at all (snakes, etc.). Those animals that are cognitively anomalous are, therefore, the most likely to be tabooed. Cognitive anomalies are a means of distinguishing order from disorder and thus make disorder avoidable.[10] Food taboos are then normative rules which can be explained from the cognitive anomaly of an animal.

From economic to structural analysis

The explanatory approaches sketched out above each claim different forms of analysis of taboo norms: economic analysis, functional analysis and structural analysis. These forms of analysis are connected with the fundamental paradigmatic assumptions of the individual explanation strategies.

The rationalistic paradigm[11] is based on a form of analysis that applies only under restricted social conditions. This economic analysis presumes a society that has neutralized moral considerations and symbolic constraints and conceives of social norms independently of such preconditions as the aggregate effect of rational individual actions. This produces fatal theoretical problems. Particularly when construction processes of shared symbolic worlds are at issue, this theory must fail. The economic analyses work in such cases with the assumption of special boundary conditions which, however, restrict the scope of the explanations in the degree to which these boundary conditions are multiplied. The internal logic of this explanation ultimately ends in an explanatory model in which that which is to be explained is crowded out into the boundary conditions. Only this expulsion of the problems of the explanation into the boundary conditions protects the 'pure' validity of the theoretical assumptions on rational behaviour and makes the assumption of the universality of such norms plausible. The economic analysis simply presumes a cultural world that exists prior to any

---

10 Food taboos are not some arbitrary case of the symbolic order of society. They belong instead to those symbolizations which use the problem of material survival in order to make the non-material conceivable. Here nature becomes the medium of the symbolic organization of society.

11 The rationalist paradigm has not been resurrected as 'economic analysis' in social and cultural anthropology alone. It has also found a certain dissemination in general sociology and in the sociology of law. The functionalist paradigm has become part of the standard paradigm of sociology through Parsons. The theory of collective behaviour (Olson 1965) and the theory of social differentiation are only applications of these two theoretical paradigms.

psychological dispositions. That makes the economic analysis insufficient for a sociological analysis of norms. An economic analysis of food rules must therefore always fall short of its goal.

The functionalistic paradigm virtually reverses the problems of rationalistic approaches. The functional analysis of norms does not in any sense tie down the reference point in respect to which these norms can be functional. These reference points are ultimately arbitrary. Instead of proceeding from a 'hard' basic assumption (such as rational behaviour), functional analysis is 'soft'. There are always norms that are dysfunctional in regard to a chosen reference point (such as 'social integration') or are neither functional nor dysfunctional. Norms may indeed have arisen from such functional requirements, or they may possess a particular capability for survival because of such functional requirements. In order for them to be able to be identified as norms in the first place, they must 'fit' into a cultural order. They must relate to other norms and be understood from this context. The logic of such a symbolic order, however, cannot be obtained from functional considerations. The logic of a cultural order exists independently of the system character of social reality.

The structuralist paradigm takes a step toward an analysis of the logic of cultural orders. The structural analysis of norms on which it is based makes connections visible between them which neither a reductionism to functional imperatives nor a reductionism to universal psychological dispositions can bring to light.[12] Structural analysis therefore focuses on the systematic prerequisites of both theoretical strategies, the rationalistic and the functionalistic. The world in which psychological dispositions can have an effect and functional imperatives can have consequences is already a symbolically structured world, not a *tabula rasa*. The structures of this symbolically ordered world explain how dispositions and effects, imperatives and consequences, are connected. Structural analysis leads in this way to a theory that conceives of society, beyond the addition of individual actions and beyond self-complexity, as a symbolically regulated context. Structural analysis is hence presumed in economic analysis and functional analysis.

The structural method may at first appear to be a procedure of searching for coincidences. As in a puzzle, food taboos are combined over and over again until they yield a logically constructed order. Structural analysis is thus quite the opposite of a random procedure. It is a procedure that attempts to find out the structuring rules (the 'principles') of the context of a symbolic

---

12 The world of symbolic forms is more than the uniqueness of the subjective inner life and less than the complexity of the objectivized social world. It is located between a subjectivistically understood and an objectivistically understood world. It makes it necessary to distinguish a world of social facts from a subjective world of knowledge, feelings, etc. and an objective world of systems. The world of symbolic forms must therefore be conceptualized beyond objectivism and subjectivism. The concept of 'culture' as an expression of socially constructed individuality offers itself as a label for this intermediate world.

(or cultural) order. The structural method is based on the assumption that culture is a logically ordered world.[13] The logic of symbolic connections no longer reflects the logic of society. Rather, the models according to which people act in society are established in these structures. Symbolic connections are no longer the superstructure, but rather the base (and the base, according to Marxian theory, then becomes ecological environment!). The structures of symbolic connections and society behave toward one another like model and reality or orchestral score and performance (Lévi-Strauss 1964b: 24ff.; Leach 1976). Society is defined as a praxis which embodies the underlying model more or less well.

That is why the structural analysis of food taboos attempts to decipher the logical order that lies behind the various food taboos. It brings order into a chaos of phenomena by seeking out higher standpoints in order to summarize differences into classes of differences. This procedure can be repeated. One can continue looking for standpoints that reduce the differences to higher-level differences between higher classes. This regression through stages of abstraction away from the original differences ends in a fundamental difference, the difference between humans and animals in the case of food taboos. Structural analysis therefore seeks to trace the existing differences back to their organizing principles. The argumentation connected with this structuralist perspective, that animals are good to think order or disorder, extends a central thesis of Durkheim's. Classifying animals is a means of representing society. Society orders itself in the ordering of the animals. That means that when we understand the logic of the system of food taboos we will have understood the logic of the symbolic ordering of society.[14] The structuralist thesis asserts that the logic of symbolic orders is the key to the analysis of the functioning of society and the key to the explanation of the rationality of social action.

Thus a structural analysis of the food taboos of various cultures will be attempted. Cases will be cited which represent differing forms of society: the food taboos of the Jivaro Indians in central Brazil, the food taboos of traditional Jewish society and the food taboos in modern European societies. This analysis leads to the productive enquiry into the semantic

---

13 The case of 'logical disorder' is not excluded. According to the theory presented here, logical disorder ought to go hand in hand with social disintegration. In case of logical disorder, after all, there has been a failure to create symbolic connections that can be shared by everyone. No shared culture can be produced.

14 Durkheim & Mauss (1963) first formulated this thesis in 'De quelques formes primitives de la classification' (L'Année sociologique, VI, 1903). The thesis is, in brief: society orders the world in its own image. Durkheim's more far-ranging thesis was that the 'forms' of the social structure (in the sense of a morphological notion) determine classificatory thinking. The Durkheimian example (Durkheim 1968) was that of the Zuñi Indians, who allegedly had a seven-part social organization, which was allegedly reflected in a seven-part heaven. This example is of course empirically false and theoretically not compelling. This reveals a morphologistic self-misunderstanding, which for no good reason devalues the thesis that the order of society is contained in the order of the animals.

contents that are communicated through the symbolic system of food taboos. An attempt is made to correct the cognitivistic 'bias' of structural analysis and to identify the social content of these structural properties. Sociologically enlightened structural analysis consists in systematically integrating the problem of morality into a structural analysis of symbolic orders.

Comparative analyses

Food taboos among the Jivaro in central Brazil

The Jivaro[15] live in small semi-settled groups near or directly on the shores of the rivers that flow through the Amazon Basin. Their habitat is thus primarily tropical rain forest. They have the following food taboos:

1 the tapir, the deer and the amphibious capybara, the world's largest living rodent;
2 the anteater and the sloth;
3 lizards, mice and snakes;
4 predators (particularly the jaguar).

Animals generally considered edible include birds, small rodents, monkeys (apart from the guariba monkey) and South African wild pigs (peccaries). These food regulations contrast with the food norms of the Yanomamö and the Mundurucú (also living in this area), who hunt the tapir, the deer and the capybara but avoid the anteater, the sloth, lizards, snakes and predators; the Kalapalo, on the other hand, avoid all land animals except monkeys and restrict themselves to fish.

We attempt below to decipher the significance of the food taboos in these tribes. First of all a rationalistic explanation is discussed. Then an attempt is made to identify the function of these taboos in fostering solidarity. Finally, the semantic context in which the prohibited animal species receive a certain significance, that is, the cognitive classification system underlying the food taboos, is discussed.

An economic analysis of the Jivaro food taboos   An economic analysis of the taboo norms of the Jivaro was presented by Ross (1978). According to Ross, food taboos are the result of the attempt to produce an ecological equilibrium among natural environment, hunting techniques, size of a group and form of settlement. The adaptive advantage of food taboos consists in restricting the protein supply of a population to animals that permit an economically optimal provision under given natural boundary conditions.

---

15 For the ethnographic literature on the Indians in the Amazon basin in general and on the Jivaro in particular see Ross (1978); Karsten (1926); Chagnon (1968, 1974); Zerries (1983).

The following proposed explanations result from these assumptions. Populations that live in the vicinity of rivers with plenty of fish will tend to taboo the animals living on land. Populations living at a certain distance from rivers must hunt animals, and face several alternatives. They may hunt all animals, including big game, but then they must pay the price of low population density and high geographic mobility (with special social consequences, which cannot be further discussed here). Or they may hunt only small animals, which permits a more settled mode of life, but at the same time limits the size of the settlement. A third possibility is to rely partially on fish and to hunt small game as well; in this case the morphological limitations on social organization prove least restrictive. These connections can be well illustrated with the various tribes that live in the upper Amazon Basin. The Achuraians, for instance, with relatively small villages, taboo the deer and the tapir and concentrate on hunting small animals. The Yanomamö hunt big game and form only relatively unstable settlements. Ross concludes from this that those groups which have specialized in big game tend to be forced more into a nomadic life than those which specialize in small game.[16]

Why, however, are the animal species not used in each case prohibited? The explanatory logic sketched out above explains only the ecologically meaningful concentration on the eating of certain animal species. An alternative proposal is to explain such taboo norms from the perspective of the danger of overhunting. In that case, taboos would be attempts to avoid maladaption. If larger communities were permitted to hunt big game, which reproduces only slowly, it would very soon be extinct. The reproduction rate could no longer be brought into agreement with the necessary hunting rate. The minimal necessary protein supply would consequently be endangered. Taboos are then elements of a prospective care for the ecological equilibrium, strategies of anticipatory adaptation to a habitat.

There are cases of tabooing, however, which make little sense from this standpoint. There are always maladapted practices. The hard version of the ecological explanation (taboos as rational answer to problems of survival) would have to be replaced by a softer version. Carneiro proposed one in a critique of Ross.[17] The softer version starts from the idea that each society normally has more possibilities of survival than it minimally requires. Most societies can therefore afford maladaptive practices. Such maladaptive practices can be explained by an inertia inherent in symbolic restrictions. Taboos simply continue to be valid, even after the environment that led to their emergence has changed and the taboos have become superfluous or even counterproductive.

---

16 Thus Ross argues: 'The focus on small animals makes possible a more stable residence pattern which has shifted much of their energy investment to a horticultural regime more compatible with labour intensification than is the procurement of large game.' (Ross 1978: 9).

17 Among the critiques of the essay by Ross, that by Carneiro is particularly helpful. See Ross (1978: 19f.).

The taboo on anteaters seems to be neither adaptive not maladaptive, so that this additional assumption makes little sense for anteaters. There are also difficulties attached to the question of why animals which are difficult to hunt, such as the tapir or the deer, are tabooed even when they are no longer needed for the protein supply.[18] A final source of difficulties is that the concentration on hunting small animals is connected with the taboo on animals such as lizards, mice and snakes. What could be the reason why these animals are excluded as a possible source of protein if they are indeed a functional equivalent to the renunciation of hunting big game?[19]

A functional analysis of the Jivaro food taboos   It is scarcely surprising that hunting animals is subject to economic restrictions. That does not imply by any means, however, that the animals not hunted must be tabooed. For that reason the question arises how the scope provided this way is filled out in normative terms and what the consequence is for the social organization of hunting. The functionalist explanation of food taboos comes down to identifying solidarity-fostering processes triggered by taboos and attributing socially integrating functions to them. The different distribution of food taboos among the individual tribes is part of this. If the Yanomamö and Mundurucú hunt and eat large animals, while large animals are taboo among the Achuraians and the Kalapalo, then that simultaneously implies a social distribution of opportunities for material reproduction among the tribes. Food taboos here regulate an area of social relationships that lies outside the reciprocity networks of the individual societies. Food taboos make living together possible. Their function is to preserve a social order in this special case: the reproduction of the segmentary differentiation of society.

As members of the upper Xingú tribes, the Kalapalo are distinguished from the lower Xingú tribes, who eat everything. They are distinguished from the other upper Xingú tribes by their peacefulness and generosity, by a certain way of marking themselves as people. Being peaceful and not eating the meat of large animals distinguishes them from their hostile neighbours, who eat everything and are aggressive. The maintenance of a culinary practice thus protects the uniqueness of one tribe against the others. Delimitation from the outside and protecting internal solidarity are the socially integrative standpoints with which a functional analysis operates.

Food taboos also possess differing validity inside a tribe. Taboos can vary by season or in ways specific to the group. Wagley (1977) has demonstrated such specific taboos among the Tapirapé Indians of central Brazil. Among the Tapirapé, women, children and the fathers of children are those not allowed to eat the meat of certain animals (Wagley 1977: 77ff.). The

---

18 This does not cause difficulties if one assumes that these animals taste particularly good, which is why consumption must be prohibited by the taboo. This, however, leads to a tautological explanation, since that which tastes good is only defined by taboos.

19 One need only think of the Aztecs, who intensively used these tiny animals all the way down to ants for their own food supply. Cf. Harris (1977).

forbidden animals for them include the deer, the guariba monkey, the tapir and the small anteater. Generally taboo among them, as among the Jivaro and other neighbouring tribes, are the capybara, the sloth, snakes and the opossum. These 'special' taboos have a function within the tribe which is analogous to that of the 'general' taboos between groups: they produce social solidarity by producing social relationships between groups.[20] And by symbolizing the seasonal rhythms, they protect social integration over time.

In the functionalist perspective, food taboos therefore appear as a means of expressing prohibitions. Prohibitions generalize behavioural expectations. In that way, they protect social integration. At the same time, they also have an integrative function spanning space and time. They structure relationships of social groups in a given social space, and they structure the time in which the group lives. The issue of why these functions should be fulfilled specifically by the medium of food taboos, however, remains contingent in the functionalistic perspective. What is of interest is not why food taboos are suited to the reproduction of social systems, but simply that they are suitable. That leads ultimately to a tautological explanation:[21] the constraints of social order are what leads to the social constraints. Food regulations are what leads to a dietary regime. But food taboos are more than this analysis makes of them. They are also, and above all, a way of conceiving of the social world.

A structural analysis of the Jivaro food taboos   If one inquires into the significance of food taboos, not just into their function, then that leads to the necessity of first reconstructing the interpretations that are given for the food taboos by those who observe them. The Jivaro give the following answers to the question of why some animals are not edible:

1   the tapir is prohibited because it utters a peculiar whistling sound and moves soundlessly; the deer is prohibited because it can scarcely be heard when it moves and it is unbelievably fast (Karsten 1926: 285);

---

20 Wagley interpreted this as follows: 'A man who was the father of an infant and thus prohibited to eat armadillo, for example, would kill such an animal if he encountered it, even though it was also taboo to his wife and daughters. He would bring it to the village as a gift to a brother-in-law, a sister's son, or a special friend (anchiwawa) who did not have an infant child and perhaps had growing sons (boys can eat armadillo). He would not expect immediate payment of any kind, but in time he would expect his relative or friend to remember his gift. Thus, if the recipient had chances to kill a peccary, he would have reciprocated with a choice piece of meat. In consequence, the limitation on diet resulted in cementing social ties. Unless it was an animal which all Tapirapé found repugnant, such as the sloth, there was always someone anxious for the meat.' (Wagley 1977: 67).

21 These problems of explanation cannot be cleared up either by a division of the analysis into the surrounding systemic and life-world conditions. It remains to be shown what the cultural or symbolic prerequisites of any functional analysis are. They remain unproblematic as long as the cultural prerequisites of functional analysis are uncontroversial. As soon as the latter vary, however, the functional explanation loses its explanatory power. The classical critique that functionalist explanations possess an inherent orientation towards stability is not the result of the theory's conservatism, but rather of the insufficient theoretical conceptualization of the cultural system.

2 the anteater and the sloth are not edible because they have no anus, and
   the guariba monkey is prohibited because it continually farts (Lévi-
   Strauss 1968a: 393);
3 snakes and predators are not edible because they are monstrous, because
   they have a shocking nature; the Kalapalo call this quality 'itseke', which
   means 'the unusual' (Basso 1972: 643).

These animals somehow deviate from that which is felt to be normal. This
includes land animals which move best in water. It applies in particular to the
amphibious capybara, which, with webs between its toes, is optimally
equipped for swimming. The unusual thing about these animals is thus that
they can live both on land and in the water (according to the rule:
quadrupeds belong on land and fish belong in the water).

This ambivalence is less central to the deer and the tapir (although it may
be part of the frustrating experiences of hunters that both can easily escape
tracking by swimming). What strikes the Jivaro about the tapir and the deer
is their motion mechanism, their eating habits and their language. Special
modes of behaviour are conspicuous. These animals live alone and are active
only at night. They do not live socially and they do not sleep by night. In that
sense they are unusual in a very special way. What is conspicuous is the
ability to live and/or move in water and the solitary and nocturnal way of life.
These are joined in the view of the Jivaro by additional types of conspicuous
behaviour. The tapir speaks falsely because the sounds it produces consist
chiefly of unusual whistling sounds. The deer is hypernervous because it runs
away too swiftly.

The anteater and the sloth have a special status alongside these large
animals. They are avoided equally by all tribes. Both animals belong to the
class of the *dasypodidae*. Within the mammal group they display an unusual
quality: they belong to that class of mammals who violate the rule that at
most seven molars may be present on one side of a jaw. Both the anteater
and the sloth have many more molars on one side.[22] Another characteristic
of these two animals that the Amazon Indians mention is based on their
mode of digestion. The Indians express this by saying that these two animals
have no anus. Because the anteater has no anus, it must live on ants
(otherwise it would be able to eat larger creatures). The sloth has no anus; it
was plugged up with earth because that creature was constantly farting.[23]
This ambivalence applies analogously also to the guariba monkey. It is not
edible since it must constantly defecate. It has an excessively open anus.
Here it is peculiarities of the mode of digestion which make these animals
conspicuous. Wild cats, finally, are distinguished from the other animals in

---

22 Cf. Romer (1970: 582ff.). Incidentally, in African societies the counterpart to the
anteater, the pangolin, a scaly predator of ants, is also a highly ritualized animal. Cf. Douglas
(1966).

23 See Lévi-Strauss (1968a: 393). That other symbolic elements also play a part in the myths
reported about the sloth will not be disputed here. Here we are concerned only with the position
of this animal in the system of problematized animals.

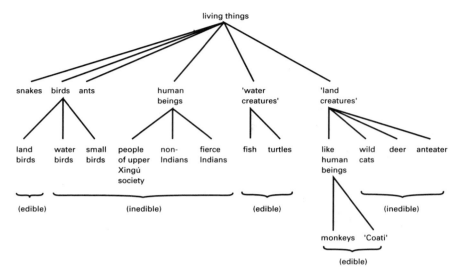

Figure 3.1   *The system of food taboos among the Kalapalo*

that they attack people. They have a special status as predators which distinguishes them from other animals. Snakes likewise belong to a special class of animals. They are felt to be sinister quite simply because of their body shape.

The logic of this system of food taboos will be reconstructed in a double manner. First we shall investigate the classification system of the animal world used by the Kalapalo, who have the most extensive food taboos in the field of interest to us here. An attempt will be made here to reconstruct the internal logic of the system from the nomenclature of the classification categories. Then this logic will be confronted with the attributions which the Amazon Indians bring to the animals classified in this way.

Basso (1972: 630) described the structure of this classification system in an analysis of the Kalapalo food system. Morphological characteristics, ways of eating and habitat are external properties of their classification. The 'living creatures' are organized and named accordingly (see Figure 3.1).

The edible category includes birds that live on land, land animals that are like people and water animals. The inedible category includes human beings, land animals not similar to people, birds that do not live on land and, finally, snakes. Why is it permissible to eat monkey meat? Because, as the Kalapalo say, it is similar to a human being. An animal is edible because it most closely approaches the idea of human-like behaviour. Animals that are like the Kalapalo, that is, peaceful, can be eaten. One parameter of this classification is the similarity to human beings. It applies to birds that live on land (they are also two-legged animals after all) and it applies to monkeys. Fish are negatively defined creatures. They are the opposite of two-legged land animals, namely animals living in water. They are as far removed from people as the other animals are close. Only these two categories of creatures, those very close to people and those very remote from them, are edible. The inedible categories of animals are those that are dissimilar to people, but not so dissimilar that they have nothing human about them (in which case they would become edible again).

This implicit logic makes sense if one analyses the explanations that the Jivaro give for their food taboos (Karsten 1926). The animals most feared by the Jivaro are the jaguars and other members of the feline family, as well as the anaconda, a poisonous giant snake. Both animals are characterized by their ability to kill. The Jivaro express this quality by explaining that both animals are the reincarnation of the spirit of medicine men and conjurers, who are said to be trying to harm or even kill their enemies with the assistance of these animals. This is not a personification of the tiger or the anaconda, but rather an expression that such animals are part of a disorder, that is, part of an antisocial world. Both animals are to be avoided as much as possible.

If one takes the talk of the spirits inhabiting animals as a metaphorical way of expressing a social disorder, as the examination of a 'symbolic disorder' of society, then the prohibition of the other animals also makes sense.[24] Evil spirits are attributed to the inedible animals. These spirits are of a human nature. They use the external form of the deer or the tapir, not so dissimilar to the human being, in order to harm people. Such attributes would never be associated with fish. The animals are connected with evil spirits: the evil spirits of conjurers, of murdered enemies and of women. The connection with the evil spirits attributed to women is most extremely marked among the Yanomamö, who also physically mutilate their women. Obviously, the distinction between edible and inedible draws a symbolic border between society and non-society, between symbolic order and symbolic disorder.

The explanation of the taboo on the anteater and the sloth also makes sense as a metaphoric expression of symbolic disorder. It is an ancient mythical theme that it is the lot of humanity to be either constipated or incontinent. It is part of the order of the world (and this applies equally to animals and humans) that they should have an opening with which they can

---

24 The Jivaro list the following as reasons for the special taboos on the tapir and the deer: 'The tapir is looked upon by the Jivaro with superstitious fear as being the incarnation of the spirit of an evil sorcerer. The animal is supposed to bewitch people by means of whistling sounds that it produces. Its flesh is therefore never eaten. The same in a still higher degree holds good of the deer, which is one of the most dreaded demons (iguanchi) known to the Jivaro. The souls of persons particularly feared in life – for instance, those of enemies killed in battle – may reappear in the shape of a deer. The souls of women are also believed to reincarnate themselves in this timid animal which, in its noiseless movements and the mysterious rapidity with which it disappears in the forest, easily suggests to the Indian mind the idea of a ghost. The Jivaro therefore never eat the flesh of the deer, believing that if they do eat it they will certainly die.' (Karsten 1926: 285). On the indigenous explanations of the significance of the tabooed animals among the Yanomamö cf. Zerries (1983: 160ff.), who reports the creation myths concerning these animals. This, however, is already leading us into issues of the analysis of the morality of food taboos.

excrete what has been eaten, without losing it undigested.[25] Everything that is too closed (constipated) and everything that is too open (having to defecate constantly) is disorder. Animals that do not conform to this order fall out of the system of natural order. One must have nothing to do with them. They must not be eaten.

Critical limit cases of social integration are symbolized with this contrast between too 'closed' and too 'open': the centripetal and centrifugal tendencies of a kinship system. The society is too open if the reciprocal obligations between relatives are too broad. It is too closed if the obligations are demanded directly. Lévi-Strauss (1967) showed how this logic operates in the marriage regulations of simple societies. Marriage systems tend to develop in the direction of generalized exchange of women (marriage with the daughter of the father's sister) since the restricted exchange of women produces only closed systems. The generalized exchange of women opens an order; it makes the integration of many units possible. This system, however, can easily break apart; it can be too open. The exchange of women can collapse, the order can be disrupted. Just as people avoid constipated animals, so do they avoid the logic of the restricted exchange of women.[26] The logic of constipation and diarrhoea is thus a metaphorical mode of conceiving of an order that is not closed, but also not so open that the individuals can no longer relate socially to one another.

Food taboos in Old Testament Judaism

The norms that establish the Jewish food calendar are formulated in two books of the Pentateuch: Leviticus and Deuteronomy. According to these regulations it is forbidden to eat the meat of pigs, hares, camels and the rock badgers.[27] The rule listed for this is that one may not eat animals that only have a cloven hoof or only ruminate; only animals with both features are edible. The taboo on pork has achieved a particular significance. It has become the quintessence of the dietetic regime in the Old Testament. That is why most of the attempted explanations have restricted themselves to this

25 A myth of the Guyana Indians justifies this criterion for normality as follows: 'At one time neither people nor animals had anuses, and they defecated through their mouths. Pu'iito, the anus, slowly walked around, farted in their faces and ran away. The angry animals joined together. They pretended to sleep and when Pu'iito approached one of them and farted as usual, they ran after him, seized him and cut him into pieces. Each animal received his part, larger and smaller, according to the orifice one sees in it today. This is the reason why all living creatures have an anus, without which they would still have to defecate through the mouth today so as not to burst.' (Lévi-Strauss 1968a: 393)

26 The restricted exchange of women is empirically rarer than the generalized type, which can be viewed as a statistical indication for the validity of this interpretation. Cf. Lévi-Strauss (1967) on this diagnosis.

27 A classic interpretation is Noth (1965). Mary Douglas has reopened the debate on these prohibitions (Douglas 1966, 1975: 276–314). For a discussion and critique see Carroll (1977). A brilliant interpretation of the dietary laws of the Jews is found in Soler (1979).

taboo. It will be shown that the restriction to the taboo on pork hampers the explanations of the food taboos in this society and even makes them impossible.

Rationalistic, functionalistic and structuralist explanations have all been given for these prohibitions, especially the taboo on pork. The following analyses will be discussed below: the economic analysis of Harris (1977), functional analyses of varied theoretical provenance and the structural analysis of Douglas (1966).

An economic analysis of Jewish food taboos   The question of why pork is prohibited has moved interpreters for a long time. The orthodox answer is that pigs really are dirty. This answer has little in its favour. There are, after all, many other animals which eat excrement and roll in their own filth, just like pigs. Moses Maimonides, Saladin's court physician in Cairo, developed the first serious non-religious theory in the twelfth century: pork is unhealthy, since insufficiently cooked pork contains trichinae. Thus there is a 'natural' reason to avoid pork. The orthodox opposed this with the argument: if Yahweh had really acted for health reasons, then He would have only forbidden eating insufficiently cooked pork. Yet He prohibited all pork (and, one must add, many other animals as well). So Yahweh must have had other reasons.

Modern scientific explanations pick up on and continue this dispute. In his 'cultural materialist' approach, Harris (1977, 1978) presents an improved version of the Maimonides argument:

1   Pork tastes good and if it is useful to prohibit it, then the sanctions must be set very high; people cannot on their own resist a temptation harmful to them, so there must be high costs at stake in order for a net benefit to result which can explain the prohibition of pork.
2   The ecological habitat in which the ancient Hebrews lived was unsuited to swine husbandry; the 'energy base' of this society was not sufficient to support swine production; the ecological and economic costs would have simply been too high.
3   The function of such norms is ultimately to be able to be distinguished positively from others, to protect a group identity without harming the 'energy base', the ecological adaptability.

The fact that other animals, such as vultures, falcons and shellfish, are also forbidden along with swine causes a certain difficulty for this explanatory strategy. The birds mentioned are insignificant to the nutritional supply. Shellfish were scarcely available in the Hebrew environment and therefore irrelevant. Thus there is nothing irrational from the standpoint of utility in prohibiting these animals as well. It is irrational at first sight to prohibit such a tasty animal as the pig. A utilitarian explanation can explain this apparent irrationality as rational behaviour if it can show that the costs of pork consumption exceed its benefits.

How do these high costs of pork consumption arise? According to Harris, the costs of feeding and caring for swine under the given ecological conditions are too high, compared to the costs of raising cattle, goats or sheep. The Hebrew habitat was semi-arid; pigs are adapted to forests and shaded river banks. They depend on nuts, fruit and the like; they cannot live on grass alone. Above all, however, the pig is poorly adapted to the hot, dry climate in thermodynamic terms: it cannot sweat sufficiently; it has too little hair in its coat to be able to remain in the sun for long periods. That is, it needs either shade or opportunities to get moisture from outside.[28]

Thus the pig was a difficult animal to rear, and this had been the case since about 7000 BC. It was a luxury animal for which shade and puddles had to be provided, an animal that produced no milk, only meat. Besides that, it ate the same things that people ate. Moreover, as the population rose between 7000 and 2000 BC, the forest was largely destroyed, which further increased the costs of swine production. The pig increasingly became an ecological and economic luxury. This appears to explain the genesis of the prohibition on pork. The costs of raising pigs had become too high because of ecological conditions and the demographic development. Yahweh's hearing that pigs are unclean, which led him to prohibit pork, means nothing other than that society understood that it had become too expensive to raise swine under the given conditions. This explanation solves the riddle of the seeming irrationality of this norm. What is more, it also confirms the general assumption that ecological and demographic conditions determine cultural development.

Numerous empirical objections have been raised against this explanation.[29] The central objection is that it is not climatic or topographical conditions that explain the taboo on pork, but rather religious reasons. Under similar conditions, after all, there are taboos on pork in one area and the culinary enjoyment of pork in others. As far as the pig is concerned, it is much more adaptive than Harris assumes. It eats wastes that people can no longer sell. It has a relatively high efficiency (35 per cent) with regard to the relationship between 'food intake' and 'meat production'. All these standpoints tend more to make an antithesis seem plausible. The taboo on pork is ecologically arbitrary. There are no ecological or economic interests that can provide a satisfactory explanation for the existence of this taboo.

A functional analysis of Jewish food taboos   The fact that the taboo on pork is not sufficiently determined by ecology makes it necessary to introduce additional variables to determine the 'adaptation value' of this taboo. If it is

---

28 This is the reason for wallowing: the warmer it gets, the more often pigs must wallow in a damp medium and, of course, the dirtier they become.

29 Cf. Diener & Robkin (1978: 496ff.). This discussion does nothing other in terms of the history of theory than reproduce the thesis of the early Durkheim (the Durkheim of the division of labour). The critique which follows on that is also found in its essentials in the later Durkheim, that is, the Durkheim of the *Elementary Structures of Religious Life* (Durkheim 1968[1912]).

not the costs of food production, then it is social (and thus sometimes non-rational) reasons that result in adherence to a taboo (no matter how it may have originated). That is the starting point of a functional analysis.

A historically specific context serves as the starting point for a functional analysis of the food taboos in Old Testament Judaism: the distinction between clean and unclean meat coincides with the end of the Egyptian captivity of the Jews and the beginning of an independent history of their own, with the transition from a natural order of independent nomadism destroyed in captivity to a desired, politically based order (Kippenberg 1977: 313ff.). This political order was precarious, considering the permanent threat from more powerful peoples (Egyptians, Persians, Greeks, Romans). Maintaining a Jewish identity under those conditions became the central problem of the reproduction of a governmental order. On the level of cultural symbolizations, this permanently-threatened collective identity leads to a special emphasis of the difference between clean and unclean. Animals labelled unclean receive a special significance and are therefore tabooed. The tabooed animals represent enemies threatening the collective identity of Judaism.[30]

This explanation gains plausibility when one compares Jewish history to that of Mesopotamia and Egypt. In those societies there are no prominent taboo norms that ascribe such a central position to ideas of purity as are characteristic of Judaism.[31] Those societies were expansive, as is understandable from their history; they did not confront the problem of self-preservation as a collective in the way Jewish society did. Their external boundaries are indistinct. Relations with groups on the boundaries of the empire could only be useful, whether for the purpose of expanding the empire or as a bulwark against even more remote enemies. The mixture of belonging and not belonging was thus socially integrative. Hence the difference between purity and impurity becomes insignificant; there is no functional reference for such distinctions.

A test case for such a theory is the taboo on pork in Islam and the relaxation of the taboo on pork in Christianity (Diener & Robkin 1978: 504ff.). Islam and Yahwism are similar in their beginnings. The origin of the state on the Arabian peninsula takes place under conditions analogous to the emergence of a state in ancient Palestine. A series of nomadic groups, subjected to foreign tribes for a time, organizes itself in an autonomous political unit. That implies a clear differentiation against the outside. The clear differentiation, codified institutionally by the distinction

---

30 For an excellent functionalist interpretation along such lines see Davies (1977). This explanation follows the classical functionalist schema of social differentiation and the corresponding cultural transformation. It leaves unanswered, however, how this correspondence arises. On this theoretical and methodological issue see particularly Luhmann (1980, 1981).

31 One need only think of the numerous animal divinities in Egypt and Mesopotamia. For a survey, see Müller (1983).

between the faithful and the unfaithful, between those who follow Mohammed and the others, leads to the adoption by Mohammed of certain things from the Jewish tradition, particularly – this is the thesis – the emphasis on classificatory purity regulations. The fact that Mohammed also pursued an anti-Jewish policy (making Mecca the centre of the faith rather than Jerusalem) is not incompatible with this. With the emergence of a politically organized society, in both cases the world-view is reorganized in a way that the taboo on pork now fits into.

Why then is the taboo on pork not continued in the Christian tradition, apart from a few exceptions? The explanation lies in the different manner of continuing political history. Christianity first became a political institution inside the already established Roman Empire. It did not, therefore, need to lay down rigid borders against the outside, but rather to keep borders open. That resulted particularly from the cultural self-definition of Christians after the Pauline turning point. The decisive difference lay in the fact that even heathens could become Christians. Purity criteria had become dysfunctional. The impurity of the pig no longer had to lead to a taboo. It led instead to indifference.

The central significance of the taboo on pork for Jewish identity was fortified to the extent the political existence of the Jewish people was called into question. In that way, the taboo on pork received a historical and political significance at the time of the Greek conquest and the revolt of the Maccabees. The consumption of pork was used at that time as a test of loyalty to the Greek masters. For the first time, one of the many Jewish dietary prohibitions became a central criterion of identity: being a Jew meant not eating pork (Douglas 1973: 60f.). Here pork becomes the means to the end of calling foreign domination into question. The taboo on pork received the significance at that time of justifying the special nature of the Jewish people, its unwillingness to submit to other peoples, and was thus the basis for a specific relationship of Israel to neighbouring peoples. Internally these taboos also served an integrative function, namely, protecting the power of a priest class (and the kingdom allied with it) against heretical tendencies in the people.[32] The foundation for the power of the priests is precisely their function of supervising the following of the taboos and also of testing the meat to be eaten for purity. That places them at the centre of a system of social control.

According to the functionalist explanatory logic, pork is not prohibited because it is maladaptive. It is prohibited on the one hand because the others eat it, because it serves to delimit a collective identity against the outside. Forbidding it also creates a medium which makes the preservation of the power structures in society possible. Food taboos stabilize a collective

---

32 This aspect applies particularly to societies organized as states. In them food taboos exercise an eminent control function. The priestly control over what the people eat and when they eat or fast is among the elementary forms of political and social control.

identity and simultaneously reproduce social power. They protect the reproduction of political dominance.

A structural analysis of Jewish food taboos The need for delimitation against the outside does not explain the Jewish food taboos sufficiently. Above all, it does not explain why the pig and not some other animal was suited to this purpose. The structuralist answer to the question of explaining the taboo on pork is that the anomaly of the animal in the classification system of animals is what singled out the pig and predestined it for functions like those mentioned above. To answer in this way is to occupy a methodological view opposed to the functionalist perspective; for this means that one has to become involved with descriptions and explanations, with the form of the cognitive organization of the world. One must first of all attempt to understand, why Yahweh forbade pigs and one must take the explanations of the rabbis regarding Yahweh's motives seriously.[33]

To what extent does the pig appear particularly anomalous in the interpretations of the rabbis? Why does the pig appear as a monster in the ancient Hebraic classification system?[34] In Leviticus 11 the pig is forbidden along with the hare, the camel and the rock badger. What these animals have in common is that they either have cloven hooves or they ruminate, but they do not have both features at once. Thus they do not fit into the classificatory subsystem of the ruminants. Cattle, sheep and goats have cloven hooves and ruminate. The underlying rule is: a clean animal must have all necessary criteria of its class; otherwise it is revolting and unclean. This rule also applies to the mode of locomotion: only those animals are clean which have the appropriate characteristics for movement in their habitat: fins in water, wings in the air, four feet on land. Animals that live in water without fins or that have wings but do not live in the air are anomalous. Animals are anomalous if they live on land and have many feet or no feet at all. Animals that are associated with the wrong element (waterfowl, for instance) are anomalous. Finally, animals must be complete, that is, they must possess skin, feet and arms. For fish, this means that they must possess fins and scales. Therefore, all molluscs and shellfish are unclean. Also unclean are worms (because they have no feet) and centipedes, because they have either no feet or too many feet, depending on how one views it. The fundamental principle of this classification system of clean and unclean foods has the function of defining a cognitive order of the world. The structure of this classification system can be represented in a simplified way as shown in Figure 3.2.

In the classification of the animal world, only a few animals appear to be

---

33 That is to say, one must not consider the rabbis mere fools. One must instead make their perspective the starting point of a more adequate explanation attempt.

34 In answering this question we refer back to the analyses and interpretations of Davies (1977), Carroll (1977) and Soler (1979).

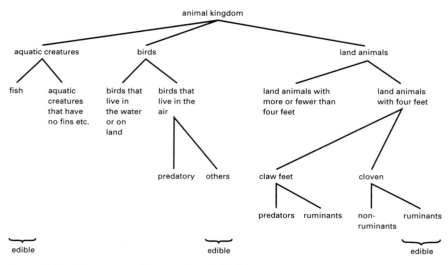

Figure 3.2   *The system of food taboos in Judaism*

edible. Their edibility is constituted by the fact that they belong to clean classes. Land animals that have cloven hooves and ruminate are clean. Birds that live in the air and are not predators (that is, do not have talons) are clean. Water animals are clean if they live only in the water and have fins (caudal, pectoral and dorsal). All these animals are suitable for the table. Among the clean animals there is furthermore the distinction between the animals that are suited for religious sacrifices and those that are only good for eating. The cleanest of the clean animals among the birds are turtle doves, doves and sparrows (Douglas 1975: 264), and among the land animals the cleanest are the first-born of domesticated cattle, goats and sheep. These animals symbolize domesticity (which is why domesticated animals and not fish are sacrificed) and peacefulness (the Assyrians, by contrast, sacrificed wild animals).

The social logic of this classification[35] becomes visible when one reads this classificatory system as a social classification:

1   Shunned animals are unpeaceful (like the hostile neighbours).
2   Edible animals are not predatory (like adherents to the same law), which does not mean that they are peaceful.
3   Sacred animals are domestic and peaceful (like the Levis, the holy representatives of Yahweh).

Thus it is possible to construct parallel series between inedible, edible and sacrificial animals on the one hand, and classes of people on the other (see Figure 3.3).

---

35 The stimulus for constructing the connection between the logic of the classification and the social classification of people comes from Leach (1964). Bourdieu has expanded this explanation strategy to the sociological analysis of modern societies (Bourdieu 1980, 1984b).

Social classification of people	Levis	clean people	unclean people
	first-born Jews	Jews as chosen people	non-Jews
Edibility of animals	sacrificial animals	edible animals	inedible animals

Figure 3.3 *The social classification of the animals in ancient Judaism*

The classificatory logic for animals is a means of constructing the classificatory logic for the social sphere. In this view, animals are a means of conceiving of society. The classification of the animals allows the structuring of the social space. It still remains an open question, however, why the pig received a prominent role in the system of food taboos. In order to understand a special taboo, such as the taboo on pork, one must have understood the entire system. If one has understood the system, then one sees that the pig represents a particular anomaly in the classification. The pig crosses the boundaries of a taxonomic class; it belongs half to one class and half to another. And this crossing of boundaries is what makes it so offensive.

On the background of the historical experience of this society we can now understand why violations of classificatory boundaries can become significant. The condition that cognitive anomalies are foreseen in the symbolic order of a society must be joined by the condition that boundary violations endanger that society. It is part of the negative historical experience of the Jewish people that its boundaries, objective as well as symbolic, have always been endangered. Old Testament society gives positive value to perfect categories, categories that precisely divide what belongs and what does not. A precise boundary, which presumes a rigid collective identity, cannot permit something both to belong and not to belong.[36] The pig's classificatory anomaly, deriving from the logic of the culture, is therefore the prerequisite for the fact that the taboo on pork was able to achieve such a central historical and political significance in the context of Jewish society.

Food taboos in modern societies

Modern European societies, just like others, have a number of taboos. Prominent among these are the taboos on horse, cat and dog meat. The taboo on dog meat, in particular, distinguishes European culture from cultures in the Asian-Pacific area, which consider dog meat a delicacy

---

36 This can be shown particularly well by the example of the marriage rules of the ancient Israelites. It was permitted to marry female prisoners of war from distant peoples, but it was problematic to join in matrimony with half-blooded Israelites. And the pig is just as much a semi-belonger. It is the only one of the four explicitly prohibited animals that has cloven hooves, whereby it almost belongs to the class of ruminants. This makes the pig particularly repulsive.

(Ishige 1977). The explanation for this difference is obvious. Because of the pastoral tradition in Europe, which did not exist in the Asian-Pacific countries, the dog became man's 'friend', an attitude which is foreign to non-pastoral cultures. The inverse of the prohibition on horse, cat and dog meat is the high valuation given to beef and pork. Even modern culture seems to continue having symbolic forms that cannot be adequately explained in terms of social structure, as an expression, for instance, of strata-specific nutritional habits (Herpin 1980; Ferber 1980; Grignon & Grignon 1980). Associated with this is the hypothesis that modern food rules also presume a symbolic order, the clarification of which makes it possible to see how animals are valued and how this determines their edibility.[37]

Despite all the disenchantment in the modern world, therefore, modern European culture continues to have taboos on meat which set limits to the instrumentalization of the meat of animals. The subsequent analysis of the food taboos specific to modern European culture permits us to draw conclusions on the cultural certitudes in which the process of 'moderniz-ation' is refracted. Here one should look for the bases of that which we today call the 'reenchantment of the world'.

An economic analysis of modern food taboos If things went according to the logic of modern utilization rationality, then the modern food taboos would be only an increasingly superfluous superstructure over the rules according to which people eat what is made available through the development of productive forces by means of animal husbandry. What counts is the exchange value of animals; it determines their edibility. Those animals which are 'still' tabooed are also meaningless in economic terms. Dogs, for instance, simply have an excessively unfavourable relation between protein input and protein output. Those animals considered optimally suitable in economic terms, by contrast, become part of the utilization process which is regulated by way of the market (cyclical changes in pig prices) or the state (farming subsidies).[38]

Even when this system runs up against ecological and psychological limits (for instance, in the wake of the increasing industrialization of meat production), the economic system reacts rationally. The trend is increasingly

---

37 This symbolic order of the consumptive appropriation of nature is increasingly expanded in the modern era. The taboos on animals are joined by the taboo on other forms of appropriation of nature: on those substances that intoxicate and ruin discipline. Taboo norms are extended from 'meat' to 'drugs'. This is characteristic of a culture that rewards achievement and punishes intoxication, that rewards rationality and frowns on irrationality. Such additional taboos include for instance the tabooing of drugs as 'narcotics', in contrast to the non-tabooed drugs 'tobacco' and 'alcohol'. Cf. Schivelbusch (1980: 235ff.) as well as Hess (1987). One can understand this as the dialectic of enchantment: disenchantment goes hand in hand with an increasing enchantment.

38 Typical of this logic of utilization is the expansion of pork production. The pig is in fact best suited for industrial meat production. This, however, presumes that the pig – as in Europe – is not tabooed.

to utilize animals with the next-best relation of protein input to protein output, such as lamb or game. Such an economic theory must assert that modern food taboos which contradict this rule (the taboo on horse meat, perhaps) are simply traditional relics from a time when economic circumstances were such that the taboo made sense. In the context of a modern culture which makes instrumental rationality its fundamental cultural orientation, however, these taboos lose meaning. The taboo on horse meat and dog meat is only a contingent boundary condition for modern capitalistic agricultural production (Sahlins 1976). The logic of capitalistic production increasingly reshapes the symbolic logic manifest in food taboos. It universalizes the logic of maximizing the appropriation of nature. The rationality of capitalistic production is only restricted by taboos, but not determined by them. The taboo on horse meat is a case that argues for the assumption of a restrictive role for such a symbolic logic. The horse is being increasingly utilized because it is suitable for eating. This increasingly causes the taboo to disintegrate. The logic of utilization pushes aside those relics of taboos that hinder it excessively.

Empirical evidence alone contradicts this image of a society maximizing collective utility (Sahlins 1976: 171f.). An outsider, particularly one from the Pacific area, who studied daily life in the Western world would certainly be struck by the numerous cats and dogs (as well as other animals) filling the streets of the cities, fouling the pavements, climbing on to chairs, climbing into bed with people and sharing family meals. The most surprising phenomenon to him or her, however, might well be that they are not eaten. What sacred cows are to the Indians, dogs and cats are to Western culture. They stand for a conviction that structures everyday life. This example shows that animals which are not eaten have a use value. Even in modern society, the eating of animals is tied to a symbolic logic that gives animals a social significance.[39] The form of appropriating the animal kingdom by humanity will remain incomprehensible so long as the symbolic logic of social construction is not understood.[40]

A functional analysis of modern food taboos   As the modernization of society proceeds, food taboos lose their social function. A functional analysis of modern food taboos must therefore cite specifically 'modern' functional reference points that can reveal the contribution of food taboos to the reproduction of modern society. A first such point is the symbolic

---

39 An excellent analysis of this logic and its development in modern culture is found in Rittvo's analysis of the English discourse on animals. See Rittvo (1989).

40 The argument that capitalist production destroys this symbolic logic and replaces it with its own logic of utilization, is an assumption that overestimates the economic logic. In particular, it causes the critique of the appropriation of nature to focus on the economic logic and thereby systematically overlook the irrationality of symbolic logics (which are no more immune than is the economic logic). Not every 'Green' is rational. And not every economic viewpoint is irrational.

representation and cultural reproduction of the model of equality which distinguishes the organizing principle of modern societies from that of traditional societies. When everyone becomes equal in the capitalistic economy and in the eyes of the modern state (without of course receiving the same things), a specifically modern problem of the reproduction of differences arises. The problem is that society must act as if it is treating all of its members equally. Stabilizing this systematic deception (this 'as if') is the central ideological function of modern symbolic orders.

This precipitates an extensive transformation of the culinary milieu. Its rules must fulfil an ideological function that is decoupled from conventional religious traditions. Food taboos lose their function of institutionalizing a hierarchical order (and the associated primarily vertical differentiation). They now draw boundaries around that region of the animal kingdom in which the animals may be eaten by anyone, without reservations. Animals now serve 'conspicuous consumption' (Veblen 1953[1899]). Outside those boundaries, that is, in that part of the animal kingdom in which animals may be eaten only with reservations, food taboos serve a 'conspicuous non-consumption'. Here an interaction with animals arises which is based on the interaction with people.

Food taboos thus have the function of symbolizing a functional differentiation as well as enabling and reproducing the egalitarian competition of the members of modern society. The social function of modern food taboos thus consists in upholding distinctions. Modern people are what they eat. And if they wish to be something special, this can be accomplished by highly individualized eating habits. The earlier rise of restaurants in cities (Aron 1973; Mennell 1985) and the recent formation of a gastronomic culture through the *Larousse gastronomique* or the *Guide Michelin* are phenomena that build upon this modern form of appropriating nature. Each person can eat in his own way and thus increase his cultural capital. Social differences in 'egalitarian' society are being created by means of increasingly differentiated strategies for dealing with the norms that regulate eating.[41]

A second point of reference for a functional analysis of modern food taboos is the external delimitation of modern societies against one another. This can be shown particularly clearly in the national differences between individual modern societies. Thus, national gastronomic cultures of the various modern European societies serve to stabilize external delimitations, to maintain national differences and to protect national identity. That is the function underlying the labelling of the French as 'horse-meat eaters' by Germans. It is also the basis for the negative image of the Italians as people

---

41 This new significance of dietary regulations is connected to the commercialization of nature. If people can no longer differentiate themselves emphatically enough by that which they have or do not have, then the way they eat becomes a criterion for internal delimitations. People have to shift to symbolic strategies. Cf. Bourdieu (1984b).

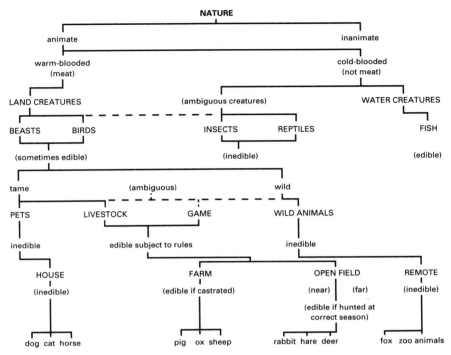

Figure 3.4   *The system of food taboos in modern society (from Leach, 1964: 41)*

who will eat almost anything. Modern food taboos serve as key symbols of identity and difference.[42]

Modern food rules can be explained only insufficiently by these functional relations. The symbolizations underlying these functions and the symbolic logic of modern society which precedes them go uncomprehended. That motivates the attempt at a structural analysis here too.

A structural analysis of modern food taboos   If one wishes to understand the significance of animals from the cognitive order that is projected onto the animal kingdom in modern times, then one must not rely on the scientific classification of nature. Linnaeus does not determine the collective image of nature and the order of the animals. Closer to the structures of everyday life are popular zoological lexica: books that do not contradict the classifications of biological science, but nonetheless introduce those parameters relevant to life experience. The consequence (not the cause) of those parameters is

---

42 That food is among the aspects in which attitudes towards the respective other nationality are expressed most clearly is one of the classical findings of research into national prejudice. What people eat defines their otherness – Italians eat spaghetti and Germans eat sauerkraut.

certain affective structures with respect to the various species. A structural analysis of this practical logic is found in Leach's study in cultural anthropology, which attempts to identify the concepts of an ordering of the animal kingdom that structures everyday life. Leach (1964) reconstructed the system of food taboos in English culture on the basis of the distinctions between 'living creatures' in English.[43] In Figure 3.4, which reproduces that of Leach with slight modifications, the edible and inedible animals are found in the bottom row, graphically grouped together under a line. They are the result of a logical 'derivation' that starts from the concept of nature and arrives at the identification of inedible animals by way of conceptual dichotomies.

Insects and reptiles are not edible (with certain exceptions resulting from the recent exoticizing of European cuisine). Among the edible quadrupeds there are restrictions with regard to general edibility. Domestic animals which are closest to people in their capacity as 'pets' cannot be eaten. Predators must likewise not be eaten. Fish, birds and quadrupeds are edible under certain conditions. Domestic animals that are not pets can be eaten, as well as animals other than predators that live in the wild. Thus the edible animals are those that occupy an intermediate position between those closest to human beings and the predators. The pig, for instance, is a stall animal and not a pet, while the horse or goat is much closer to people. The field hare is edible because it lives in the wild, but the fox as a predatory animal living in the wild is taboo.

In order to identify the structure of this system, Leach attempted to explain food taboos by the proximity or remoteness of the respective animals from human beings. Animals closest to people are prohibited, as are those furthest from human beings. This explanation makes an explicit normative assumption, an anthropomorphic one: the animal kingdom is classified from the reference point of a self; near and far are conceptualized relative to a self.

Why are predators the most remote from the self? As already mentioned above, predators are among the universally tabooed (or shunned) animals. Predators are defined as very remote from the self, and as a 'non-self' in the extreme case. They are distinguished by being 'inhuman' in a specific sense. The 'close' animals are pets or those which have an affective significance for people. In this respect they are very human, that is, related by nature to the self. Such an interpretation remains arbitrary, however, so long as it cannot be related to interpretations by the agents themselves. Predators (and in our case that encompasses mainly martens, foxes and wolves) are animals that kill. In fairy tales and fables these animals are characterized as killers that must be kept away from society (whether by tricks or by force). As in other

---

43 Leach's analysis of the anthropological aspects of language starts from the connection between animal categories and cursing (Leach 1964). Cursing can be considered a way of expressing distance, the most extreme form of which would then be the taboo.

cultures, the modern myths that give predators a significance pick up on their bestial nature, which is opposed to that of human beings. Domestic animals that are an immediate part of households are treated, on the other hand, as interaction partners of humans (this goes for the dog to the cat to the horse; goats are a borderline case, although here too the fairy tales tend more to emphasize the human side). This 'interactive' relationship to humans is cited in modern stories as being characteristic of their nature. An interpretation of these animals as 'close to people' is thus backed up by the perspective of the agents themselves.

If one looks for the parameter in this classification logic that distinguishes the edible from the inedible animals, then it must be a common denominator for domestic animals that are close to us and for predators. This parameter of a binary schematism of edible/inedible can be connected to the dichotomy similar/dissimilar. Pets and predators are the most similar to humans in the sense of being either interaction partners or hunters and carnivores. Farm animals and non-predators living in the wild are most dissimilar to people because they are herbivores and objects, whether of human care or of the hunger of predators. This parameter separates those animals which, like people, are subjects from those which are objects, unlike people. While close animals and predators take on the character of subjects for various reasons (they are active creatures), the other animals become objects that are subordinate to humans. Thus they are 'objectively' suited to be the object of human culinary needs.

The modern practical taxonomies that distinguish the edible from the inedible distinguish between those animals that are very close to or very far from people and those that are neither close nor far. That is, they define a (cognitively neutralized) category of animals that are viewed instrumentally, as objects of human action (as meat). Secondly, they define a category of animals that are taboo. This includes, first, pets and close domestic animals, which are viewed as interaction partners of people. It also includes those animals one avoids, which are not pursued so long as they do not pursue people. The fairy tales and fables of wolves and foxes deal with precisely this type of negative reciprocity. Not being permitted to eat certain animals is connected, first of all, with the fact that they are viewed as if they were people. These are the animals that are not simply used, but instead earn a special kind of sympathy. Secondly, the prohibition on eating certain animals is connected with the fact that they are to be left in the state of nature. 'Wild' animals are the other world, which becomes an object of curiosity (one need refer here only to the invention of zoological gardens) or childish fright. People do not eat that which they admire, conquer or spin yarns about.

This classificatory order (as described by Leach 1964: 43f.) can be presented in graphical form (see Figure 3.5). This classification assures the edibility of that part of the animal kingdom which largely differs from human beings. All the animals which are not so remote represent cognitive anomalies. In what sense are dogs, horses, cats, donkeys and the like

distance to the self	pets	livestock (farm animals)	game (field animals)	wild animals
food taboos	+	-	-	+

Figure 3.5   *The classification of animals in modern society*

anomalous? They are anomalous because they are situated at the boundary between animal and human, the boundary which makes the world of human beings different from that of animals. That these animals are like interaction partners with us puts them in a precarious position. And pets endanger this difference more than any others. Why then are predators taboo? Because they act analogously to people, namely, they make themselves master over other animals and kill them. In that sense they threaten the privilege of human beings to make the environment subject to themselves. They violate the boundary between animal and human in a different way. This boundary is respected in the intermediate categories of animals. They do not hamper the free availability of animals for human needs. This means that the food taboos can be reversed. Eating (permitted) animals becomes a culinary delight. Such animals become means for the culinary appropriation of nature. Our classificatory system permits us to make these 'intermediate' animals the object of culinary enjoyment. The edible animal receives a use value that results from its symbolic suitability for culinary use.

An analogous series of norms exists on the level of marriage regulations (Leach 1964), which indicates that the logic for classifying the animals is a means for representing the logic of the society. Those who are too close to a person, that is, to the self, are taboo as marriage partners (incest taboo). Those who are further away from the self, or are unlike it, are potential marriage partners. These include sufficiently distant relations (cousins) as well as neighbours in general. Difficulties arise in interpreting marriage rules with respect to outsiders. The criterion of excessive geographical or cultural distance as a disqualifier has been relativized as a result of increasing modernization to such a degree that the differentiation *vis-à-vis* an outsider is scarcely permitted anymore.[44] The differences shrink to one fundamental difference: that between near and far, between familiar and unfamiliar.[45]

Even in the modern era, there is a symbolic logic which determines the practical action of people prior to any ethic or any calculation of utility. It

---

44 Where differences can still be experienced is more likely the result of not knowing exactly whether the outsider is a relative or not. The outsider can potentially always be a relative; there is no shared social context, which could decide this question. An indicator of this problem would be modern literary figures such as Brother Medardus in E.T.A. Hoffmann's *Elixiere des Teufels* ('The Devil's Elixirs').

45 This cannot fail to have consequences for the theoretical descriptions of society and the dichotomies that characterize it. Thus the difference between life-world and system seems to belong to the category of distinctions that shrink to exactly the extent the symbolic logic of modern society can explain them.

results from the symbolic social construction of nature and the associated process of constructing a 'natural' order of society. Modernity has not transcended the practical logic attributed to 'primitive' societies. Its symbolic order is interspersed with this practical logic just as much as are those of other societies.

Culinary culture and morality

Normative implications of the structural analysis

The structural analysis of food taboos shows that they can be adequately understood only from the cognitive order on which they are based. The problem remains, however, of why this cognitive order can motivate practical action. The structural analysis of food taboos which Mary Douglas proposes runs up against this problem. She ultimately solves it 'psychologically'. For her, food taboos result from a universal aversion to 'anomalies', from a mental compulsion to produce a cognitive order. This assumption, however, only sidesteps the problem of why cognitive anomalies should be avoided in the first place.[46]

It is natural to want to solve this problem 'psychologically'. The motivation to do what the logic of the symbolic order of society requires appears to be something that society can no longer control. It appears to be a problem of the personality system. In taking this approach, however, structural analysis pulls the ground out from under its own feet. The system of food taboos is based on structures which precede psychological dispositions. This results in a plea against a psychological solution of the problem of the transition from the logic of a symbolic order to the practice of a symbolic order. The alternative is a plea for an elucidation by cultural theory of the structural analyses of symbolic systems.

An explanation of food taboos with the aid of psychological dispositions necessarily gets caught in a tautological circle. Every society – so goes the psychologizing argumentation – has affective problems that result from individual dispositions. This argument implies the assumption that people universally find certain things nauseating, that they are afraid of them. Such a (more or less) universal distaste would then underlie food taboos as well. Psychological explanations proceed, furthermore, from the assumption

---

46 Cf. Douglas (1966). The radical sociological interpretation of symbolic logic, which Douglas is able to demonstrate, consists in defining the contextual conditions of symbolic logic as part of this logic. This leads to defining symbolic logic as practical logic. See the chapter on 'Praxis und Geschichte' in the German original of this volume (Eder 1988).

that, above all, ambivalent feelings towards filth[47] are projected onto natural phenomena that are significant to people, such as foods. Hence the taboo on pork among some peoples has often been interpreted as a psychological distaste towards a dirty animal, specifically, one that eats excrement. The pig symbolizes affective distastes which can be compensated for by according it an anomalous status in nature and deriving a taboo from that.

This theory confuses cause and effect. The pig as such does not produce any emotion. We eat pork, as do other people, even though pigs eat excrement. It is only the ritual relation to the pig and its tabooing which produce a disposition towards fear, and this disposition can then be occupied by general psychological emotional attitudes. Far from being the cause of the tabooing, the emotional fears are only a product of this tabooing.[48] Thus, psychological explanations of food taboos are ultimately based on a tautology: one claims to explain food taboos from psychological dispositions, and yet these dispositions must first be explained in order to make food taboos comprehensible. The emotional attitude towards a tabooed animal is the result, not the basis, of its logical position in a (culturally defined) world order. The animals which may not be eaten produce emotional attitudes only secondarily.

Such a tautological false conclusion also underlies the idea of a general ability to empathize with animals – as suggested by Rousseau and Bentham, the capacity for 'compassion'.[49] This emotionally determined relationship to animals makes eating the meat of these animals a problem. Any meat that is eaten, after all, implies the killing of an animal. Killing animals, however, has never been without problems for people. This practice has always been the peg on which an extensive symbolism and regulatory practice were hung. That is why the eating of animals must be regulated and restricted. In the extreme case, it is avoided altogether. Then the problem is solved by the

---

47 Another psychologizing explanation attempts to connect the distaste for the meat of certain animals with the class of phenomena that provoke negative mental reactions. This includes any kind of excrement: urine, semen, menstrual blood, sweat, saliva, shed hair, fingernails and so forth. At times even mother's milk provokes nausea. Yet even these phenomena are subject to a practical logic. As excretions of a person they are border violations of a self. What was previously part of a physical identity has now separated from it. How precarious these border situations between self and non-self are, can be seen on one level of the euphemization strategies: people speak and write of excrement, not shit, and urine, not piss (Leach 1964).

48 Lévi-Strauss applied this critique to the theories that base magic and ritual on fear: 'As affectivity is the most obscure side of man, there has been the constant temptation to resort to it, forgetting that what is refractory to explanation is ipso facto unsuitable for use in explanation.' (Lévi-Strauss 1964c: 69). Anxiety is not a cause; it is 'the way in which man perceives, subjectively and obscurely, an internal disorder. If an intelligible connection exists, then it has to be sought between articulated modes of behavior and structures of disorder, of which the theory has yet to be worked out, and not between behavior and the reflection of unknown phenomena on the screen of sensation' (Lévi-Strauss 1964c: 68).

49 Cf. in particular the works by Singer (1976). It is obvious that the consequence of such reflections can only be vegetarianism.

vegetarian lifestyle. Here too, cause and effect are being confused: compassion with animals is the effect, not the cause, of taboo norms. How far compassion goes, why it is narrow in one case and broader in another, depends on the socially determined relevance of taboo norms. Therefore, far from being a cause of taboos, compassion is a consequence of society, a moral position towards animals which is produced by society.[50]

Yet this argument of a moral attitude towards animals is simultaneously a key to the problem of the collective avoidance of cognitive anomalies. Food taboos have a moral significance, and their motivating power is based on it. A consistent structural analysis must, therefore, go one step further. In the logic of the cognitive classification of animals it must also demonstrate the logic of moral sentiments with regard to animals. Such a structural analysis describes the moral motifs that underlie the symbolic practice of observing food taboos. Observing food taboos is not the result of dispositions that can be explained psychologically. It is the result of collectively valid moral notions that are transported and communicated in the cognitive order of the world. Food taboos are the result of a cognitive order which makes a moral order conceivable. They are a possibility of conceiving of a moral world.[51]

The ability of food taboos to symbolize the logic of moral relationships (the differentiation into near and far, above and below, friend and enemy) has already been alluded to several times. However, that does not sufficiently determine the relationship between the cognitive logic of food taboos and their moral logic. The fundamental question still comes up as to why animals are particularly suited to be means for the moralization of the world. That is why a structural analysis of food taboos cannot restrict itself simply to exhibiting the cognitive relations between the animals that must not be eaten. Rather, the logical relations between the taboo animals simultaneously stand for moral relations. The world of animals (= nature) is always a moral world and one which at the same time can serve as a metaphor for the world of people (= society). The metaphorical relationship between nature and society is a means for reflecting society back onto

---

50 Cultural materialism (Harris 1979) works primarily with a pseudo-exactness. This becomes possible because people always make their arguments based on the result of social processes. If one always knows the results in advance, then the result of a theoretical construction can never be false. One can then only point out that the theory is insufficiently complex. One can react to this in turn with the 'refinement' of the theory (that is, by additional hypotheses). The theory itself can never be called into question. It is also possible to argue analogously against the psychologizing assumptions which are characteristic of the 'cultural-materialist theories'. They require improbable assumptions on the nature of human beings. They start from a rational model of strategic action. Here it must be explained sociologically under what (very special!) conditions strategic action is possible at all. Any strategic action is tied to practical logic, which is peculiar to the context of action.

51 An excellent analysis in these terms is found in Walens (1981: 67ff., 97ff.). The modern environmental debate is beginning to open this connection to reflection. It identifies the interaction with nature as social praxis and the description of nature as the focus on a societal relationship with nature. On this, see particularly Chapter 2 in this volume.

nature. A moral significance is given to natural differences. The moral order characteristic of the society is projected back onto the state of nature. Food taboos stand for a model of the appropriate relationships between individuals and groups. The classification of the animal world into edible and inedible is also based on the idea of a correct order of society.

The model of a moral order contained in the classificatory order of the animals can be reconstructed with the assistance of assumptions that return to the purported moral 'quality' of animals. The following two assumptions can be cited as keys to the reconstruction of this moral order:

1   The taboo on the meat of predators is connected to the problem of killing. Predators are taboo because they are killers themselves. Killing is one of those actions which require special ritual and symbolic control, treatment and justification. Predators do not fit into a cultural order which seeks to regulate killing. Eating such animals implies in a certain sense incorporating disorder and endangers the socio-cultural distance between people and nature.
2   The taboos on non-predators share the quality that the tabooed animals belong to a culturally defined world and contradict it at the same time. Animals are taboo if they contradict an order that people have projected onto nature. For instance, they are taboo if they call an order of creation into question. They are also taboo if they are similar to people in any respect, that is, if they transgress the cultural definition of the boundaries between the human and the animal orders.

The first assumption refers to the taboo on eating the meat of predators, and the second to the taboo on eating the meat of certain animals which are not predators. The metaphorical relationship that results from these assumptions is that between hunting/killing nature on the one hand and peaceable nature on the other. The key to explaining the moral logic of food taboos is found in these projections of morality onto nature. They justify the way these societies leave behind the state of nature and enter into society. They are found in particularly informative form in creation myths which narrate and explain the transition from nature to culture. Theories on the origin of a moral order in the world are also found in these myths. The morality which is the basis for food taboos is formulated there. In the creation myths we can reconstruct the practical logic which explains why people obey the cognitive logic of symbolic orders. One need only decipher this logic in the myths.[52]

---

52 That does not mean that social theory would now be reduced to myth analysis. The point is instead to attempt to decipher the rational and irrational elements in the explanations which are supplied in the modern era for the validity of various types of practical logic. This is the opposite of a mythologizing of modernity. This is demythologizing by means of 'mythological analysis' of social theory.

A structural analysis of morality

Food taboos are obviously based on a practical logic and they are particularly emphatic, in comparison to other norms. They regulate moral behaviour and they can only do that by virtue of the morality already present in them. All food taboos contain an elementary moral problem, the problem of killing. In the relationship to nature, and particularly in the relationship to the animals that are to be eaten, the problem of killing is inescapable. This problem of killing can be projected into nature; then nature appears as a world in which people, 'like animals', are permanently engaged in a struggle of all against all. Society must keep its distance from this nature. Or one can assume a 'fall from grace' in which the paradisiacal coexistence of the animals among themselves and with people has been destroyed by the killing of an Other; then coexistence must be produced all over again in society. In order to solve the problem of killing, explanations and justifications for killing are sought in the form of theories of the transition from nature to culture. Every society has interpretations and explanations for how it evolved into society from the state of nature. And it has explanations for why people are allowed to kill animals in society.

We shall attempt in the following sections to reconstruct the forms for examining the moral problem of death on the examples of the creation myths of the Jivaro, the ancient Hebrews and modern Europeans. In a continuation of the structural analysis of food taboos, it will be shown that a specific moral significance is inherent in the cognitive constructions of nature – one which makes it possible to grasp the practical significance of cognitive anomalies theoretically.

Myths of creation among the Jivaro   The idea of a right and good order among the Jivaro is expressed in those myths which narrate the forgotten past in which people and animals were still one. Animals were once gifted with human speech, had human emotions and human intelligence, were organized in tribes, made war against one another and held victory celebrations as the Jivaro still do (Karsten 1926: 284). This idea of a time in which all living creatures were people is a backwards projection of the world the Jivaro define as the morally good world into a paradisiacal past. In this world, animals were not eaten, nor did animals eat people. Paradise is rather a state of natural harmony among all living creatures. This paradisiacal past does not get lost in the transition to culture. The Jivaro denote the connection between humans and animals as 'mana', a physical force that is inherent in all creatures.

This mana was morally differentiated in the transition from nature to culture. There is good and evil mana. Predators have evil mana because they kill. The tapirs and the deer have evil mana because they act like those medicine men who wish to do evil to people with their secretive behaviour. That is why these animals are tabooed. By contrast, those animals which share a feature with (good) people have good mana. These are animals that most closely conform to the human order. The Kalapalo, for instance, eat (besides fish) only those land animals which they themselves classify as 'similar to people' (mainly monkeys, which also have a morphological similarity to people).[53] The tabooed animals are, therefore, those which do not fit into a conception of natural harmony. In their own way, they disrupt the order which once existed, and humankind can only maintain this order by avoiding these 'disorderly' animals. On the other hand a person can eat those animals with which he or she can live in natural harmony.

Now a problem arises, namely the contradictory demand on people of conceiving a unity with animals on the one hand (by excluding the tabooed animals), while on the other hand eating the non-tabooed animals, which first implies killing them. Killing animals destroys that cultural order which was made possible by the distinction between good and evil mana. Not the eating of meat, but rather the associated shedding of blood is what brings the new disorder into the world. This results from the notion that the life which is characteristic of animals resides in their blood rather than in their flesh; the 'soul' of the animal is in its blood. Taking blood means taking life. This is seen most clearly in those situations where people come into contact with blood, whether in the case of bloodshed in war or in the case of menstrual blood: both require purification rituals in which the blood is once again 'washed free' so that the person can become clean again and no longer be taboo (Karsten 1926: 482).

Because of these implications of bloodshed, the Jivaro slaughter domestic animals by strangulation. These animals are sometimes subjected to a ritual in which they are begged for forgiveness for the fact that they are about to be killed. The Bororo have developed the ritualization of the killing of hunted animals most extensively. They beg every captured animal or fish for forgiveness before they kill it. This ritual treatment of the edible animals ensures that killing for purposes of food does not destroy the natural order of the world which was instituted with the transition from the state of nature to society.

Myths of creation among the ancient Hebrews   For ancient Judaism, as for the Jivaro, the idea of a right and good order also contains the idea of a good relationship with animals. The information on this point is provided particularly by the book of Genesis, which narrates the paradisiacal state and the gradual loss of it. In this tradition, God originally forbade killing without exception. God was life and taking life was tantamount to killing God. For both people and animals, Paradise had a vegetarian character (plants were not considered living things). This order was shattered by

---

53 The Kalapalo draw the limits of this similarity very broadly. The realm of the edible is very limited in this way. The Jivaro and the Yanomamö draw narrower limits, presumably for environmental reasons. The unclean animals are reduced to a few central cases, which represent social disorder.

people. Then came the flood and, after the flood, the new social order.
Killing, and thus the dietary regulations, were reinterpreted. God permitted
Noah to eat any kind of meat, but he forbade the consumption of animal
blood. Blood became the essence of life; it belonged to God. The boundary
between order and disorder, between life and death, was therefore drawn
with the symbolic distinction between blood and flesh (Soler 1979).

The system of dietary regulations of interest here did not originate until
the time of Moses: the distinction between clean and unclean, and thus
between edible and inedible, animals. The commandments God had given
to Noah applied to all people. The commandments he now gave to Moses
applied only to his chosen people, the Hebrews. To the universal separation
between blood and flesh was now added a separation which was distinctive
for a certain people: that between edible and inedible meat. This specifi-
cation of food taboos requires the introduction of additional moral
perspectives on which the new system of food taboos can be built. The
system of food taboos is becoming more complex. The specific feature on
this level of complexity is derived from the linkage of three previously
unconnected structural elements. Here, as in the example of the Jivaro, the
difference in meaning between flesh and blood is constitutive: blood = life,
flesh = death. This difference is confirmed in ritual over and over again.
Eating an animal presupposes the sacrifice of its blood.[54] Only in that way
does the flesh become clean. That is how people escape the law: he who kills
will be killed. But not every type of flesh is clean. A second difference is
added: that between clean and unclean. Now this difference is constructed in
a novel and more complex way. On the basis of the books of Leviticus and
Deuteronomy, it is based on three criteria. Animals are clean: (a) if they
have hooves; (b) if they ruminate; and (c) if they have cloven hooves.

The first criterion quite clearly separates herbivorous animals from
carnivorous ones. Only herbivorous animals are clean. Animals with hooves
cannot take prey. Only animals with claws can capture and eat other
animals. But why are herbivorous animals clean? This follows stringently
from the logic of God's creation, because carnivores and hence carnivorous
animals (including dogs, cats and birds of prey) were not contained in the
plan of creation. The second criterion is rumination. Why this criterion? It is
a reinforcement of the first criterion. Rumination is an unambiguous
criterion that the species in question is indeed herbivorous. It excludes the
pig because the pig does not ruminate. The third criterion, cloven hooves, is
the criterion for domestic animals: cattle, sheep, goats. Why this third
criterion? It is a reinforcement of the second criterion. Ruminants do not
simply eat plants; they even eat them twice. Besides the characteristic
'rumination', the ruminants (sheep and cattle for instance) possess another

---

54 At first this ritual had to take place in the temple of Jerusalem. Later it could be conducted
representatively in every household, which was certainly a way of adapting to society's
becoming more complex.

specific anatomical feature: cloven hooves. This triply protected symbolic system obviously has the purpose of providing optimally precise and restrictive criteria to ensure that these really are herbivorous animals. This additionally excludes the horse, the donkey, the camel and the rock badger.

Why then is the pig specially emphasized? The basis lies in its anomalous status. It belongs among the clean animals according to the third criterion, but not according to the second. So it is both clean and unclean, and according to the logic of cleanliness it is both a herbivore and a carnivore. Thus it slips through the logic of the morally motivated distinction. It endangers the logic of the order which the ancient Hebrews constructed in the mythological reassurance of the transition from nature to culture. The particular distinctive feature of the moral order that was created here and finds its absolute negation in the pig is based on the rule: man must only sacrifice to Yahweh the blood of those animals which are unambiguously herbivorous. This defines a social reality which makes the principle of not killing, symbolized in the primacy of the herbivorous part of the animal kingdom, the moral reference point for that which separates culture from nature.[55]

Modern myths of creation   Modern myths of creation are contained in the theories of a social contract which have determined modern social and political thought since the seventeenth century.[56] They describe a (more or less) fictitious transition from the state of nature to society, which becomes possible by a contract concluded among the participants. The people agree in this contract on a moral order which is valid in the sense that it is binding upon all of them. The consequences that result from making this contract are in turn dependent upon how the condition that is to be overcome by the contract is conceptualized. This state of nature also defines the conditions under which the contract is made.

The idea of a state of nature has been determined by two factors in modern Europe. The first factor has to do with the emerging modern natural science and the second with the emerging capitalistic economy. Since the late seventeenth century, natural scientists have been pointing out the similarities in anatomy and intelligence between people and anthropoid apes. Darwin finally demonstrated the common ancestry of humans and animals. Our relationship with the animal kingdom has become increasingly problematic as a result of these genealogical insights. The Industrial Revolution, on the other hand, has made people increasingly independent of animal labour. The more marginal animals become for the economy, the

---

55 This separates this society for instance from Greek and Roman society, which occupy the other pole of the symbolic organization of society. See Chapter 4 in this volume.

56 Labelling modern theories of the social contract as myths of origination does not mean negating the specific rationality that characterizes these stories. They have become part of the practical discourse which was only separated out in modern times and therefore built by definition as a reflexive construction. Cf. Eder (1986a).

more an empathetic attitude towards them has been able to develop. Like children, animals have become emotional partners.

Since the sixteenth century, these changes have been the triggers for a cultural movement that has reformulated the model of a proper relationship between humans and animals from an anthropological perspective. Animals are viewed like people or – less often – people like animals. The latter characterizes Hobbes's view of the state of nature. Rousseau, by contrast, speaks of a state of nature in which people and animals are of the same type, in which all living creatures are treated equally. The common point of these positions is that animals are no longer conceived of from the perspective of Yahweh, but on the basis of human feelings and sensibilities. The theological argument in favour of animals as part of the order of God's creation is reinterpreted anthropologically in these positions.[57]

One way of 'anthropologizing' the older theological argument is the utilitarian doctrine that the happiness of all those who can feel and suffer ought to be maximized. This anthropologization has established a philosophical tradition that reaches from Bentham all the way to Singer (1976, 1979).[58] The utilitarian tradition articulates a moral sentiment that we can feel with respect to animals, namely that we should not make them suffer. Perhaps the most extensive attempt to ground such a sentiment in moral terms is found in the 'radical egalitarianism' of Singer (1979), who ascribes rights to all sentient creatures and, therefore, condemns not just the mistreatment of animals, but also the killing of them for food. If it is possible for human beings to satisfy their hunger without meat, then eating animals is an action that can no longer be morally justified. It is immoral. This

---

57 An interesting field of modern mythological analysis is to be found in the literature which uses animals in order to describe the world of people. One example is Carroll's *Alice in Wonderland*.

58 The utilitarian position against killing animals has been the most effective position, viewed historically. Bentham gave it the following eloquent justification: 'The day may come when the rest of the animal world may acquire those rights which never could have been with-holden from them but by the hand of tyranny. The French have already discovered that the blackness of the skin is no reason why a human being should be abandoned without redress to the caprice of a tormentor. It may one day come to be recognized that the number of the legs, the villosity of the skin, or the termination of the os sacrum, are reasons equally insufficient for abandoning a sensitive being to the same fate. What else is it that should trace the insuperable line? Is it the faculty of reason, or perhaps the faculty of discourse? But a full-grown horse or dog is beyond comparison a more rational, as well as a more conversable animal, than an infant of a day, or a week, or even a month, old. But suppose they were otherwise, what would it avail? The question is not, Can they reason? nor Can they talk? but, Can they suffer?' (*Introduction to the Principles of Morals and Legislation*, Ch. XVIII, Sec. 1, note; quoted according to Singer 1979: 49f.) Singer worked out this position tending towards an animal ethics (Singer 1976) and attempted to develop it further philosophically (Singer 1979). For criticism of the systematic attempt to combine classical utilitarianism with preferential utilitarianism, cf. Hart (1980). On Singer's practical intentions see his preface to the new edition by Salt (1980). Clark (1977) offers a position avoiding the problems of a utilitarian zoophilia by denying the uniqueness of the human moral status and beginning with a moral community encompassing humanity and the animals.

inversion of the transition from nature to culture manifests a novel form of producing a moral order in the society 'the wrong-way-around'. If people reformulate their relationships on an 'anthropological' basis they will be forced to apply egalitarian principles. That implies conceiving of the difference between humans and animals as the difference between two egalitarian systems. Just as people must treat one another as equals from the moral point of view, so are animals equal among one another. Still at issue is how the difference between these two egalitarian ranks ought to be conceived.

This problem has levelled the way for a new turn of thought. Rather than being anthropologized, the state of nature is made an a priori. Kant made such an attempt by speaking of duties to animals as indirect duties to people. The way one acts towards animals is the way one acts towards people. Kant elaborates this argument using the example of the loyally serving dog whose owner cannot simply kill it, from the standpoint of humanity (not from the standpoint of an obligation to animals, since animals cannot make judgements). This justification of a moral relationship to animals argues from human expectations of the animal. If one expects the animal to relate to people in a quasi-human way, then that results in 'obligations of humanity' *vis-à-vis* the animal. Since animals cannot think and judge, they cannot be ascribed any moral rights *per se*. Those rights do pertain to them to the extent human beings incorporate them into their expectations of the animals.

Respect for animals is dependent in these theories on what we expect from the animals' behaviour. We kill flies and insects with no moral reservations. We are inhibited in doing the same with higher animals, particularly with dogs and cats, and sometimes also with horses, donkeys and goats. We have different expectations of that which is edible. Food taboos are thus a result of a differential construction of 'indirect' duties (as Kant puts it). However, it is insufficient to derive the non-edibility of animals only from the principle of understanding duties to animals as indirect duties to people. It is no coincidence that Kant's justification of a moral treatment of animals (that is, that one cannot just kill them) is elaborated on the example of the dog. Kant's attempt at a justification, therefore, already presupposes a relationship to animals that is regulated culturally in a special way.

The relationship to the part of the animal kingdom defined to be edible (and exploitable) can be rationalized with such a justification of the relationship to nature,[59] because it delegitimates the sacrifice ritual. The consecration of slaughtering has become impossible in modern times. The ritual sacrifice, which sanctified the killing of animals, is replaced by making

---

59 That the Kantian justification can objectively fulfil this function is due to the fact that it no longer remembers its own cultural premises and, instead, traces them back to the a priori conditions of practical reason. Hence it remains indifferent to practical logic. It is not a critique of practical logic, but only a self-critique of practical reason. This does not suffice to grasp the self-legitimation of social praxis.

slaughtering unrecognizable, by the privatization or, better, the de-publicization of slaughtering. Slaughtering of animals is taken back into the slaughterhouses, it is de-publicized to such an extent that the meat lying on the table no longer has anything to do externally with the animal being eaten. The apotheosis of this ritualization of the interaction with animals is the hamburger.

Modernity solves the problem of killing in a new way, by organizing the killing 'professionally' so that non-butchers are no longer affected by it. Making the butcher a professional substitutes for priestly ritualization. 'De-publicizing' the relationship to nature is the complement to the instrumental rationalization of the relationship to nature. The ritual act is demystified into the professional act of the practical distribution and utilization of meat. In this rationalization process of the relationship to nature, the myth of creation is destroyed. Nature is subjugated to society. At the same time, however, the state of nature catches back up with society, objectively in the sense that society reaches the limits of nature, and subjectively in the sense that nature rebels against the instrumentalization of nature in an irrational act of resistance.[60]

A theory of moral evolution

Types of moral evolution

The myths that report on the production or reproduction of a morally regulated world describe an evolutionary learning process. Their object is the social evolution of a societal state. They are not only 'reports' on this evolutionary learning process; they are also theories about this learning process. Myths that tell a story of creation are thus always mythologies that at the same time contain their own (indigenous) theory of social evolution. Each of the three societies discussed above has a mythical account and a mythological theory of the transition from a state of nature to society. The food taboos that receive their explanation and justification in these myths apply to this day in these societies. They are not ground down by natural evolution (that is, because of the development of productive forces or the increase in complexity), but rather by cultural contact and cultural assimilation. Myths of creation are competing, not mutually reinforcing transitions from the state of nature to society.

The transitions will be described theoretically below as forms of special moral evolution. These forms of moral evolution differ in the following

---

60 These cultural definitions supplied the connection points for various types of modern radicalism (Schäfer 1985). The moralization of nature as a 'social nature' is a component of Green protest movements. The juridification of life is an example of a radicalism of the instrumental attitude to nature. And the aestheticizing of nature is part of the basic pattern of romantic escape movements (Schimank 1983; Weiß 1986).

respects: in the degree of differentiation from nature and the corresponding type of social differentiation that they set down, and in the organizational principles of the moral order they generate on this foundation. This also prohibits us from interpreting these special processes of moral evolution as stages of a general moral evolution, that is, in the sense of a universal history.[61] Instead, they are treated equally and with a comparative intention as possible forms of moral evolution.

These forms of special moral evolution can be reduced to three types, each of which has a specific societal relationship to nature as its starting point. These three types are based on the idea of society as (a) a natural order, (b) a hierarchical order, and (c) an egalitarian order. These three types start at differing degrees of differentiation of society away from nature. One can in turn classify these varying degrees of differentiation of society away from nature in an evolutionary way according to their disposition over resources. The theory that results is a theory of the evolutionary increase of power. It describes how societies, that have increased their productive forces and their complexity, have received and then used the opportunity to subjugate other societies and draw them into the process of their own respective form of social evolution. This kind of natural evolution of society virtually rules out the inference of a social evolution of society.

These forms of special moral evolution produce competing models of a moral order. They can be characterized as a savage morality, a holistic morality and an individualistic morality. *Savage morality* is characterized by the tying of culture and society to a natural order which minimizes the evolutionary speed of the increase of social power. Law continues to be tied to 'custom', to conventional ways of life. With the assistance of the natural order, the moral order puts limits on power-based organization of social relationships. The modes of stratificatory and functional differentiation are not differentiated away from the savage morality, but remain bound to it and therefore restricted. *Holistic morality* dominates only where the law can free itself from the conventional context of customs and habits and establish an order beyond a natural order, that is, a supernatural order. It favours, within social evolution, stratificatory differentiation based on the idea of a hierarchical order. *Individualistic morality* survives in societies in which the individual is set free, that is, cut off from traditional bonds (as in the capitalistic economy). That sets functional differentiation free. There is no longer any 'justice', only 'interstices' between fully differentiated systems which steers moral evolution towards more abstract provisions of a social

---

61 This takes up once again the question of the relationship between general evolution and specific evolution. The concept 'evolutionary learning processes' gives a greater significance to the aspect of 'special evolution'. This is connected with follow-on problems for the idea of a 'general evolution' that calls into question the concept of a cognitive developmental logic in general evolution. On this classical distinction in need of correction, see Sahlins & Service (1960).

order. The normative premises of a social order are radically simplified. They are founded on the (fictitious) equality of those who belong to the order. The 'de-hierarchization' of the world, which is connected with the premises of an equal opportunity for participation and involvement, sets free the inherent dynamism of social system formation, especially the mechanism of functional differentiation. Morality is transformed into an abstract procedural moralism (Eder 1986a, 1987). This has accelerated the evolution of modernity into a 'counterfeit' egalitarian order.[62]

These three types of moral evolution produce moral orders which are once again in competition today. They have been 'successful' in different ways within the natural evolution of society characterizing the natural history of society. The most 'powerful', not the 'highest', form of special moral evolution has triumphed in this natural history.[63] The end of the natural history of society (and modern society with its environmental crises seems to announce this) does not imply the victory of the so-far prevalent form of moral evolution. On the contrary, this end of natural history has produced the preconditions for the evolutionary competition of these forms of moral evolution. And the outcome is more open than ever.

Natural order and savage morality The mythological explanation the Jivaro provide for their social order, and for the dietary regime in particular, starts from the notion of a self-evident order of the world present in the nature of things. The connections between animals and people are ultimately based on the conviction that animals are neither better nor worse than people, nor fundamentally different from people; rather, they are like people. This idea of treating animals as if they were people allows them to construct the model of the animal kingdom by analogy to the model of the world of people. The order of this world is therefore equally binding on animals and people. The transition from the state of nature to society is not connected with a breakup of the state of nature. The societal state is characterized instead by the fact that people are prevented from destroying this state of nature.

This idea is diametrically opposed to our own. While, apart from a few relics, we orient our dietary norms today according to whether we can digest meat, whether it is beneficial to our health, the idea underlying savage morality is characterized by the fact that the individual must not sully the 'purity' of the order.[64] Culture and society are upheld by protecting them

---

62 Something analogous goes for the differentiation of a 'professional' knowledge of nature out of the 'savage' systems of knowledge and for the differentiation of 'theoretical' systems of knowledge out of professional knowledge.

63 For further discussion, see Chapter 1 in this volume.

64 Lévi-Strauss formulated this relationship of subject and object world as follows: 'Instead of good manners protecting the inner purity of the subject from the external impurity of creatures and things, as we believe, they serve among savages to protect the purity of creatures and things from the impurity of the subject'. (Lévi-Strauss 1968b: 418f.)

from the subject. The undifferentiated state of nature is upheld in society by institutionalizing a system of taboos and purification rituals. The undifferentiated state of nature is culturally stabilized because the concepts of nature and morality focus on the direct connection with nature. Anyone who violates these rules corresponding to the state of nature destroys the harmony of nature. He departs from the natural order and thus from society. He dies a social death. His spirit remains behind in those animals that are taboo to people. In this way, the order that was called into question in the formation of society is restored.

Hierarchical order and holistic morality   The system of Jewish food taboos is a logical consequence of Yahweh's plan of creation. This plan contains the fundamental moral rule to which His people must submit. Paradise is a primeval world without killing, a world conforming to the plan of the story of creation, that is, a vegetarian world. The way out of Paradise, the transition from the state of nature to society, is a breach with Yahweh's order of creation, that is, mankind's fall from grace. Killing entered the world with this breach. The return to a state of nature has now become impossible. The production of society is no longer related to the protection of a state of nature. The state becomes instead a 'second-best' order.

This second-best order is characterized by the fact that society likewise returns to Yahweh's plan of creation, but now directly rather than derivatively. That does indeed mean the subordination to Yahweh's will. Only this subordination can compensate for the contamination of paradise by mankind. Subordination is connected with a reconstruction of the societal state. The society appears as a logical transformation of the state of nature on which Yahweh's plan of creation is based. This double structure of being simultaneously tied to Yahweh's plan of creation and yet setting up a new society, explains the specific complexity that characterizes the system of food taboos in Old Testament society. Food taboos are a means of reconstructing a universe reconciled with Yahweh. They purify the universe of the contamination by mankind, but they acknowledge at the same time mankind's presumptuousness in taking the right to kill from Yahweh's hand. This solution has become precarious because society is still tied to the state of nature and at the same time seeks to emancipate itself from nature. This ambivalence explains the rigid enforcement of food taboos, which regulate the distance between nature and culture.

The connection between state of nature and society, animals and human beings, sets the 'traditional' type of social evolution in motion. In this social evolution, animals serve to symbolize the differences between people which can form a hierarchy. Clean and unclean animals stand for domination and subjugation, for higher and lower. Animals themselves are incorporated into this hierarchy, specifically as an extension of the hierarchy downward. Animals now become legally responsible, just like people; they too can be sentenced and punished.[65] Not only domestic animals were convicted. Amira's interesting typological findings (1891) show that punishments of animals for murder that were called for by secular tribunals in Europe were restricted to domestic animals (pigs, cattle, horses and the like) and that trials of animals convened by episcopal tribunals for damage to the community were restricted to rats, mice, locusts and similar vermin. The explanation is obvious. Animals that are not under human control, and therefore cannot simply be summoned to court, require the intervention of the Church, applying forms such as exorcism or excommunication.

The examples show that animals are similar to people in a very special way. The animal is like the human being by being subjected to the same law. People treat animals as equals in one very special respect: as part of an order of creation. People and animals are equally subject to this order, but the animals occupy the lowest rank in the order of creation. They are not merely special creatures, they are the lowest-ranking people in the order of creation. They are at the bottom end of the hierarchy that distinguishes society from the state of nature.

Now one can see how savage morality is distinguished from the morality of subordination to a divine plan of creation – a hierarchical morality, that is. In the context of savage morality, the social order was self-evident. The order had to be prized more than the subject. In the new hierarchical model, the subject penetrated into the natural order and, by the standards of savage morality, contaminated it. The paradise, the unbroken unity with nature, can no longer be restored, in contrast to the logic of savage morality. The production of a society presupposes ascribing the social order to an absolute subject outside the empirical subjects, an absolute god. The breakthrough of subjects into history is compensated by the subordination of the subjects beneath the absolute god. There is no longer any self-evident order, only a god-given order, which is conceived of beyond any nature, and is 'supra-natural' in that sense.

Egalitarian order and individualistic morality   The system of modern food taboos is based on the idea of a subject furnished with rights. The system's central features are equal treatment of each individual and the acceptance of

---

65 In Exodus 21:28 one reads for instance: 'If an ox gore a man or a woman, that they die: then the ox shall be surely stoned'. In Leyden a dog that had bitten a child was arrested in 1595; since it did not deny the deed, there was no need for an ordeal; still he was executed by the hangman (Rensch 1973:246). As late as 1906 a dog was sentenced to death in the town of Delemont in Switzerland because he and two men had murdered another man (Evans 1906:334). In the *Süddeutsche Zeitung* (8 May 1980:47) it was reported that in the western Indian city of Ujjai a man had filed charges against a monkey for murdering his wife.

each particular individual as an embodiment of humanity.[66] Animals do not fit into this world. In traditional conceptions of an order of creation the animals still belonged to the social order (albeit as the lowest form of creation). In the modern era the animals lose even this status. They become the environment of the human social order, with which one can interact caringly, exploitatively or aggressively. They become objects to the same extent people seek to make themselves the subject of the society. Animals are no longer subject in the modern era to a divine law that applies equally to people and animals. The animal kingdom is subjected to law in a different way. Animals become legal subjects in the various animal protection laws in the sense that these laws seek to minimize the suffering of animals. This applies equally to animals that serve as pets and to those that are eaten, kept in zoos or serve the pleasure of hunters.

This legal codification of a duty to treat animal life appropriately goes hand in hand with an extension of the right to deal manipulatively with nature.[67] This implies a transition from the legal treatment of animals according to a criminal law applying to all of God's creatures to an administrative treatment of animal life. The first steps toward the juridical management of living nature have already been taken. In a US Supreme Court ruling of 16 June 1980 (*Diamond* v. *Chakrabarty*, US 103), the issue was whether it was possible to patent the discovery or production of a certain micro-organism which is capable of degrading petroleum. The court's positive ruling means expanding the administrative management of nature to living nature. This judgment is the opposite side of the development that attempts to minimize the suffering of animals by legal regulations; it stands for the maximization of the instrumental management of living nature. There is now a juridical management of life which unleashes the manipulation of that life. The artificial nature that human beings are adding to natural nature corresponds to the ideal of a cultural relationship to nature which is no longer with nature but against it (Bonß 1990).

The transition from the state of nature to society experiences a further radicalization in this cultural context.[68] Society is no longer only a 'second-best' order. Nature is also no longer 'preserved' in something supra-natural. Instead, society is the order that breaks with nature and

---

66 Locke, for instance, speaks in his Second Treatise of the 'great and natural Community' (§ 128) that each individual would embody in the ideal case (that is, if human beings were not evil). In contrast to the holistic notion of an order of creation (see the Book of Genesis) in which everyone is assigned his place, here an individualistic universe (Dumont 1970) is constituted, in which everyone is theoretically equal to everyone else.

67 This is the reason for the renewed debate on the old theme of animal rights. For a recent contribution on that issue, see Bosselmann (1986).

68 The actual debate about genetic technology is to be seen in this context. It has brought together the new sub-disciplines of the sociology of technology and the sociology of risk. For an interesting and theoretically relevant discussion, see Bonß (1990) and van den Daele (1993, 1994).

subjugates it. The criterion that separates the human world from nature is reasonability. Reason is a part of society. Unreason belongs to nature. Those who do not fit into the social order are unreasonable; these include animals, but criminals and the insane as well. This separation of reason and unreason makes it possible to make the unreasonable the objects of the reasonable, whether by eating, pampering or shooting the animal representatives of unreason or by locking up and disciplining the human representatives in jails and asylums.

The reasonable subject takes the place of anthropomorphic nature and the absolute god. Society is no longer being constructed because the subject can destroy and contaminate a natural order or violate a supernatural one. Once constructed, society instead serves for the reasonable subject to produce the natural order. The construction of a supernatural representative of social agents, and the assumption that society is preserved by his plan, is broken up in favour of the idea that the social agents themselves determine the 'plan' according to which the society can be produced.

The evolutionary rationality of food taboos

What criteria of rationality can such a theory of moral evolution provide for the problem of the rationality of food taboos? The classical enquiry into the rationality of food taboos cannot be decided quantitatively. There is no connection such as: the fewer food taboos, the more rational the society (with the implication that the decrease in food taboos would be an indicator of the transition from magical to rational ideas). There is no connection such as: the more optimally adapted to the habitat, the more rational the food taboos (with the implication that survival crises cause social self-construction). Both indicators are insufficient. Even magical practices can be rational. And economically optimized practices can be irrational. How then can the rationality or irrationality of food taboos be decided?

First of all, this forces us to introduce the social and cultural context into the rationality issue. People then enquire into the 'ecological rationality' of food taboos.[69] Are the food taboos rational in view of the natural environment of a society? What are the consequences of food taboos for the reproduction of society in nature? Do food taboos destroy this natural environment or do they contribute to its reproduction? Of course, this naturalization of the rationality issue runs the risk of an unrestrained relativism. It comes down to the idea that there are as many criteria for rationality as there are different natural environments. If one does not share the consequences of such a relativism, then one must specify restrictive conditions for rationality. One must conceive of 'ecological rationality'

---

69 On this concept see the introduction to this volume. The concept of 'ecological reason' first signifies only a rational form of adaptation to an environment conceived of as objective and external. The key to a 'critique of ecological reason' is the concept of adaptation.

more narrowly. Two rationality criteria beyond an 'ecological rationality' can be specified: the criterion of successful cooperation and the criterion of successful communication.[70] Cooperation is the reaction to the degree of differentiation away from nature. The further differentiated, the greater the demands placed on the reproduction of cooperation. Food taboos can then be assessed from the standpoint of how they protect or hamper cooperation at a given level of differentiation away from nature. All cooperation is socially constructed by communicative organization and is placed under further demands for rationality. Successful communication given the differentiation from nature is the only rationality criterion left. Food taboos are rational to the extent they enable and protect communication under the conditions of differentiation of society away from nature.

Successful communication produces social relationships without conflict and solves disputes without force and repression. In simple, as well as in traditional and modern societies, we find rationality and irrationality in the sense of successful or failing communication. Revenge is not limited to simple societies. In some advanced countries the penal code still recognizes a logic of revenge. And discursive agreement is not typical of modern societies. It is found just as frequently or just as rarely in the procedures for dispute resolution in simple societies (Nothdurft & Spranz-Fogasy 1986).

The analysis of the food taboos in various societies has shown that in this respect the Jivaro and the ancient Hebrews developed a system that was able to initiate successful communication. This has become rather dubious in modern societies. The analysis of modern food taboos shows that modern culture is based on premises that obstruct such a rationality. The opposition movement against these premises and the changed interaction with animals, as well as the movement against the mere exploitation of nature, show that the rationality issue is undecided. Whether the 'modern experiment' of the radical differentiation of culture and society away from nature is rational has become the core question of highly developed modern societies. It need not be irrational *per se*. It is obvious, however, that the communicative forms that would be appropriate to this experiment have not yet been found. We continue to act as if what we eat had no communicative significance.

---

70 A rationalistic standard for successful cooperation is found in the rational choice approach in sociology (Raub & Voss 1986; Axelrod 1984; Elster 1989). A non-rationalistic concept of cooperation has been developed in the framework of the theory of norm-oriented action (Habermas 1984, 1987; Eder 1985; Miller, M. 1986, 1987). For a rapprochement of the two positions see the discussion in Elster (1991).

4

CARNIVOROUS AND VEGETARIAN CULTURE: TWO MODELS OF THE SYMBOLIC ORGANIZATION OF SOCIETY

The communicative structure of symbolic practice

The ethnographic perspective

Social and cultural anthropology are among the social sciences that have always irritated the self-understanding of the society from which they originated. The study of cultures foreign to us does not simply force us to reflect on the cultural preconditions of the perception of foreign cultures. The alienation effect connected with the study of the 'foreign' (Leiris 1930, 1950) also caused the issue of 'understanding' to be pushed into the centre of methodological self-reflection at an early date (Kippenberg & Luchesi 1978; Douglas 1975). Conducted with sufficient thoroughness, such a self-reflection leads to the questioning of the cultural preconditions of one's own thinking. Sociology, by contrast, has so far preferred to deal with its cultural preconditions as a problem of a 'sociology of knowledge'.

To the extent that the ethnographic perspective is turned back on one's own society, the alienation effect also seizes hold of sociology. The ambivalence and lack of clarity of this 'reference culture' become visible. The culture of modern society appears to be a culture that has lost all culture, one that attempts to reduce its logic to instrumental rationality, to 'utility as the cultural order'. As soon as this culture no longer really works so well (and this phenomenon is relatively new) this self-description begins to falter, and with it the theoretical self-certainty of sociology, which is built upon it. The ethnocentrism suggested to sociology by its own object breaks out as the society in which sociology lives calls these prerequisites into question. The reactions to this are varied. One reaction is to treat the cultural presuppositions in a culturally relativistic way. Another is to naturalize society, to reduce it to anthropological constants of human action.

The culturally relativistic tradition has always had to struggle against its own logical inconsistency. Even cultural relativism has to be subjected to its own verdict. More significant in systematic terms has been the naturalistic theoretical tradition, appealing to utilitarian theories of action.[1] An important debate in this connection is under way in social and cultural anthropology: the debate between the cultural materialists, whose main exponent can be considered to be Harris, and the symbolic structuralists, whose main exponent can be considered to be Marshall Sahlins (Harris 1968; Sahlins 1976). Both authors ask themselves the same question: what is the concrete life, the concrete praxis that determines the reproduction and evolution of historical social formations (consisting of base and superstructure)? Harris answers this question in a way that closely approaches a familiar variant of historical materialism: it is the utility-optimizing of the appropriation of nature, the development of productive forces which set a mode of production with its entire political/legal and cultural superstructure in motion. Sahlins answers this question in a way that is unusual in the context of historical materialism: it is the symbolic practice of appropriation of nature, the transformation of nature into culture via society which establishes the conditions for the reproduction and evolution of historical social forms. Harris explains the origin and transformation of institutionalized practices (of an economic, political or ideological nature) from the net utility (benefits minus costs) that results when the needs for food, sex, health and approval are supposed to be satisfied. Whether costs or benefits are present can be measured on the basis of rising or falling death rates, calorie or protein input, the frequency of illness or 'energetic balances' (ecological equilibria) and the like. Sahlins, on the other hand, explains the origin and transformation of institutionalized practices from the way in which the relationships between the people and the relationships between people and nature are symbolically organized.

These theories thus contain competing explanations for the genesis and reproduction of a social order. A utility theory of culture (culture as profit) leads one to base the explanations of the genesis and transformation of cultural norms on a naturalistic logic. This naturalistic reductionism thought out to its logical end culminates in the thesis of the sociobiological foundations of social order.[2] A communicative theory of culture (culture as language) leads one to base explanations of the genesis and transformation of cultural norms on a logic inherent in cultural orders. That leads one to decipher the rules for constructing a social order and to identify the 'developmental logic' invested in that order. This does not imply assuming a universal developmental logic on the level of the history of all of humanity. It only implies reconstructing the underlying logic of symbolic order, the

---

1 These theoretical traditions are again being disseminated under the title of 'economic theory' in sociology and social anthropology. For sociology, cf. for instance the works of the new Chicago school. Fundamental to this is Coleman (1990). See also Lindenberg (1986).

2 This process of thinking things through to the end should of course be taken with a grain of salt. Such theorizing at least suggests protecting the basic assumptions on human behaviour as long as possible. And what science would offer a better 'scientific' foundation for such assumptions than biology?

cultural prerequisites, for each specific culture and identifying the developmental opportunities opened by them.[3]

Utility-oriented action presupposes a presocial condition. Theories of utility must always proceed from a zero point of social self-construction when they seek to explain social matters. The ideal zero point, and that which provides the conditions for the application of these theories, would be the state of nature. The alteration of this state of nature and its transformation into a society are precisely the object of sociological analysis. Sociological theories start at the point where the state of nature is abandoned. A communicative theory of culture, in contrast to economic theories, makes this difference from the state of nature its field of enquiry. Only such a theory can comprehend the complexity of a societal relationship to nature. Economic theories of culture distinguish societies according to how 'advantageously' they adapt to their economic and other environmental conditions. They underestimate the problem of implementing such an adaptation. The premise of an economically rational interaction with nature acts as if economic rationality could be communicated without problems. And it acts as if economic rationality were the only rational aspect of human communication. The perspective of communication theory shows that such insinuations contain false generalizations just as they miss the meaning of communication.[4]

This communication-theoretical perspective – and the utilitarian theory of action baulks at such a perspective as a matter of principle – will now be directed at a type of practices which represents both a societal relationship to nature and a specific structure of communicative relationships in society: the

---

3 This contrasting of utilitarian and symbolic theoretical explanation strategies is, of course, not intended to conceal the differences within these theoretical positions. In both positions, minimalist and maximalist variants can be distinguished. Minimalist utilitarian theories explain only those norms which protect survival; anything beyond this minimum is contingent. Maximalist utilitarian theories explain the origin of all types of norms as the result of an optimization strategy (somewhat on the model of micro-economics); this theory functions, however, only under the stipulation that all other action variables remain constant (this is the *ceteris-paribus* stipulation) (Opp 1983). Minimalist semantic interpretations maintain that an inherent symbolic logic can only be ascribed to those norms which make fundamental problems of human life bearable, in particular the problem of death; whatever goes beyond that is ascribed to material compulsion or the genius of a culture. Maximalist interpretations explain the origin of all types of norms as the logical result of a communicatively organized symbolizing process, in which all aspects and elements of the world are integrated into a cognitively consistent system, an 'image' of the world. With a slight displacement, the underlying model can be described in its conceptualization of the 'social' as a Durkheimian sociological determinism.

4 These communication-theoretical reflections follow up on the concept of communication developed in structural anthropology (Leach 1976). This permits us to move the communications concept developed theoretically by Luhmann (1984) and Habermas (1984, 1987) closer to macro-sociological phenomena.

practice of sacrifice.[5] We shall be concerned in particular with the practice of blood sacrifice, which extends from cannibalism to animal sacrifice all the way to certain types of self-mutilation. Loeb (1974) called this the 'blood sacrifice complex'. It is possible to demonstrate with such sacrificial practices that the sacrifice is a type of appropriation of nature which fulfils communicative functions beyond its economic function. Such practices illustrate in exemplary fashion the blindness of the economic perspective and the acuity of the communication-theoretical perspective.

Sacrificial rituals and social self-construction

The sacrifice is a form of ritual practice that is found in simple societies. It is part of a ritual practice that gives back to the spirits that which they have given to people. The spirits are not necessarily in a favourable mood; one must attempt to win them over. One must only preserve the mutuality that characterizes simple societies in relation to the spirits as well. In state societies, such ritual forms become a sacrifice that is given to the gods in order to influence them positively. The restrictive communication of the ritual (Bloch 1974) is reorganized in the direction of higher degrees of freedom. The social evolution of the sacrifice has also been accompanied in traditional societies by excesses that deprive this evolutionary process of its straightforwardness. In order to make the gods who grant power, prestige, law, wealth and health favourably disposed, the gods are given as a sacrifice the greatest sacrifice people can give: human beings. All of the more complex societies have known human sacrifice. The mythic accounts of those societies which no longer have human sacrifice (having replaced it, for instance, with animal sacrifice) tell of human sacrifice in their prehistory. The extent of human sacrifice varies among the archaic traditional societies. And the extent to which this sacrifice has been civilized also differs between societies.

One result of this civilizing process with eminently evolutionary consequences is the shared sacrificial feast which became the model for the organization of the Greek polis.[6] The community of sacrificial participants defines the mode of communication on which the society is based. The rules of the sacrifice represent the rules of social communication in the polis. This sacrificial feast, combined with Judaeo-Christian elements, then serves as the transitional formula into modernity. The sacrificial feast is replaced by

---

5 Sacrifice has played an important part in theory formation in sociology and social anthropology. For theoretical discussion of sacrifice cf. the classical works of Hubert & Mauss from 1899 (Hubert & Mauss 1968a, 1968b), Loisy (1920) as well as the newer approaches of Girard (1972) and Turner (1977). Here the foundations are laid for a simultaneously structural and communication-theoretical analysis.

6 See the works of Detienne & Vernant (1979), who have drawn new interpretations of the connection between culture and society in ancient Greece by tying together approaches of social anthropology and history.

the communion of those who work for God and live together. The Protestant sects take over the evolutionary role that the sacrificial community played in the evolution of state societies. Even in the modern era, the evolution of sacrifice has been accompanied by excesses. Attempts to give a 'modern' meaning to sacrifice extend from the witch hunts through nationalistic and colonialist repression all the way to the Holocaust.

Bourgeois society is the attempt to civilize this form of communal construction, to make it into a model of society which is able to control these excesses.[7] The Enlightenment societies were a crucial result of this evolution for the modernization of some historical societies. Their mode of communication follows the ideal of 'discursive understanding'. This form of communication became the model for what we know as 'bourgeois society' (Eder 1985). The group of those communicating with one another in a milieu determined by work is reduced to its most naked form, the form of 'discursive' debate. Whether and to what extent this model is capable of civilizing such forms of communal construction has of course become dubious after the experiences of modern history. The civilizing effect of communication is obviously independent of the degree of complexity a society has attained.[8] The following reflections aim to show what it is that determines the evolution of communication in these societies of varying complexity for simple, traditional and modern societies.[9]

The end of cannibalism

The discourse on primitive cannibalism

Cannibalism is a derogatory concept for practices pertaining to the interaction with dead or killed human beings. What the phenomenon that has been labelled cannibalism in the anthropological world-view really means presupposes an understanding of the contextual conditions. Unless corrected, the concepts which a culturally-imperialist view employs to comprehend these phenomena systematically lead us astray. Cannibalism is

---

7 Thus one can also conceive of the history of the origin of modernity as a new evolutionary start towards a 'civilizing process'. On this programme cf. Elias (1978, 1982). A further development is found in Mennell (1990), who points out decivilizing processes in modern societies. This idea connects well with our concept of a limited civilizational competence of (European) modernity.

8 Such levels of complexity are defined by the level of development of the forces of production and the degree of differentiation of society away from nature (on this, see also Chapter 1). The civilizing process is largely independent of this. Only the demands on it rise with increasing complexity.

9 Let us emphasize once again that this distinction of societies implies no assumption on their rationality. It is only a matter of differences with respect to the degree of differentiation of society away from nature. In this sense modern societies are farther removed from nature than are simple ones. This is independent of whether the form of ritual communication emerging in these different societies is rational or not in a 'practical' sense.

a symbolic practice that is found in some societies and can be made comprehensible from the logic of these societies.[10]

If one reconstructs the discussion of cannibalism, then the difficulties begin already where the anthropological world-view would presume to find the most cannibals: in the prehistoric proto-history of mankind (Andrée 1887; Roper 1969). The archaeological material presents a particularly clear example of ignorance of cultural theory. Systematic injuries to the human body are taken as indicators of deliberate intrahuman killing, with the objective usually being suggested or even explained by a hint at cannibalism. The self-evidence with which people attempted to interpret such phenomena as cannibalism was bound to provoke the suspicion that there is no cannibalism. Cannibalism is said to be a mere invention of anthropologists; it is a result of the anthropological world-view and thus a part of modern ideology (Arens 1979). This argument is indeed true, but the conclusion that there never was any such thing as cannibalism is an exaggerated effort to defend the honour of humanity. It is indubitable that 'cannibalistic' beliefs did exist. Nor is there any argument a priori why these beliefs should not (rarely or rather frequently) have been put into practice.[11]

Even at an early stage of human culture, that which is labelled as cannibalism probably had something to do with the fact that people are intensely interested in the bodily remains of their fellow human beings. This can express itself in different forms, whether in the form of burial rituals, in the form of head-hunting cults or in the form of the cannibalistic appropriation of the Other's body by eating it. If one wishes to know what cannibalism is, one must understand what it means in its details, in the form of eating, for instance. One attempt to explain anthropophagy consists in suspecting and identifying an objective advantage, which people need not be

---

10 There is a connection, then, between slight differentiation away from nature and cannibalism, a connection that suggests a culturally-imperialistic view, where it strikes us politically and culturally. One example of this is the 'ethnographic study' on anthropophagy by Andrée from the year 1887. Two quotations show this more than clearly. He writes: 'Anthropophagy certainly appears most revolting to us where any sort of feeling is so dulled that it becomes a pure delicacy . . . If – as various credible observers consistently report – the Fan on the Gabon river and the Obotschi on the Niger dig up foreign bodies and devour them, we do not find that any better.' (Andrée 1887: 103). Apart from the fact that the enjoyment as such is already suspect, the civilized consciousness articulates itself as repulsion to such practices. At the same time this civilized consciousness can console and congratulate itself: 'It is gratifying to see how anthropophagy is losing more and more ground and how, even in the short span of historical time that has passed since the great age of discoveries, cannibalism has already disappeared in a very significant area . . . Of course, in many places anthropophagy disappeared along with the people [who practised it] and, where only a hundred years ago in the area of the North American Great Lakes cannibalistic redskins were still engaging in the hunt and vengefully dismembering and consuming the enemy tied to the war-pole, the Anglo-Saxon race is now proliferating, flooding powerfully across the country.' (Andrée 1887: 105f.).

11 This entire discussion owes more to ideological struggles than to scientific analysis. Since theoretical interpretation has a relatively free scope, because of the problematic character of the empirical material, improbable interpretations easily spring up.

conscious of, behind the cultural ideas that people connect with these rituals. It is obvious here to consider the food value of cannibalistic practices. An early version of this thesis is found in Dole (1961). It does not restrict the food value only to that which it calls 'gastronomic endocanni-balism'. It also sees the food motive in existence in 'ritual cannibalism' (Dole 1961: 570).[12] This argument has been refuted by Garn & Block (1970). In remarks in a discussion they point out that the minimum ration for a group of 60 men would have to come to at least one man per week. That would mean that this group would have to eat itself up in a year in order for a significant effect on protein intake to result. This argument did not prevent the debate that took place in the 1970s (Harris 1977, 1978; Dornstreich & Morren 1974).

Lévi-Strauss's theory of cannibalism marks the structural counter-movement to this ecological objectivism.[13] It is precisely anthropophagy, he notes, which provokes the most horror in our culture, which in itself says something about it. If one sets aside those forms of anthropophagy which are forced by emergencies (and they exist everywhere), then what remains is the problem of the ritual consumption of body parts of a relative or an enemy in order to appropriate or neutralize their power. The condemnation of such customs already presupposes belief in the resurrection of the flesh, certain ideas on the connection between spirit and soul. However, such ideas are also the basis for ritual anthropophagy. Nor can one accuse these practices of lack of respect, considering that we do not treat bodies any differently in our anatomy laboratories than do individual simple cultures.

Beyond an idea of the connection between soul and body which is widespread in all cultures, the difference between simple and modern society consists in the fact that those cultures ingest that which is considered dangerous, while in our cultures it is egested ('spit out'). The first case is anthropophagy, the second anthropemia (Lévi-Strauss 1955: 447–8). These are thus two opposing models of symbolic practice, two models of the symbolic organization of society, which cannot be distinguished in moral terms or ranked in a hierarchy.[14] Cannibalism has to do with deep-seated

---

12 The cultural model behind this interpretation becomes obvious when Dole assigns the eating of human flesh to an early phase of ritual endocannibalism, whereas symbolic practices, such as drinking bone meal of the dead stirred into water, are interpreted as a remnant of simpler forms of cannibalism. See Dole (1961: 572).

13 Cf. Lévi-Strauss (1964a) as well as (1968a: 395–411). The intellectual premises for this approach were already formulated in 1955 by Lévi-Strauss in *Tristes tropiques* (Lévi-Strauss 1955: 377ff.) in a chapter entitled 'Un petit verre de rhum' ('A small glass of rum').

14 Lévi-Strauss compares the ritual practice of consumption with our practice of punishment and reaches the following conclusion: 'And the peak of absurdity is reached when, as we do, people treat the guilty party on the one hand as a child, in order to punish him, and on the other as an adult in order to deny him consolation, and moreover believe they have attained a great advancement of the spirit because they prefer to mutilate some fellow citizens physically and morally instead of consuming them.' (Lévi-Strauss 1955: 449).

cultural definitions, which as such cannot be moralized (only the practices resulting from such cognitive presuppositions can be moralized).

The thesis of the 'culinary triangle' (Lévi-Strauss 1964a) was a first step in the analysis of these cognitive presuppositions. The specific thesis that there is a connection between endocannibalism and boiling and between exo-cannibalism and roasting has been disputed (Shankman 1969). In the subsequent revision by Lévi-Strauss of the 'culinary triangle' (1968a: 395ff.), the dichotomies have been modified. The contrast is no longer between boiled and roasted, but between raw and cooked. Roasting is only a partial transformation of the raw. This implies that the cooked tends more to be associated with culture and the raw or roasted with nature. Cannibalism, to the extent the flesh is cooked, would be a cultural practice; to the extent it is roasted or eaten raw, it is 'natural' practice obeying the constraints of necessity. Lévi-Strauss's attempt to explain cannibalism with the culinary triangle is probably a case of misplaced concreteness. How the logic of preparing ritual meals is connected with the logic of the culture is an open question. No direct relationship can be demonstrated empirically. That is why it is advisable to return to the classic structural hypothesis, to proceed from the dichotomy 'ingest/egest', and to leave the connection between this dichotomy and the culinary dichotomies open.

In this way one can formulate a more promising structural explanatory strategy. It does not tie symbolic practices to the universal need to still hunger and have good food, nor to envy and hunger for prestige; instead it associates those practices with the logic of a culture at a specific level of differentiation of society away from nature. One could then investigate how much the specific harshness of the natural living conditions of simple societies varies along with this difference and causes differences in the cultural practice of anthropophagy (or anthropemia). This proposed analysis thus amounts to first identifying the structural alternatives that are presented by the symbolic organization of society at a low level of differentiation away from nature, and then, in a second step, identifying the contextual conditions that select one developmental path from among these alternatives.

The world of the Kwakiutl

The culture of the Kwakiutl Indians is an especially instructive example of how the state of nature manifested in cannibalism is collectively processed and symbolically overcome.[15] Ecological and economic theories in cultural and social anthropology have made the culture of the Kwakiutl the privileged object of their theories. The institution of the potlatch, in

---

15 Cf. Walens (1981). In addition, the ethnographic reports on this culture are among the most outstanding documents of ethnographic field research (they were collected by Boas).

particular, has stirred the fantasy of economic theorists and methodologists over and over again (Harris 1977: 81ff.). It has become an equally privileged object of theories with a structural approach. Walens (1981) has presented an interesting study, very ambitious in terms of cultural theory, of the structures of the symbolic organization of Kwakiutl society. The following reflections follow on from that study.

The world of the Kwakiutl is full of mouths, the mouths of people talking, the mouths of hungry animals eating, the mouths of killer whales, the threatening teeth of wolves and bears, of cannibal birds that crush human skulls, those of savage women with pendulous breasts and projecting lips who seek out careless travellers and naughty children and devour them. The world of the Kwakiutl is an oral culture. It is based on the fear of being devoured.

The apotheosis of the power of hunger occurs in the *hamatsa*, the 'cannibal dance' (Walens 1981: 15). All the forces that can destroy society are represented by the desire of the cannibal to eat human flesh. The cannibal must therefore be tamed and that is the basis of the cannibal dance. So obsessed is the cannibal dancer with the desire to eat human flesh that he continuously grinds his teeth. He first attacks all the people in his vicinity, bites them and is driven away by the bear dancer. After a while he returns, since the old hunger for human flesh has seized hold of him again. Then a naked woman (his real sister or the classificatory equivalent) appears with a body in her arms and dances lasciviously for him. Even this incestuous offer cannot restrain the cannibal from his hunger for human flesh. He grabs the body and devours it. That satisfies the hunger, but does not negate it. That can only happen in the last dance. The other dancers hold a smoldering cloth impregnated with menstrual blood in the cannibal dancer's face. As soon as the sacred smoke reaches the cannibal's body he is satiated, because his primary need is allayed by the menstrual blood. At that moment, the cannibal becomes a child who must be taught everything, eating and drinking, talking and sleeping, all over again. Once the cannibal dancer has put this re-initiation rite behind him, he has conquered the destructive power of the original hunger.

This dance solves the fundamental problem of Kwakiutl culture: to rid oneself of the unchecked hunger to eat one's neighbour and put eating into a symbolically regulated form. However, this does not simply civilize cannibalistic desires. Such a psychological explanation would not be able to explain why eating plays such a great role (and cannibalism is only the most ambivalent form of getting nutrition). This becomes clear when one interprets eating – like cannibalism as its most radical symbolization – as a form of communication. Eating is the medium for communicating with the spirits on which people depend. The spirits provide the food, and people must give it back. Here they transform even this giving-back. They do not return bodies; they return objects that represent souls. Only this meaning of food makes it comprehensible why cannibalism has become the organizational principle of Kwakiutl culture.

The symbolic economy of the potlatch

If the food problem plays such a great role (and for that there are certainly convincing ecological explanations), then one can characterize Kwakiutl culture as a culture that has learned how to regulate this problem ritually and thus civilize it. This phenomenon allows us to understand a phenomenon that is of great economic significance for the society of the Kwakiutl: the potlatch, the ritual of the collective destruction of wealth. What appears to be an irrational destruction of goods to the eye of the naïve observer acquires a rational meaning in the symbolic system of the Kwakiutl. By destroying animal skins and blankets (which are homologous to leather), one returns to the spirits what they previously gave as food.

It is also possible to see a calculating rationality at work behind this manifest irrationality, especially when one views the potlatch from the perspective of a feast in which the participants strive to outdo one another in what they offer to the feast. That this mechanism could take effect in the potlatch is the outcome of a ritual but not its cause. If one joins in a ritual, one does so because in that way a cultural norm is followed which makes certain practices possible (and others impossible).[16] Thus the point of the feast is not the lavish banquet, but something which at first seems quite senseless: the destruction of goods. This practice contradicts the idea of a redistribution from those who have too much to those who have too little. And the prestige one acquires by being able to destroy large quantities of goods is not based on the fact that the have-nots are able to acquire them, but on the fact that there is a communally shared belief in the spirits which leads to this 'destruction' (which is nothing of the kind for the culture).[17]

The merely material motive is largely neutralized by the structure of the symbolic universe of the Kwakiutl. The example of the cannibal dance shows precisely that the need simply to appropriate nature, to devour it, is highly problematic. The appropriation motive is virtually tabooed by the culture. In that way, the Kwakiutl culture is capable of controlling its cannibalistic past as well as the excesses that threaten it with the increasing complexity of society. In that sense, the significance of the potlatch is precisely the opposite of that ascribed to it by economic explanations. The potlatch is a mechanism to neutralize the very motives that are imputed to it by the economic explanation. In an involuntary irony, the potlatch protects the reproduction of a non-utilitarian culture.

Kwakiutl culture can be interpreted as the result of a social evolution in which it was possible to 'civilize' the complexity level of pre-state societies. It

---

16 Harris explained the potlatch as 'a nearly universal mechanism for assuring the production and distribution of wealth among peoples who have not yet fully acquired a ruling class' (Harris 1977). The symbolic competition is thus explained from the lack of a ruling class.

17 How much this destruction can meaningfully be connected with prestige depends on whether the material motive plays a central part for the spirits. This in turn is a question of the cultural code of a society. Among the Kwakiutl at least, this connection is not present.

differs in that way from other simple societies, whether from the Ya-nomamö, whose control of aggressivity had scarcely developed, or the headhunter societies in New Guinea, which act out aggression against others to the detriment of strangers and enemies.[18] These differences also accompany the evolution of society on the level of state societies, as the subsequent analyses of Aztec and Jewish society demonstrate. The central problem for explanation is: why was human sacrifice maintained in more complex societies, and what were the reasons that led to the abandonment of human sacrifice in some societies?

Human sacrifice and cultural order

Aztec human sacrifice rituals

The existence of the Aztec human sacrifice rituals, with their subsequent distribution of human flesh for consumption, has sometimes been ques-tioned in the literature.[19] The objection is based on a reading of sources, the reports of Spanish chroniclers, in the light of ideology critique. In summary form, the argument against the reality of Aztec cannibalism runs: in order to cause the highly developed Aztec people to appear to be barbarians, the Spanish embellished them with the most barbarian qualities they could imagine. That made a justification of the exploitative and annihilationist policies of the Spanish conquistadors possible.

This argument is, of course, nothing more than a variant of the self-description which is characteristic of modern western culture, that it is the embodiment of everything non-barbarian. The argument that the barbarian aspects were only fictional additions to other cultures assumes that they are in reality just as non-barbarian as western culture. There is no questioning of the distinction barbarian/non-barbarian, but that is precisely what is at stake. One cannot work with the self-evident cultural certitudes of modern societies if one wishes to measure how barbarian a culture is. One must reconstruct the cultural significance of what we call 'barbarian' from the logic of the respective culture. Otherwise one obtains only the inverse of classical cultural imperialism (Diamond 1974).

---

18 On these examples cf. Chagnon (1968, 1974) as well as Rappaport (1979). In these societies, a different cultural evolution takes effect on an analogous level of differentiation of society away from nature, an evolution which relies on force and not on communication. The example of the Guayaki remains ambivalent (Clastres 1972: 229ff.), since they continually fight against the dead and take refuge in anthropophagy, but also kill fellow tribesmen and strangers for different reasons (this is the case, for example, among the incestuous Guayaki) in order to subsequently eat them.

19 The motives for this are multiple, perhaps to justify the actions of the conquistadors, perhaps to remove the empirical basis for the moral devaluation of the Indians. There is a copious discussion on this. Cf. Arens (1979), Sahlins (1979), Séjourné (1971).

The empirical facts from which we must work (and which we consider 'barbarian') are these:[20] roughly 20,000 people were sacrificed during the four-day dedication ceremony of the main temple in Tenochtitlan in 1487. From the sixteenth century onwards, some 15,000 to 20,000 people were killed and eaten per year. The sacrificial ritual itself was extremely elaborate. The victims (usually prisoners of war, occasionally slaves as well) were ornamented and brought into the city in a kind of procession. They were presented as if they were gods. During the preparations for the sacrificial ritual they were served sacred bread and sacred wine. The killing took place on the great pyramid. The hearts removed from the bodies were held out to the sun, the blood poured over the divine sanctum. The bodies were finally thrown down the western steps of the sanctum, the arms and legs passed out to be eaten by those gathered there, and the trunks of the bodies were fed to the animals in Montezuma's zoos (Sahlins 1978; Erdheim 1973; Séjourné 1971).

Three questions arise in analysing and explaining these practices:

1   What significance did these practices have?
2   What objective prerequisites must be fulfilled in order for these practices and the norms governing them to have the supposed significance?
3   What function did these practices have for the reproduction of the social system?

The starting point for an explanation of the human sacrifice rituals is the question of the objective significance of these practices. This question has analytical primacy over the others, because the enquiry into the objective conditions or the functions presupposes a culturally constituted practice. That does not rule out the possibility, however, of this practice being modified by its objective conditions and functions. In fact, these productive questions are crucial to the problem of the 'direction' of the evolution of symbolic practices in various societies.[21]

On the logic of human sacrifice rituals

An economic analysis   Harris (1977, 1978) attempted to explain the significance of the human sacrifice rituals from a utilitarian theoretical perspective. People act in a certain way because the benefits of so doing exceed the costs. Applied to food, this implies that people eat certain things because the benefit from them exceeds the cost implied in preparing them.

---

20 Particularly after the careful edition of the numerous volumes of Father Sahagún (Sahlins 1978: 45), it is becoming necessary to take the chroniclers more seriously than a projective ideology critique would wish to do.

21 The concept of evolution is thus not framed in terms of universal history. It designates instead the dynamism and direction that determine the development of historical societies at a given level of differentiation of society away from nature. The problem of whether these initial conditions themselves contain a universal evolution is excluded here.

Exaggerating a bit, one could say that Harris explains the cultural norms of the Aztec human sacrifice ritual by the stomach's needs: the point of the ritual is provision with protein-rich food. That immediately solves the issue of the meaning of these practices. Eating human flesh is the more or less efficient solution of a nutritional problem in society.

These naturalistic interpretations of meaning are expanded in a second step into an ecological explanation. The 'energy base', the maintenance of a natural equilibrium under given ecological conditions, determines the formation and reproduction of these cultural practices. Thus Harris attempts to show that this ritual activity actually made sense under the prevailing ecological conditions of Aztec society. Because of a permanent population growth and the intensification of food production for over a millennium, the number of cattle, swine, birds and fish declined in the central Mexican highlands, with the result that there was no longer enough animal protein available per capita. Unlike other high Indian cultures of the time such as the Incas, who had the llama at their disposal, the Aztecs faced the problem of not having enough edible animals available.

However, it is not as if the Aztecs would have had to invent the possibility of eating human flesh. Quite to the contrary. Ritual cannibalism was widespread in pre-governmental societies. It was a reward for loyalty and bravery in battle, according to Harris. A comparison with other societies on the level of organization of governmental societies shows that a different type of utility analysis prevailed there. Ruling classes find it more profitable, as a rule, to use prisoners of war as slaves and servants than to eat them. This utility analysis does not apply to Aztec society. They eat their prisoners of war. If one is to remain in the logic of Harris's explanation, cannibalism must have had a different net utility. Aztec cannibalism, according to his conclusion, must be explained by the specific ecological conditions of Aztec society. For ecological reasons, the consumption of human flesh was not prohibited, but virtually encouraged. In fact, he concludes, Aztec cannibalism solved the problem of provision with protein-rich food.

The thesis in this general form, however, cannot be correct. Fifteen thousand human sacrifices per year compared to a population of two million in the Mexican highlands comes to less than one human sacrifice per hundred residents. Distributed among all the residents of the Mexican highlands, this would amount to less than one kilogram per person per year. This amount would probably have appeared meagre even to a cannibalistic chieftain living under pre-governmental circumstances. Harris therefore introduces two qualifications: first, the argument that the human sacrifice rituals took place only once a year, and then at a date when the already meagre provisioning with meat had reached a minimum for seasonal reasons. This argument does not produce more meat per person per year either. That is the reason for the second argument: human flesh was distributed only to the ruling classes, not the mass of people. Only the warriors and the nobility received human flesh. Warriors were privileged participants in the sacrificial feast, as Harris showed elsewhere, because for them ritual cannibalism had the function of maintaining or positively improving their ability to fight by comparison to competing tribes. The nobility were privileged participants in the sacrificial meal because human flesh had prestige and power-protecting functions for them. This was of particular importance to the merchant class among the Aztecs. Merchants, after all, cannot take prisoners of war. They had to purchase slaves in order to be able to sacrifice human beings. The expenses involved with this, including those for the preparation of the ritual, could rise so high that the merchants had to sell themselves as slaves and perhaps be eaten themselves.[22]

This at least relativizes the ecological argument. Even though there may have been no premium in the ecological sense for eating human flesh, it is still useful to privilege warriors in order to preserve the tribe in competition with rival tribes. The integration of the merchants, whose number increases with the increasing complexity of Aztec society, into this privileged class only amplifies this effect. That raises the question of the social function of these practices. What function did the human sacrifices and the consumption of human flesh have? Harris implies that such norms made it possible to create relationships of exploitation. The relationship between eaters and eaten represents the most extreme conceivable exploitation of man by man.[23] This usage context protects the stability of norms even beyond the context in which they originate. They apply even when their original prerequisites (that is, being useful to an individual or the group) are no longer valid. The cultural norms that originate in such a way are nothing more than 'spiritualized' forms of natural restrictions.

It can be seen from this very example, however, that 'cultural materialism'[24] is an insufficient attempt to explain the origin and change of a culture. This social theory explains cultural practices as the result of a rational calculation with the resources available to satisfy natural needs. There is a rationality in these practices, but it should be sought inside, not outside, this culture.

A structural analysis   In his critique,[25] Sahlins disputes the interpretation by Harris that the meaning of ritual human sacrifice lies in the latter's 'nutritional value'. Instead, he claims the meaning is that these rituals are sacrifices, actions that have a peculiar symbolic meaning. A sacrifice creates two types of relationships: those between sacrificers and sacrifices, and those

---

22 This is – as Harris (1979) notes in his critique of Sahlins – the logic of the profiteer: 'Dog eats dog wherever you go'.

23 As Harris remarks with reference to modern forms of exploitation: 'Even bourgeois businessmen refrain from dining on their workers.' Cf. Harris (1979: 52).

24 This is the self-identification of this theorizing strategy; cf. Harris (1968, 1979), who in turn falls back on Harner (1977a, 1977b).

25 The critique by Sahlins has not remained entirely within scholarship. Even in its publication strategy it aimed at having a public effect. See Sahlins (1978, 1979).

between the sacrifices and the gods. The sacrifice is identified with the gods; in a certain sense, it becomes divine. And those conducting the sacrifice identify themselves with the sacrifice. They address it as 'dear son'. They are not eating the flesh of their sacrifice, since one cannot eat 'one's own flesh'. The sacrificer eats flesh from another sacrificer. The sacrificial ritual then makes it possible to create a relationship between people and god by way of the two relationships above. The human sacrificial ritual represents a sacred communication, a communication with the gods.

In a comparative sense, this symbolic meaning is not so terribly unusual. As a functional equivalent, the Jewish tradition has the sacrifice of a lamb, which is in turn a substitute for the sacrifice of Isaac by Abraham that was first demanded and then prevented by Yahweh. Human sacrifice in the form of the self-sacrifice of Jesus becomes the central topos in the Christian tradition. 'Holy communion' (the eating of bread and wine) is understood by the Christian church as the consumption of the flesh and blood of the son of God. Here too, it is a human sacrifice which makes the relationship between people and the one God possible.

The meaning of this symbolic practice should be sought in the overcoming of the problem of death.[26] By sacrificing and then eating the offering it is possible to transform death into life. This attempt to overcome death is not a sufficient explanation of sacrificial death. Sacrificial death is also a mechanism for repairing a disrupted relationship between the person and the god to whom the sacrifice is given. A symbolic order is reaffirmed by repairing the communicative relationships between god and people through sacrificial death. Sacrificial death, therefore, protects the medium of social communication, and the logic on which it is based has nothing more to do with cost-benefit calculations. This is a logic to enable interindividual communication, not individual utility maximization.

In this communication-theoretical context, the question then arises of why in the Aztec case it is human sacrifices that are supposed to serve to create the relationship between god and people and thus enable communication. Sahlins seeks the cause for this in the specific symbolic imagery characteristic of Aztec culture, the images of the gods in particular. Gods are viewed as something that transcends the social order, something outside the control of mankind. In that sense gods represent potential enemies. One must appropriate the gods in order to bridge this distance and ward off the danger presumed to lie in the gods.

The conquistadors experienced this view personally. They were received like deities, and as soon as they could be seized, they were eaten – that is, their divine power was appropriated. The creation myths of the Aztecs report what the people later re-enact: only by destroying themselves did

---

26 The connection of sacrifice and death is already part of early speculations on the meaning of sacrifice. The psychologizing speculation usually obstructed a revelation of its meaning. See especially Leach (1976).

they become gods. Their own sacrificial death was what made them gods. That set the sun in motion and 'created' the world. The cosmology underlying the Aztec culture was set into motion by the self-sacrifice of the gods and is kept in motion by additional sacrifices. The value orientations of this culture are attuned to this cosmological notion. Someone who is a warrior is honoured (because he takes prisoners who can be sacrificed). Mothers are honoured for having children who can be sacrificed to the rain god (because the tears of children are like raindrops). Blood must flow in order to keep the world going.[27] The fundamental notion on which this culture is based is, therefore, based on blood. The flow of blood is equivalent to the motion of the world.[28] Sahlins reduced the logic of this system to the phrase a 'potential disaster'. The rituals were a permanent bloodletting for society. This is a ritual of a large-scale destruction of life, the significance of which was anything but 'economic' in nature.[29]

The function of such cultural practices for the reproduction of society is based on their protection of the solidarity of groups and of the social integration between social groups in an ever more hierarchical society. The problem that such societies confront is how to guarantee social integration under the condition of an increasing social inequality. The function of ritual is not – as Harris assumes – the maximization of the possible exploitation of the underprivileged by the privileged, but rather the protection of social cohesion. The human sacrifice ritual tied the emerging privileged classes (warriors and merchants) into a cycle of reciprocal obligations, which was still constitutive for the overall system in pre-governmental societies. The formation of bureaucratic forms of political rule found its cultural and legitimatory basis in the human sacrifice rituals. The Aztecs set a social evolution in motion there which becomes tangled in its own evolutionary logic. The form of social communication established by such sacrificial rituals no longer assures its own continuation. At the same time it cannot stop it because of the dynamism this society had set into motion.[30]

The legitimatory function is given by the prestige which warriors, in particular, were able to acquire in the sacrificial ritual. It is an often

---

27 Thus birth is accompanied by the midwife with the cry: 'The woman has made a captive.' The trader was defined analogously to the warriors. Purchasing slaves was reinterpreted as a hidden form of conquest.

28 On this point cf. Sahlins (1978); Erdheim (1973: 47ff.); Séjourné (1971: 176ff.).

29 Cf. Sahlins (1978: 48). Something similar applies to the South Pacific cannibals, where the arrival of the Europeans influenced the logic of symbolic representation in such a way that cannibalism was strengthened, although the population rate sank rapidly and sufficient food was available.

30 This formulation assumes that societies which differentiate increasingly away from nature have an increased need for communication opportunities The function of social evolution then consists in expanding these communication opportunities. In this way sacrificial rituals can be interpreted as a form of protecting such communication opportunities and can be evaluated for their suitability in respect to the reproducibility of communication.

remarked fact that the state and its social classes did not arise from naked power, but indirectly through charismatic forms of rule, such as that based on special moral prestige. Success counts among non-privileged groups as a justification for privileges, and in the context of Aztec culture this would be the number of prisoners of war taken or slaves bought. Religious rituals as means of domination are a self-destructive mechanism in the social evolution of state societies, however. Sometimes they are only transitory phenomena on the way to the state (Eder 1976; Service 1962, 1975). Often they are also the end of evolution for state societies. Aztec society blocked this evolution by clinging to sacrificial rituals and then further developed these forms to excess. But in so doing, it did not solve the central problem of this type of society, that is, the stabilization and reproduction of a form of legitimate political rule.[31]

The end of human sacrifice

The non-sacrifice of Isaac

The analysis of Aztec sacrificial ritual has shown that a new cultural identity was produced in a traumatic way in the course of the social evolution of the state. This has to do with a certain form of social evolution, so that it is not a transitional evolutionary stage which all societies must pass through. The Aztec example is an example of a possible course of evolution. The fact that things need not go this way can be seen from another, equally extreme example: the cultural assimilation of the transition from a tribal society to a state society in the history of the Israelite tribes. The key to an understanding of this form of cultural processing is the story of the non-sacrifice of Isaac by Abraham.

This event founds a tradition that places the killing of people under quite different and, especially, very restrictive conditions. It leads to a limitation of killing, which obviously can easily slip out of all control in the transition to more complex stages of evolution. The experience of political rule leads to symbolization strategies that provoke and culturally elevate the return to the logic of killing and being killed. Only through the medium of such symbolic practices, it seems, is the ruler able to preserve that status which raises him above all others and assures him recognition. Through the non-killing of Isaac, which installs a specific type of killing taboo in the society of ancient

---

31 One could describe the central problem of this social type as the protection of the primitive accumulation of political power. Until this accumulation is successful, there is no social structure that makes it permissible to monopolize the resources of power (land ownership, control of labour power) and employ them strategically. The discussion on clientelism (Eisenstadt & Roniger 1984; Roniger 1983) gives a good notion of these problems. On this point, see also Mann (1986).

Israel, this society occupies a special position in its historical environment.[32] This taboo contradicts the social order that was central to the cultures of Egypt, Mesopotamia and Syria. All those cultures shared the practice of human sacrifice at the time when the culture of the ancient Israelites had already abandoned human sacrifice (Green 1975). In other cultures, people continued to be sacrificed to celestial deities that were supposed to assure rain, sun and so forth. Human sacrifice was supposed to ensure (as in Aztec culture) that the sun would not deviate from its orbit, the moon would not grow dark or that rainy seasons would arrive. The break with such notions was presumably set in motion by cognitive learning processes. As soon as the logic of the celestial movements is understood, as soon as people realize that observed movements are somehow self-actuated, the sacrifice of people to influence celestial deities is unnecessary. The non-sacrifice of Isaac could also be connected to this, as Heinsohn (1979) asserts. The idea of an omnipotent god, after all, underlies the monotheistic conception of the one God. This innovation shortens the evolutionary dissolution process of ideas to which human sacrifice is tied.

Yet the taboo on killing in the culture of the ancient Israelites cannot be sufficiently explained as the effect of the cognitive rationalization of the knowledge of nature. What is required is an explanation of the development that makes such cognitive insights possible. Cognitive rationalization may accelerate social evolution in a certain direction. The problem to be explained is: how does this specific discontinuity arise? What predestines this society to it? What are its social and political prerequisites?

On the logic of the taboo on killing

A rationalistic explanation   Heinsohn (1979) supplied an interesting explanation of the killing taboo among the Israelites. It consists of two parts: the killing taboo was set up in order to encourage growth among a decimated group ('Be fruitful and multiply') and at the same time it served to mark the difference between the ancient Israelites and their (former) oppressors. These utilitarian-motivated explanations can then be linked with assumptions on the functions that could be fulfilled by the killing taboo. Such a functionalism no longer formulates the utility preferences in purely physiological terms (for protein supply), but sociologically. The explanation model itself remains untouched. The lack of cannibalism makes a physiological explanation impossible. Where nothing is being eaten, no hunger can be sated.

Such externalist explanations slip beneath the central problem. Why are identity problems situated so centrally in the first place and why are hopes placed in population growth? Why is a fertility morality enlisted? Making

---

32 Cf. Laum (1924: 82ff.). Parsons also uses this society as a special case, but for other reasons; see Parsons (1971).

assumptions here on rational behaviour implies presupposing what is to be explained. Why are the people of Israel more 'rational' than their neighbours? Why are they the ones who seek a special identity, when there were many more oppressed cultures than oppressor cultures? Why is it possible to work with such a rationale in this case?

A symbolic interpretation   The solution of this problem should neither be sought in connection with the rise of monotheism, as Heinsohn (1979) suspects, nor in connection with social contextual conditions. First of all, there is an empirical argument against that. Human sacrifices continued even after Abraham's decision not to sacrifice his son (Davies 1981: 64). Children, in particular, were sacrificed to Baal, the Moloch, and the more such things are condemned in the Old Testament, the more obviously that reveals their empirical reality. Abraham was a 'premature' attempt to 'rationalize' symbols and the associated symbolic practices, with which people seek to communicate with their gods.

In need of explanation is why that process starts in Israel, which replaces human sacrifice by animal sacrifice (the lamb), then by sacrifices of fruits of the field (cucumbers, for instance) and finally by the paltry sum of five shekels which were to be paid to the sacrificial priests. Social structures are obviously present here which no longer require symbolic mediation by sacrificial actions. A rationalization in the direction of a more abstract form of social communication is taking place: communication with the one God. This abstraction now takes the path of a legal, no longer a religious, structuring of societal relationships. The material devaluation of the sacrifice is not the decisive factor (although it is the necessary condition for its self-abolition). Rather, the break with the sacrifice occurs where legal regulation takes the place of sacrifice. The word, not the ritual action that stands for the word, becomes the medium of communication. The commandment to kill is transformed into the taboo on killing. It is characteristic of Old Testament tradition that it placed the killing of people under conditions regulated in a legally very complex way. Killing could now be permitted only by appeal to universal principles, to a law given by God. The *lex talionis* limited the killing of people to precisely definable cases, cases of injustice that fundamentally endanger coexistence.[33] The justification for

---

33 Sources of these rules are primarily the Pentateuch, which contains the laws of ancient Israel. The law of reprisal is fundamental. That law is: 'The revenger of blood himself shall slay the murderer' (Numbers 35: 19). Do unto your neighbour as he has done unto you: an eye for an eye, a tooth for a tooth. In Numbers this principle is limited to the case of killing: 'Moreover ye shall take no satisfaction for the life of a murderer, which is guilty of death, but he shall be surely put to death.' (Numbers 35: 31).

why murder should be punished with death is derived from the sacredness of the life as the gift of God.[34]

The struggle between these competing principles of social communication was subsequently radicalized and then decided in the case of the prophet Jesus. Here we have a human sacrifice that is simultaneously a result of legal proceeding: the judgment is a human sacrifice and vice versa. The sacrifice becomes a self-sacrifice, which loses its earlier logic. The sacrificer and the sacrifice become identical. The sacrifice is no longer compelling *per se*. It becomes individualized and reflexive. The power inherent in the sacrifice is shifted to the law and civilized there institutionally.

The direction this evolution took consists in the detachment of the sacrifice from the context of mere legitimation of domination. It leads to the tying of communication to the society that already exists before any legitimation: the congregation of the faithful. This way of anchoring communication in forms of communal construction outside of governmental communities is the condition for why this society succeeded in holding the excesses of political power under control. The social evolution of Old Testament society produced the conditions for a 'communicative' organization of societal relationships that was appropriate to the realm of necessity, the complexity of 'traditional societies'.

Human sacrifice in modern society

The Greek sacrificial feast

Modern society, which has taken form since the sixteenth century, retains only a very broken connection to the Jewish tradition of the bloodless sacrifice. It does not so much develop a model of social communication restricting killing, rather, it continues a different traditional evolutionary line of the sacrifice: the tradition of the sacrificial feast. The Greek sacrificial ritual 'civilized' the earlier blood sacrifices in a different way than the Jewish tradition. It did not abolish blood sacrifices, retaining them instead as a sacrificial feast in Delphi, against the resistance of Pythagorean and other groups that attempted to call this central symbol of the polis into question. If one wishes to understand the culture of modern society in Europe, one must relate equally to the bloodless tradition of Judaism and to the bloody tradition of ancient Greece. Only reference to this double cultural tradition makes the ambivalence of modern culture comprehensible.

The 'bloody' Greek sacrifice was the cultural foundation of the polis. To the extent the polis becomes the model for political modernity, the bloody

---

34 This justification can be understood as an evolutionary transition formula: 'Whoso sheddeth man's blood, by man shall his blood be shed: for in the image of God made He man.' (Genesis 9: 6).

sacrificial feast also becomes a key to those forms of *communitas* that are the basis of the process of political modernization.[35] The symbolic forms that were characteristic of the community participating in the Greek sacrificial feast are reproduced in those forms of sociation that have supported the modernization of European society, specifically the Protestant sects and the Enlightenment societies.

This symbolic role of the Greek sacrificial feast for the social evolution of modernity is addressed in the thesis of the Greek sacrificial meal as a symbolic enforcement of a social contract (Detienne & Vernant 1979). The culinary practice of the sacrificial meal is the 'constitutive session' of a social contract. When one takes account of this line of cultural tradition, the modern social contract appears to be nothing other than the continuation of a bloody culinary operation. The Greek sacrificial meal is thus also a key to the pathogenesis of this aspect of modernity. The ability of the Greek sacrificial meal to integrate the Dionysian and simultaneously exclude the Pythagorean may have still been possible in traditional societies. It collapsed, however, as the social power that was to be tamed with the assistance of this symbolic form grows. That means that this symbolic form was no longer capable of civilizing the excesses of the growing power of evolving modern societies. This symbolic form made the beginning of modernity possible by offering models of communication on the level of modern societies, but it can no longer assure the reproduction of this modernity.

The ambivalence of modern types of sociation consists in perpetuating, under the conditions of modern social self-construction, the precarious equilibrium between bloody sacrifice and the bloodless countermovement against sacrifice that created the polis. Modern society has not been able to withstand this ambivalence. Instead, the rise of modernity is a process in which the civilization of power and the excesses of power are increased in equal measure. To the degree that the civilization of power has failed, a

---

35 The importance of the sacrificial feast has been pointed out by Simmel: 'The cults of antiquity, which in contrast to the world religions tended to be addressed only to limited circles of local adherents, were able for just that reason to concentrate themselves in the sacrificial feast. Particularly in semitic antiquity, this signifies the fraternal relationship through the shared access to God's table. The shared food and drink . . . sets free an enormous socializing force, which permits people to overlook the fact that they are not really eating and drinking 'the same things' at all, and creates the primitive notion of producing common flesh and blood in that way. The Christian communion, which identifies the bread with the body of Christ, was the first to create the real identity of that which was consumed on the basis of this mysticism and in that way a quite unique type of connection among the participants.' (Simmel 1957: 244). Weber's thesis on the connection between types of communal construction and modernity, the 'Protestantism thesis', can pick up on this thesis and be reformulated. The communication-theoretical description of such 'communities' resulting from the logic of the sacrificial meal can systematically produce a connection between types of communal construction and social change.

social evolution has been set in motion which can be described as the pathogenesis of modernity.[36]

The cultural trauma of the witch hunts

The evolutionary problem of modern European societies can be defined in two ways. It is determined on the one hand by the general problem of protecting communicative structures and processes under the conditions of increasing social power. On the other hand, it is determined by the ambivalence of the cultural traditions that are the basis of the forms for modern communicative relationships.

The institutional form that marks the beginning of modernity is the absolute state. It is an attempt to control and reproduce the growing complexity of society. One of the most important institutional innovations was the attempt of the modern state to monopolize the production of knowledge (among other things, by founding universities over which it had and continues to have sovereignty). That implied at the same time excluding and oppressing all those forms of knowledge that could not or would not submit to this monopoly. This claim to the control of knowledge made the absolute state the starting point of a 'new' form of societal evolution. This is a revolutionary experiment that contains the attempt to civilize possibilities of social power which were not previously possible and to make them controllable by communication, an experiment that advanced the evolution of modernity and is not yet finished. This experiment, however, hardly seems up to the requirements that have arisen along with the origin and establishment of this society. The expansion of productive forces and the immense expansion of the possibilities for exercising social power, as well as the associated new forms of conflict (which have made world wars possible), obviously cannot be controlled by the cultural institutions that have developed historically in the social evolution of modern Europe. The cultural traditions that should have supported this experiment have obviously been unable to fulfil that purpose. Otherwise it would scarcely be explicable that the origin of modern society is associated for Europe with a cultural trauma: the persecution of Jews and witches in their own societies and the persecution and extermination of other cultures in the non-European societies.

---

36 On the interpretation of modernization as a pathogenic process affecting communicative understanding, cf. Eder (1985). The criterion for the evolutionary rationality of these types of community consists in the form of communication which they institutionalize. One possible field of application is the law. Serving as prerequisite for law are cultural certitudes which enable or hamper communication. The important point is the symbolic practices that are rehearsed in these groups. They establish the conditions for communication and with them the conditions for the success or failure of communication in modern society.

Witches, Jews and Indians were sacrificed on the altar of modernization. The institutionalization of a 'universalist' morality has taken the path of merciless persecution, not only of those who 'think differently' but also and especially of those who 'live differently'.[37] The institutionalization of universalism in the early modern state raised the problem of how to deal with those who did not submit to that morality. The modern solution was to kill the body in order to save the spirit. Mass murder was therefore the prerequisite of modern universalism. *Raison d'état* (first implemented in the Church) symbolized the universality of morality. The social contract that was concluded in the Greek sacrificial feast provided the cultural pattern for the social contract which establishes modern society, and in that way the modern state allies itself with the 'bloody' cultural tradition.[38] The sacrificial feast is replaced by its functional equivalent, the Inquisitorial trial. The fact that, in this modern sacrificial ritual, the killing of people first of all became the medium for concluding the social contract recalls the excesses that accompanied the social evolution of Aztec society. Witches and unbelievers are the modern equivalent of the Aztec human sacrifices. Modernization in Europe thus represents a form of social evolution that made an institution of collective bloodletting in a way quite similar to Aztec society.

It is impossible to dismiss this phenomenon with economic explanations (and this applies equally to classical Marxian ones and those of more modern political economy). This phenomenon has deeper roots, anchored in the logic of the culture. It cannot be reduced to problems of the labour market.[39] It cannot be reduced to problems of underpopulation either.[40] The persecution of heretics and witches may have had such latent functions, but that no longer applies to the persecution of Jews and Indians. It seems rather that the economic explanations are themselves part of the ideology that is

---

37 This does not imply condemning 'universalism' as such. It only implies the assumption that universalism *per se* does not guarantee rational social structures by any means, nor does it necessarily imply successful communication.

38 The rational justification of the persecution of witches comes characteristically from the father of the modern doctrine of state sovereignty, Jean Bodin. Cf. Heinsohn & Steiger (1985). The cultural prerequisites of the early modern doctrine of sovereignty become manifest in precisely these problems. They are a key to the communicative forms that are assumed in such doctrines.

39 Thus the inquisitorial penal practices cannot be explained solely from the function of exterminating the indigent members of the population who cannot be absorbed by the job market. Cf. the analyses by Rusche & Kirchheimer (1981). This assumption collides with the fact that under market conditions a reserve army of the unemployed is always functional for the rulers.

40 Heinsohn, Knieper & Steiger assert such a thesis. The persecution of witches is explained from the fact that the witches held knowledge of contraception. The state had to exterminate the witches in order to assure population growth even in times of great material want (where people as a rule forgo having children). See Heinsohn, Knieper & Steiger (1979); Heinsohn & Steiger (1985). For a critique cf. Jerouschek (1986) and the reply by Heinsohn & Steiger (1987).

used to justify these persecutions.[41] Economic explanations cannot identify the essential bases of these persecutions because those bases are simply not of an economic nature. One ought to look for the basis in the 'cultural code' of modern society. This cultural code continues a specific, older tradition: the bloody culture of Hellenistic antiquity.

The cultural trauma of the persecutions of witches and Jews in the early modern era is part of the modern continuation of the 'bloody' tradition. It is part of a culture that has continued the Greek tradition of the blood-sacrificial feast mediated by Christianity and the Renaissance. Modern society continues this bloody course on a more complex level of social evolution. What characterizes modern culture, is a radicalization of its built-in ambivalence in both directions, drawing sustenance not only from the Greek tradition, but also from the Pythagorean and, especially, the Jewish tradition. It is the countermovement to bloody modernity, being also an integral part of European culture, that has given the social function of modernity such an erratic profile so far and produced the particular ambivalence of modernity (Bauman 1990, 1992).

The bloodless tradition of modernity

The sacrificial victims of bloody modernization are also keys to the 'other side' of modernity: modern 'bloodless' culture attaching itself to the Pythagorean or Jewish traditions. This 'bloodless' culture first manifested itself in a sphere of knowledge that was unofficial and outside the control of the modern absolute state. This 'alternative' culture is based on a type of knowledge[42] that obstructed the modern state's claim to a monopoly over the control of knowledge. The obstacle was the types of knowledge that reproduced themselves in social contexts outside the influence of the state: the self-enclosed religious traditions of the Jews and the lore of women.[43] Just as the polis attempted to suppress the Pythagoreans and later the Jewish sects, the modern state begins to oppress those who could question the government's monopoly authority on cultural control. The existence of such knowledge accompanies modern social evolution as a latent threat. It has made possible the cultural countermovement that accompanies modern history.

---

41 Thus the persecution of the Jews has frequently been justified with the argument of their economic power and the persecution of the Indians with the latter's economic inefficiency.

42 This knowledge was not only empirical, but also moral knowledge in the form of mystic lore. It is a different 'moral' knowledge which was passed down here and then achieved effectiveness in the modern era.

43 That it is precisely these two groups has to do on the one hand with the specific evolution of Jewish society, which was previously analysed and, on the other, with the fact that women possessed a kind of knowledge which has prolonged the oppositional tendency against traditional sacrificial society into modern times. This point is connected to the antithesis between culture and nature within which women represent more the knowledge of nature and men more the knowledge of culture.

Humanitarian opposition movements have been a second form of opposition against the 'bloody' culture of emerging modernity, which manifests itself in the form of rigorous enforcement of a universalist morality. The civilizing of the modern sacrificial rituals of the Inquisition is found especially in the movement in opposition to 'inhumane' criminal law. Its demands are freedom of opinion (which would rule out the persecution of heretics and witches) and rational legal procedures, which are intended to restrict state power.[44] It is tempting to correlate this opposition movement with the idea of a 'bloodless' culture, because it has also tended to conceive of itself as a movement in protection of 'life'. The crucial element of this opposition movement is the prohibition of killing even in the legal area, the humanitarian movement against the death penalty (Leder 1986).

This opposition movement has its obvious cultural roots in the early Christian tradition[45] that appeals to a proto-Christianity, that is, its Jewish roots. As Christianity develops into a state religion this cultural tradition is suppressed. The discourse on capital punishment falls silent. The clergy was satisfied that idolatry was forbidden on penalty of death. Yet this break with a cultural tradition has itself been interrupted again and again, as the movement in opposition to capital punishment shows. The idea of a society without killing appears over and over again, particularly in the heterodox movements of the Middle Ages. St Francis is one of those who sought to replace killing with talking, not to slaughter animals but to talk with them and approach them as people in the proto-Christian sense.[46] This opposition movement took on a more far-reaching significance in the attempts to end the trials of witches and thus put an end to persecution of them. Friedrich von Spee's *Cautio* from 1632 (Spee 1982) and Christian Thomasius's subsequent critique of the witch trials in 1701 and 1704 (Thomasius 1986) are part of that opposition movement which supported the humanitarian enlightenment against the Hobbesian enlightenment. This humanitarian opposition movement, which has directed its attention particularly against state-sanctioned killing, has been successful in only a few countries so far. And even where there is no capital punishment, the continued existence of

---

44 The consequence of this is that criminals and the insane were able to become the object of state repression. That the bloody machinery of the modern state was able to continue raging in this excluded area is only an additional indicator of the ambivalence of modernity.

45 The movement in opposition to capital punishment starts historically from the prohibitions of killing which the ancient Israelite culture produced. Early Christianity rejected the death penalty in contrast to the surrounding Roman society. Thus Tertullian (d. c. 220) makes it a principle for Christians that 'it would be more likely permitted to be killed than to kill'. Lactantius (d. c. 330) rejects capital punishment the most strenuously. In his works one reads: 'For if God forbids killing, then he not only admonishes us against robbery with murder; he also reminds us that what people consider permissible (a legal execution, that is) must not occur either . . . That is why no exception should be made for this commandment of God, since it is always unjust to kill a person whom God intended to be a holy creature.'

46 In that sense it is no coincidence that Saint Francis is cited as a symbol of the anti-nuclear movement. Cf. Bahr, Mahlke, Mahlke, Sölle & Steffensky (1981).

that situation is precarious. The majority of the population continues to urge the death penalty. All that prohibits the death penalty so far are culturally unprotected institutional norms. The cultural 'code' that supports this prohibition of killing continues to be an 'alternative' modernity.

These examples of modern opposition movements against the 'bloody' culture of modernity show that the symbolic foundations of modern society have not unambiguously set the direction for the social evolution of modern society. Yet modern cultural ambivalence is the only chance this culture has. The resurrection of a 'bloodless' nature as opposition movement against modern 'bloodiness' is a possibility that is contained in the ambivalent cultural code of modern Europe. The consciousness of this ambivalence is not, to be sure, part of the 'disposition of society', it is not something that is collectively familiar. The more society slips into crisis situations, the more its specific ambivalence comes to the fore.

The ambivalence of the cultural tradition that characterizes modernity is given by the coexistence of a carnivorous and a vegetarian culture. This opens two fundamentally different evolutionary options to modern culture. It is not possible to determine a priori, however, which option will be chosen. The choice depends upon the social struggles over the implementation of one model or the other. Drawing attention to the generally unconscious cultural presuppositions of these conflicts may change the distribution of the symbolic power in favour of vegetarian culture. This will at least change the mechanisms of the social evolution of modernity. And that distinguishes this evolution fundamentally from the social evolution of traditional and simple societies.[47]

Two evolutionary options

Carnivorous culture

Eating meat in a way that differs from that of (predatory) animals allows us to make a world of culture distinguishable from a world of nature. This makes it comprehensible why eating regulations can represent a societal condition.[48] Carnivorous culture confirms the societal condition. It symbolizes the fundamental distance from the state of nature. Thus it contains a model according to which the societal condition can be reconstructed.

Three such states of society can be distinguished. In simple societies the

---

47 Yet reflexive insight, which 'disenchants' the symbolic form and the corresponding symbolic practice, seems to be able to suspend it only at the cost of pathological consequences. Where the symbolic form has been most thoroughly disenchanted, in philosophical rationalistic culture in Germany, it has returned as a ritual of romantic communication. Cf. Eder (1985) as well.

48 For literature on the symbolic significance of food culture in various societies, cf. especially the works of Goody (1982).

eating of meat has the function of ritually reaffirming social bonds, recalling old obligations and recreating social solidarity. The ability of a society for self-organization culminates in the regulation of consumption. In traditional societies, the eating of meat serves to create relationships between equals in a system of hierarchically structured social units. 'Commensalism' assures the cohesion of a social unit. First of all, eating meat creates commonality between those who eat together. In addition, the purity criterion for that which is eaten (with the complementary, increasingly complicated eating rituals) creates the hierarchy among these groups and thus a self-evident hierarchical order of society. The symbolic form on which this order is based consists in subjecting the eating of meat to an extensive ritual at the top of a hierarchy, while those on the bottom of the hierarchy devour the meat in a barbaric manner.

Eating meat becomes a 'social' matter, a matter for 'bourgeois society'. Its characteristic and identifying mark is eating with knife and fork (Elias 1978, 1982). Eating is specified to be egalitarian social togetherness.[49] The consumption of meat (and thus also the increase of meat consumption in modern democratic societies) has cultural causes and only secondarily economic ones (as a restrictive condition). By eating meat, one reproduces a culture, a practice of consumption obeying a specific symbolic logic (Sahlins 1976; Douglas & Isherwood 1980). Modern practice adds another practice to this one: that of tautological questioning. The symbolic realm becomes economic in modern times and in this process it simultaneously covers up the symbolic foundations upon which the economic realm is always based. This is the dialectic of modern social self-construction, namely, depending on cultural prerequisites and effacing them at the same time.[50]

Forms of the shared appropriation of nature thus constitute societal conditions at differing stages of the differentiation of society away from nature. They determine the cultural logic that gives this practice its objective meaning. Whatever the participants subjectively think, their actions are objectively determined by this logic of symbolic systems, these a priori cultural conditions. This results in extensive restrictions for communication in society. The symbolic logic of such an 'objective' culture can regulate communication in the medium of symbolic practices and produce the prerequisites for its social organization.

The sacrifice is a type of symbolic practice in which the symbolic order of society is manifested. To the extent this practice uses the medium of blood and meat, we can speak of a carnivorous culture. This sets down a form of

---

49 That does not mean that differences in status cannot form again inside the subsystem of companionship. Cf. Bourdieu (1984b).

50 The vegetarian oppositional movement and the (often strange seeming) forms of love for animals connected to it are the distorted expressions of the other (largely repressed) modern cultural tradition. They find expression to the extent that the rationality of economic culture is objectively called into question in modern societies. In this volume see also Chapter 3 on 'Culinary Morality'.

communication that is built on power and oppression and not on under-standing and consensus.[51] It is the one that has dominated in evolution. It determined the social structures of communication that formed in simple, traditional and modern societies. This symbolic logic has more far-reaching consequences for the direction of social evolution than for the distinction of its cognitive representations into analogical, hierarchical or egalitarian orders. Their resort to meat separates the societies distinguished in that way from another possible culture, vegetarian culture.

The concept of a modern carnivorous culture can help explain the trauma that underlies the origin of modernity, that is to say, the killing of those who think differently. An example of the specifically modern form of the carnivorous discourse is the idea of 'reason of state'. This idea justifies killing. It assigns the responsibility for killing to agencies that are no longer responsible. All this discourse asks is not to have to worry about everything, not to overburden the system. Ultimately, all it demands is that one should be thankful for being able to go through the world wearing blinkers. The vegetarian discourse does the opposite. It defends the innocence of nature and reminds us of a lost paradise. The modern justification of vegetarian culture is the search for the purity contained in nature which is basically peaceful.[52] What an oppositional discourse would look like in an ecologi-cally and psychologically troubled world remains an open question.[53] Calls for a new animal ethics and a new partnership with nature are presumably only transitional forms from a traditional vegetarian culture to a modern vegetarian culture. What in any case contributes to the reconstruction of this oppositional discourse is the systematic reflection on the cultural tradition from which it is fed: the cultural movement against the Greek sacrificial feast.

Vegetarian culture

The cultural movement against blood sacrifice aims at a reversal of the symbolism of the sacrifice. It replaces the blood-sacrificial feast with the community of those who do not eat meat. This characterizes vegetarian culture. It negates society, and it seeks to re-create that state of nature in which the paradisiacal coexistence of people and animals still exists. The community of those who do not eat meat has no differences. The vegetarian mode of life is the negation of social power. Vegetarian ways of life

---

51 This results in a considerable remodelling for a theory of social evolution starting with communications theory. It has to initiate the evolutionary differences elsewhere.

52 The vegetarian terrorism against ('ecologically minded') butchers which has arisen in England and Germany in recent years is again a mixture of the two cultural traditions distinguished above. The logic of fundamentalist collective action adds the necessary preconditions for such a recombination.

53 A radical answer is to talk about the 'end of nature' (McKibben 1990). This question will be taken up again in Chapters 6 and 7 below.

contradict social power relationships. They count on communication alone. Vegetarianism is ultimately the negation of the social order establishing itself in the course of evolution.

This applies to all societies. In simple societies the vegetarian way of life corresponds to the economy of gathering, which is associated with 'matriarchal' societal forms. In image at least, the order of women who took care of gathering was free of domination.[54] This order is opposed to the order of men who hunt. The order of men is characterized by competition and differentiation according to abilities. The origin of social power connected with hunting demands a specific distancing from nature. To the extent people differ from one another (and thus become unequal) they become different from nature. The differentiation that becomes possible with the masculine order differentiates nature as well in its own image. The separation into a carnivorous and a vegetarian world thus symbolizes the break of a (matriarchal) world of gathering with the world of (patriarchal) hunting.

This symbolic 'differentiation' is continued in traditional societies. In it, individual fate no longer counts, but instead only status in a (religiously legitimated) hierarchy. The differentiation into rulers and ruled requires a more far-reaching symbolization. Animals are divided into 'edible' and 'inedible' according to their 'cleanliness'. The hierarchy resulting from this differentiation reinforces the distinction between above and below with that between clean and unclean. The cooking of the sacrifice is pure (Detienne & Vernant 1979); the cooking of the fruits of labour is impure. Food taboos thus acquire a central role in simple societies not only in symbolizing, but also in producing and reproducing a hierarchical order. Whoever is admitted to the sacrifice belongs to the top of the hierarchy; whoever is restricted to profane everyday culture belongs to the bottom of the hierarchy.

In these societies, vegetarian ways of life are the negation of this hierarchy. Thus Detienne reports of Pythagorean sects in Attic culture that refused to eat meat and, consequently, to participate in the sacrifice.[55] There are analogous phenomena in the Bhakti movement and in Tantrism in classical India (Dumont 1970: 33ff.). With the aid of this practice they are distinguished equally from those who eat 'clean' and those who eat 'unclean' meat. They renounce society and retreat to a state of nature that contradicts society. Social differentiation, which was produced with the construction of a 'divine' natural order, is called into question by vegetarian practice. It makes it impossible to participate in the rituals regulating the symbolic

---

54 The fact that women gather and men hunt indicates gender-specific contexts for ritual action (Moscovici 1972). The carnivorous realm is connected more with the masculine, while the vegetarian is connected more to the feminine. This notion is being taken up again in the debate on the origin and historical meaning of 'patriarchy'. On this argumentation context cf. especially Borneman (1975).

55 Those who refuse the sacrifice do not eat meat. On this Greek 'peculiarity' cf. Detienne (1979: 14ff.).

reproduction of society. Beyond that, it disrupts the model with which a social order can be produced.

This vegetarian practice recurs in modern societies. Here too, vegetarian ways of life represent the contradiction of the culture of meat-eaters and a negation of their inequality. The carnivorous culture, which has differentiated in modernity into a high gastronomic culture and an industrial food culture,[56] is doubly negated by the vegetarian way of life, which is both anti-industrial and anti-bourgeois. Society is to be re-embedded in the state of nature. The renaturalization of society contradicts the industrial culture and class structure of modern societies. Vegetarian culture articulates a collective need for 'back to nature' against this industrial class culture. It is one of the escape movements that have accompanied modernity from the very beginning (Krabbe 1974; Weiß 1986; Sprondel 1986).[57] It is not the difference between traditional and modern – this implies far-reaching corrections to a theory of modernization – but the difference between carnivorous and vegetarian, between familiar and unfamiliar modernity (Schäfer 1985), which permits the adequate reconstruction of the culturally-specific logic of modern social self-construction.[58] Only this difference makes a theory of the social evolution of modernity possible.

Finally a changed perspective on the 'prehistory' of humanity also results. The debate in modern social science that has ignited on this very example of human sacrifice and cannibalism (Arens 1979; Sahlins 1979; Brady 1982) is an example of the double symbolic logic that runs equally through prehistoric ('primitive') and posthistoric ('modern') societies. This discourse is not only a more or less adequate interpretation of 'primitive' practices, but also implies an interpretation of 'modern' practices. The discourse on the good or bad prehistory of modernity is also an attempt to conduct a discourse on oneself. The fact that the options for the good or bad prehistory are open only shows once again the fundamental ambivalence of the cultural code of modern Europe.

---

56 On the issue of class-specific food cultures in an evolutionary perspective, see Goody (1982). Grignon & Grignon (1980) attempt an empirical analysis of modern class-specific food cultures. In particular the contribution by Grignon & Grignon contains an interesting empirical analysis of the differential symbolic meaning of eating.

57 Cf. Chapter 5 in this volume on the modern natural foods movement. It becomes clear from this analysis that the symbolic difference asserted here is also of importance for modern societies. This relativizes some of the ideologically motivated explanations of such movements. Whether this relativization based on cultural theory applies to all modern social movements, is a point that can only be pointed out here as an intellectual possibility.

58 Modernity is a combination of both cultures: a culture founded on human sacrifice, and a culture founded on the prohibition of human sacrifice. Greek society rewarded carnivorous culture and differentiated itself at the same time against the bloody culture of the barbarians (the Scythians). Ancient Jewish culture rewarded vegetarian culture and differentiated itself at the same time against the religious tendencies of the Orphics and the Pythagoreans, who rejected any blood sacrifice and advocated a bloodless culture. How this complex tension is resolved in modern European society remains an open problem of the evolution of these societies.

The sacrifice as social contract

The sacrifice is a ritualized form of communication. In order to understand and explain it, one can seek to understand the subjectively intended significance of actions that are ascribed to this form of communication. One can also argue the opposite and assume that the significance of the actions taking place in such communications results from the objectively expected significance of a culture, not from the subjectively intended significance.

The simplest version of an action-theoretical explanation of sacrifice consists in explaining it from the utility that a sacrificial action has. The idea that actions can always have a utility is banal. There is scarcely an action that cannot be useful in some way or other. The fact the utility is intended, that it is the motive of an action, is a further assumption of action theory. The motive for human sacrificial rituals is related here either to material motives (the eating of human flesh, insofar as it is practised at all) or psychological motives (protection of identity or a social order). These motives for action thus become the core of an explanation of sacrifice. They find their most consistent expression in the power-theoretical variant of action theory: sacrifice, particularly human sacrifice, is the result of an instrumentally rational calculation that aims to maximize exploitation. Sacrifice is a form of deliberate exploitation of those who must serve as the objects (or subjects). Interactionist variants of the action theory do not change the logic of this argumentation. They only make less solid assumptions about motives that direct the action. In the extreme case, they no longer assume any motives at all, but leave these to the negotiation process of those participating in the interaction. These variants of action theory offer no new explanatory perspectives for an explanation of the sacrificial ritual. The sacrificial ritual is precisely a system of action in which there is nothing more to be negotiated out, a situation which cuts across fundamental action-theoretical assumptions.

The attempt to explain sacrifice from the logic of a symbolic order of society, from its 'cultural code', goes beyond explanatory attempts based on a theory of action. The significance of the cultural notions on which sacrifice is based, and which are confirmed and reproduced by the sacrifice, transcends the subjectively ascribed significance. It is objective in the sense that this cultural code makes communication possible and reproducible.[59] Only this logic of symbolic orders distinguishes society from the state of nature. So long as there are only individual actions (no matter how socially motivated), the state of nature prevails. No one needs communication in the

---

59 There is no dispute that external factors such as demography, water supply and geographic boundaries have an influence. Yet their meaning is dependent on the interpretation people give to these natural factors. It is undisputed that problems of social demarcation, distribution and power also play a part. They seldom act by means of their naturalness. Their role is instead determined by the meaning of these factors, which is given them by a symbolic order.

state of nature, because there is nothing about which people must agree. As soon as those who act generate rules for their action, the societal condition prevails. Communication is needed in the society, because commonly shared rules require a process of collective agreement or collective confirmation in the case of the violation of collectively valid norms. That which distinguishes society from the state of nature is a social contract. Detienne & Vernant (1979) formulate this pointedly and provocatively: 'Le contrat social c'est d'abord une opération culinaire'.[60] The societal condition is confirmed and reproduced in the performance of a common ritual feast. The shared ritual consumption of meat characterizes a specific cultural option in this sacrificial feast, the option for carnivorous culture.[61]

The sacrificial feast reproduces the cultural foundations of political rule in the polis (and in ancient households).[62] Even in modern societies, the social contract is celebrated and invoked again and again. Of course, the symbolic forms of expression have differentiated apart. The social contract is no longer celebrated only in state banquets, which most closely resemble the classical sacrificial feast in its external form. Culinary operations dominate the reproduction of modern social self-construction in every field of social power. The idea that the modern rationalization process has also 'rationalized' the social contract and thereby abstracted it down to its naked core, of simply being a contract, is not confirmed in modern society. Even modern society cannot do without ritual staging of the social contract.

Yet we are scarcely aware of the symbolic elements of these practices any more. The historical and comparative material for premodern societies presented above was able to establish that the empirical key to these symbolic practices is found precisely in ritualized culinary operations. The symbolic effectiveness of culinary operations in modern culture remains to be shown. The first thesis is that, even in modern society, power is determined by the interplay of carnivorous and vegetarian culture. The second thesis is that we reproduce the modern social contract daily in culinary operations. Instead of capturing the culture of modernity in its

---

60 This is the wording of Detienne & Svenbro (1979: 222). Such a thesis analogizes the sacrifice and the forms of participation in modern public life. This yields some interesting perspectives on the function of modern mass media in regard to the symbolic representation of blood, killing and the like.

61 Cf. Detienne (1979: 7ff.). The fact that meat plays such a large part in this meal makes the question of symbolic logic even more acute: what significance does meat have in the sacrificial ritual? What is being communicated in the medium of meat?

62 The theoretical model of a 'social contract' can be projected equally well onto archaic societies. Hunting together depends on solving the problems of the collective appropriation of the quarry. Without a solution to this problem it would be impossible even to think of common economic action. Here the ritual form itself becomes a social form, and not because – as Durkheim believed – elementary forms are revealed in simple societies, but rather because in these societies it is possible for society to appear to the participants only as a ritual conducted by the community.

intellectual rationalizations and self-descriptions, this implies the attempt to understand this culture in its everyday performance.

Alongside the weather, food is the most important discursive topos in processes of social interaction. When food becomes the object of symbolic conflicts, then this implicit meaning becomes explicit. In the modern natural foods movement we possess a phenomenon that can provide information on both theses. To the extent it focuses on food, this clarifies the difference between a prevailing food culture and an alternative food culture which makes lines of cultural conflict visible. The analysis of the modern discourse on edibility and the mobilization of social groups within this discourse ultimately show how the modern social contract is staged in eating and how a social way of life is constituted.

5

THE MODERN DISCOURSE ON WHAT TO EAT: A SOCIOLOGY OF THE NATURAL FOODS MOVEMENT

Two modern cultures

In the process of modernizing the traditional societies of Europe, a culture arose which made a new path of social evolution possible: the culture of the Enlightenment.[1] The rising bourgeois society gave this culture the distinction of representing the highest form of social rationality. Modernization was even equated with rationality.[2] Yet bourgeois society was not able to redeem this claim, let alone assure it. The culture of the Enlightenment was never able to control this modernization or set its direction. The culture of the Enlightenment became an 'ideology', as it is called in the self-observation of bourgeois society.

This self-criticism has not been the only critique of modern culture. The history of modernization is not just the history of social movements that supported this self-criticism of bourgeois society. It is also a history of social opposition movements to modernization that have transcended the self-criticism of bourgeois society. Bourgeois society, of course, has dismissed these oppositional movements and the critique of modernity they espouse as 'irrational'. No matter how self-critical it may have considered itself to be, bourgeois society has always viewed and denounced these movements, whether they were Luddites, sectarian movements, or Romantic escape movements, as 'irrational'.[3]

The perception of the oppositional movements to modernity as

---

1 For extensive information on this cultural transformation, cf. Eder (1985). The key to this cultural transformation is the institution of associations, as it developed since the end of the eighteenth century in Europe.

2 Max Weber provided the classical description of this rationalization process. It culminates in the formal rationality of bureaucratic forms of rule. For the debate on this rationalization process, which remains immanent, cf. Schluchter (1979, 1981) and Habermas (1984).

3 These movements have so far been of hardly any importance in the theory and critique of bourgeois society. An exception is Hobsbawm (1952, 1972, 1981). For a more recent version of this theme cf. Wulf (1987). The emergence of the 'new social movements' has reawakened this interest. As representatives for others, cf. Schimank (1983), Weiß (1986) and Eder (1986b). Older analyses of such movements are found in cultural anthropology (Lanternari 1960; Queiroz 1968).

'irrational' is nourished by an unshattered self-attribution of rationality by modern bourgeois society. So far, the self-criticism of this society has stopped short of this imputation of rationality. It can afford this less and less, however, because the self-produced ecological and cultural crisis of modernity seems to validate precisely the critiques of the opposing movements. The monopoly on rationality which this society has managed to maintain so far is becoming ever more fragile. It is becoming increasingly difficult to accuse its accompanying opposition movements of irrationality. Quite the contrary, it seems appropriate to acknowledge a rationality specific to these opposition movements, rather than continuing to disparage their alleged 'irrationality'.

What cultural traditions nourished these movements? What were their cultural sources? The classical answer, which has not been able to irritate the self-concept of bourgeois society, cites expectations of salvation arising from religious traditions as found in simple peoples (Lanternari 1976), magical traditions that make it possible to compensate for the overwhelming power of nature (Thomas 1973). These oppositional movements are said to be vestiges of traditional culture that simply have not yet broken up in the course of modernization. That they have occasionally gained strength or are gaining it now is dismissed as mere regression. This theoretical perspective on modern oppositional movements continues to follow the negative perspective associated with the imputation of rationality. These oppositional movements continue to be seen as effects of transitional crises in modernity, of overwhelmed individual existences, of economic crises and cycles. In such situations it would be natural to turn to the familiar past, that which one has lost: a world without crises or problems of meaning. The theoretical image of the modern oppositional movements, then, is that of a traditionalistic reaction against modernity.

A different image results if one does not pit modernity against traditionalism, but rather the dominant against the repressed type of modernity. That opens up the possibility of testing the thesis of a rationality specific to the oppositional movements because, from this perspective, they cannot simply be dismissed as irrational. This model presumes that such movements are nourished by an alternative model to the dominant modernity, rather than by the past. They are not retrospective reactions to the process of modernization. They are just as much exponents of a 'project' of modernity – of attempts to create a modern society – as are the 'rational' movements in the process of modernizing society. They are attempts to create an alternative modernity, an 'unfamiliar modernity' (Schäfer 1985). All the way into the late twentieth century, these movements have developed not only in opposition to the ruling elites or classes, but also generally in opposition to the modernizing social movements (thus in opposition to the labour movement as well!),[4] and they differ in more than just their goal, that

---

4 An example of such a perspective is the studies on 'primitive rebels' by Hobsbawm (1972).

is, an alternative modernity. The modern oppositional movements do not want power in modern society. They want an alternative kind of modernity in the shadow of the prevailing one.

These oppositional movements deviate from the image one usually forms of a 'modern' social movement in several respects:

1   These are movements that do not care about their own growth.
2   These are movements that are not concerned with 'organizational issues'.
3   These are movements that have nothing to do with rebellion or deviance.
4   These are movements that are not dependent upon their success for their existence.[5]

The image of these oppositional movements contradicts the familiar image of a rationally organized social movement. They are a 'fluid' phenomenon (Gusfield 1981a) that resists the analytical categories of rational collective action. From that perspective, this phenomenon can only appear irrational. Modern oppositional movements differ from 'rational' social movements in regard to the topics that guide them. They are not concerned with 'rational' issues such as freedom, equality or liberation, nor with the problem of distributing rights and goods. They are concerned instead with 'irrational' issues such as the integrity of the body, that is, precisely the type of goods that can neither be divided nor distributed. These oppositional movements raise a problem of social self-construction that is more fundamental than the problem of distribution: the transformation of nature into culture. This means that, to paraphrase Durkheim, these movements address the 'non-rational foundations of rational collective action'.[6] Therefore the relationship of man to nature is a central key to an understanding of modern oppositional movements.

Having so far generally stood in the shadows of political (constitutional) and social issues, the issue of nature has received its current significance from the experience that society is no longer making its environment, but rather the environment made by it is being reflected back in a destructive fashion. That is only an external reason, and one that other societies have also experienced. The difference today is that modern society is experiencing environmental problems with an 'alternative' consciousness of what it is doing. This is the society that defines environmental problems as societal problems. Concern with the environment has pushed the transformation of oppositional movements into a 'new' environmental movement.[7] The

---

5 Gusfield attempts to comprehend the difference between movement and oppositional movement in these dimensions. Cf. Gusfield (1981a: 320f.).

6 Gusfield (1981a: 323). This emphasis on the 'cultural' side characterizes both the recent literature on new social movements and the recent literature on class structure and social inequality in advanced industrial societies, as is particularly true for Bourdieu (1984b).

7 The environmental movement is a rather broadly defined area of research. The main focus of research has been anti-nuclear movements (Rüdig 1990) and ecological (Green) parties (Rüdig 1991). A good overview is given by Dalton (1994), Dalton & Küchler (1990) and Jamison, Eyerman & Cramer (1990).

environmental movement thus gives an opportunity to an aspect of social self-construction which has so far existed in Western culture only as an underground tradition: a peaceable interaction with nature, an expressive way of life. It is the utopia of a society reconciled with nature (Milbrath 1984; Allan-Michaud 1990). This idea of a reconciliation with nature is found in religious, messianic and intellectual movements in all known cultures. It is undergoing a rise in significance in modern society at the end of the twentieth century which appears to shift it into the centre of social learning processes.

The modern environmental movement is an ambivalent phenomenon. It combines opposite perspectives on modernity: 'familiar modernity' and 'unfamiliar modernity' (Schäfer 1985). The first of these is an economically rationalizing movement, economically motivated environmental protection. The second is the renaissance of a relationship to nature that is characteristic for what has been called the 'deep-ecology' movement (Luke 1988). It moves an unfamiliar and so far suppressed type of modernity into the self-consciousness of the prevalent modernity. Deep ecology has put on the agenda the problem of the collective identity of the environmental movement. It has helped to transform it into what we have become used to call the ecology movement.

In order to understand the phenomenon of the current environmental movement, we should not simply view it as a 'new' social movement, one which succeeds the 'old' social movements and continues their tradition. This unidimensional historical perspective is not sufficient.[8] The environmental movement is both a new social movement and a new cultural movement. The double character of the environmental movement can be clarified to the extent the historical and cultural context of these movements is made explicit. That is why the ambivalence of the modern relationship to nature will be defined more precisely in the analysis below, first historically and then culturally by an analysis of modern food culture. An attempt will be made, as a third step, to demonstrate the thesis of the double character of the modern environmental movement with an analysis of the modern natural foods movement.

The ambivalence of the modern relationship to nature

The double structure of the modern experience of nature

The inherited nineteenth-century image of the development of the relationship of society to nature is ambivalent. One image is that of an increasing

---

8 This unidimensional perspective is found especially in Raschke (1985). For a balancing view cf. Eder (1993c).

moralization of nature.[9] Without distorting the image too much, one can say that the history of western Europe is viewed as a history in which empathy with nature and equal respect for nature are increasing. Rights apply equally to everyone, and what is understood by 'everyone' tends to expand to include 'every living thing'. This development runs parallel to scientific enlightenment, the decline of magic and the formation of secular moral notions (Thomas 1973). Just as slaves, inferior races and women were incorporated into the sphere of equal protection, so ultimately even animals and their suffering were drawn into this process of 'enlightenment'. Abandoning the assumption of superiority of people over animals, constitutive for classical Enlightenment, is not necessarily implied by this attitude.

The Romantic movement can be interpreted as a continuation and radicalization of the Enlightenment. It extends morality, intended to apply to people, to nature as well. The idea of an interactive involvement with nature radicalizes the idea of Enlightenment and extends it to 'life' as such.[10] Romantic emotion turns against the artificial and contrived side of Enlightenment thought and action. In this process it appeals to nature, the natural cosmos as well as the concept of naturalness (Weiß 1986: 291). Nature becomes the binding and infallible system of reference beyond everything that is merely artificial, which is identified with the political and social spheres. The Romantic concern with the relationship to nature is directed against the objectivistic and mechanistic image of nature in modern science. An idea of an 'inspirited' nature and the notion of a 'dialogue with nature' are set against the mechanistic image of nature (Weiß 1986: 289). This movement for a non-instrumental interaction with living nature found significant intellectual expression in the nineteenth century in the philosophy of Jeremy Bentham. The foundation of a human interaction with nature finds a philosophical substantiation here that makes this interactive relationship to nature more socially acceptable.[11]

The picture of an increasing movement towards a moralization of nature is, of course, not as clear as these suggestions would lead one to believe. Not only are there exceptions to this image of a continuously increasing

---

9 This positive self-image of modern culture is to be attributed to the bourgeois self-confidence in being the exponent of a higher stage of human morality. Theories of moral evolution still breathe this spirit. Cf. Ginsberg (1956). For a historical check of this thesis see Thomas (1983), who sees a slight but difficult-to-define transformation in this tendency.

10 Literary figures from Joseph Freiherr von Eichendorff to Hermann Hesse stand for the romantic interaction with nature. Wilhelm Heinrich Riehl, one of the most widely read cultural critics of the period of restoration and reaction, shows that politically this romantic enthusiasm for nature had strongly conservative aspects. He characterized the forest as that which continued to make the dream of personal freedom untrammelled by police supervision possible for modern 'cultured people'. This culminated later in the notion that the German spirit was destined to save the world.

11 On Bentham see Singer (1976) in particular. In Germany one could mention Riehl, the father of the conservation idea in Germany, as far as function, though not philosophical stature, is concerned. On his theoretical background, see Riehl (1976).

sympathy with nature, these exceptions in fact fit together into an independent history of the exploitation of nature: nature as an object to be used, whose ability to resist can be controlled by knowledge. The knowledge for dominating nature also increases. We are confronted, therefore, with a double process of intensification, which simply does not follow the logic of a zero-sum game. Both instrumental and non-instrumental interaction with nature intensify. On the one hand, the interaction with living nature is instrumentalized. Interaction with the corporeal, which people and animals share,[12] becomes part of a history of social control. The utilization of the body finds its apotheosis in the medical, criminological and psychiatric instrumentalization of the human body.[13] On the other hand, this physicality is imbued with morality: it is filled with psyche and equipped with feelings. A new kind of sensibility towards nature arises.

Thus there is a double structure of the relationship to nature inherent in modernity. That also constitutes the ambivalence in the modern relationship to nature. This ambivalence has been manifested since the seventeenth century in Europe in two typical forms of interaction with nature. On one hand, nature becomes the object of scientific knowledge; it is spied on and its fundamental laws are investigated. At the same time, nature becomes the object of touristic devotion; as 'free' nature, it becomes a medium of recreation. Since the seventeenth century, the development of the theoretical curiosity has proceeded in parallel with the invention of joy in nature. The separation of theoretical curiosity (Blumenberg 1973) and joy in nature (Böhme & Meschkowski 1986) is one of the crucial cultural choices in the modern era. It defines the European path to modern culture. This is where the social evolution of European culture is decoupled from the social evolution of other cultures.[14]

Theoretical curiosity systematizes the learning and adaptation processes that make an efficient relationship to nature possible (Sprandel 1972: 57ff.). The result of this theoretical curiosity is the ability to intervene personally in the reproduction process of nature. That permits a control over nature and a transformation of nature into social wealth which are unique in evolution. It also lays down the cognitive foundations for the current ecological crisis: accelerating entropic growth in nature, forcing the 'death by heat' of matter.

---

12 The body is one of the fashionable themes of recent cultural critique. Cf. for instance the articles in Kamper & Wulf (1982, 1984).

13 This theoretical perspective is particularly indebted to the works of Foucault. An advancement along these lines with respect to the medical interaction with the body is found in Attali (1979), who associates this form of interaction with the body and the 'cannibalistic'. Such an interaction with nature indicates the carnivorous character of this culture.

14 This does not imply that it is also more highly developed or more capable of development than those other cultures. At first this decoupling leads to nothing other than an enormous increase in the evolutionary pace. A first issue is whether modern society can even withstand and survive this pace. And there is reason to doubt whether practical reason is also developing at this pace, or can do so.

The key phrases are destruction of the rain forests, degradation of the ozone layer, exhaustion of energy resources, chemical pollution and nuclear waste. Joy in nature, by contrast, civilizes non-technical interaction with nature. The aestheticizing of nature is the medium of this sympathetic or 'communicative' interaction with nature. The fact that joy in nature is manifested in class and strata-specific ways is then of secondary significance. The cultural choice (which can always be used for the reproduction of social power relationships) is the phenomenon in need of explanation.

The parallel evolution of theoretical curiosity and the joy in nature is bound to produce interferences between these two processes. Just as the joy in nature does not remain untouched by theoretical curiosity, theoretical curiosity cannot be immunized against the joy in nature. This leads to a duplication of the modern ambivalence towards nature. Theoretical curiosity and joy in nature receive additional elements of significance. The Romantic oppositional movement to the Enlightenment and industrialism is an example of this sort of ambivalent radicalization of joy in nature. It opposes the dichotomy between art and science with notions of a Romantic natural science and of the integration of science and art. While early Romanticism still glorifies nature, this relationship is already reversed in late Romanticism. Nature becomes imponderable, a source of pain and suffering. This negative reinterpretation of joy in nature expresses the experience that even the purest nature cannot escape culture, and a direct experience of nature is no longer possible. Experience of nature is now only the experience of its impossibility and that produces pain as a new mode of nature experience.

The neo-Romantic movements in advanced industrial societies explicitly refer back to early Romanticism (Schimank 1983). Against the idea of a disenchantment caused by science, they advance the thesis of a 'social natural science' (Schäfer 1985). This image of nature criticizes 'cerebral thinking' and the 'one-sided rationality of technology'. It argues for a sympathetic and moral relationship to nature, for communalism and an irenic concept of politics.[15] This reversion justifies the phrase 're-enchantment of the world'. Reenchantment implies reversing those factors which advanced disenchantment in modernity, and the mechanism of disenchantment was, above all, modern science. Reenchantment has so far, however, been a part of modern history that has scarcely been discussed in this society's self-description. The dialectic of disenchantment by science

---

15 An example is found for instance in Maren-Griesebach's *Philosophie der Grünen* (Philosophy of the Greens) (1982). For a critique cf. Rödel (1983), who attempts in the sense of bourgeois enlightenment to work out the theoretical implications for democracy and comes – not surprisingly – to a rather (!) negative result in his evaluation of this philosophy. The ambivalence inherent in the double culture of modernity also comes through here.

and enchantment by the critique of science shows the difference between social movement and a new cultural movement in the modern age.[16]

The double structure of the schemata of experience and perception of nature has its origin in the everyday practices that determine the interaction with nature. The concrete foundation of the double significance of nature is to be sought before any intellectual representation. The ordinary practical basis of the double significance of nature is seen in the dichotomy of city and country. The double symbolization of nature enters into the antagonism between cultivated land and wilderness. It produces the antagonism between dominance and protection of nature, and it produces the peculiar relationship to animals that is torn back and forth between meat and mercy.[17] It is seen in housing, recreation and, above all, in food.

These phenomena become themes that also nourish intellectual discourse. In part, they enter into the official intellectual history of modern society. They are the object of a discourse dominated by science. They contribute to the unofficial, 'unscientific' intellectual history of modernity. They are also the object of popular theories on the interrelation of the world from the angels to the lowest animals (Böhme & Böhme 1983). Only when we understand the everyday practical forms of interaction with nature can we correct the distortions with which modern society attempts to comprehend itself in its intellectual representations. Only then can the monopoly on rationality, which the official representations are attempting to preserve, be broken up and the ambivalence of modernity even in its self-description be made visible.

The lesser known side of this ambivalence will be analysed in more detail below. The beginning of the modern era was connected not only with an increasing domination of, but also with a new sensibility towards, nature. Nature is also perceived as benevolent. This benevolent nature can also be shown in the positive evaluation of rural life and the wilderness, as well as in the origin of the concept of prevention of cruelty to animals and the concept of humaneness.

Benevolent nature

Medieval plagues were one basis for the origin of an attitude glorifying rural life (Sprandel 1972: 66f.). The glorification of nature in Boccaccio's *Decameron* (nature on patrician estates!) was a reaction to the plague in

---

16 As attempts at a reenchantment of science, cf. Capra's *Wendezeit* (Capra 1985) as well as Berman's 'reenchantment of the world' (Berman 1984). They oppose atomistic 'Cartesianism' with the idea of a holistic and participatory relationship of humanity to the cosmos. All the evils the modern world are blamed on Cartesian rationality. Prigogine & Stengers see alternatives to the disenchantment function of modern natural scientific thinking in the discovery of nondeterministic and irreversible natural laws (Prigogine & Stengers 1979).

17 Thomas characterized these antitheses as the modern 'human dilemma'. Cf. Thomas (1983: 242ff.).

Florence. People went into the country to escape the plague in the city. Life in the country became the antithesis to the death predominating in the city. Here nature became something benevolent by reference to the plague. The plague was evil. It was the opposite of nature, but it was no longer seen as the scourge of God. It was attributed to the city and thus to an expression of society. The city, as the quintessence of society, became the quintessence of death. The country as the quintessence of nature became the quintessence of life. The glorification of nature was the compensation for the experience of the deadly city. Nature was enhanced in value in equal measure with the advancement of urban development. The city's filth, bad air and stench were contrasted with the pure air in the country (Thomas 1983: 244f.). The culturally universal classification of pure and impure was projected onto the relationship of city and country.[18]

Another change in the relationship to nature is seen in regard to the evaluation of cultivating the land. Wilderness was contrasted to cultivated land as the positive, the world made by God (Thomas 1983: 254ff.). But this wilderness must be tamed in order to be considered as an expression of the good. Nature was 'embellished' as the expression of life. Nature became a 'touristic nature'. This nature is an invention of the seventeenth century (Böhme & Böhme 1983: 34ff.). It made possible the park – nature protected against tribulations. The tourist entering this well-equipped nature can experience nature as something pleasant and comfortable. If this nature is appropriately arranged, the visitor can find peace and quiet there (Van Baal 1971: 230f.). This man-made nature separated the dangerous and threatening from the beautiful, comfortable and peaceful.

The form of hunting shows the extent of the cultural construction of wilderness and the ambivalence connected to it particularly clearly. Hunting no longer has anything to do with providing nourishment; it has become a luxury. Hunting is recuperation from society. At the same time, it is also life in wild nature, which also includes the killing of animals. The element of cruelty to animals connected with hunting is relativized by its 'naturalness'. Hunting has become useless killing. This *plaisir* clearly shows how much wild nature is culturally defined nature, differing from cultivated nature only in its purpose. Cultivated nature serves the increase of wealth. Wild nature serves *plaisir*.

The ambivalence in the relationship of modern society to nature begins in everyday practices. It is present in forms of housing; it is intensified when one is dealing with the cultural forms of the hunt. The most important key to the ambivalence of the 'symbolic' interaction with nature, however, should be sought in the way people treat animals.[19] That shows how this ambivalence is tied to guilt feelings, feelings of unease and defensiveness – in other words, to ambivalences. This is shown particularly where one is

---

18 On the issue of purity versus impurity, see Chapter 3, 'Culinary Morality', in this volume.

19 This takes up a theme that already played a central part in the comparative analysis of food taboos and sacrificial rituals: the interaction with living nature. See Chapters 3 and 4, on 'Culinary Morality' and 'Carnivorous and Vegetarian Culture' respectively, in this volume.

concerned with the eating of animals. These cultural practices require extensive cultural symbolizations which can direct the feelings that are tied to the eating of meat (Thomas 1983: 287ff.). Eating meat thus becomes the central scene for the symbolic self-presentation of modern society.[20]

The ambivalent feelings that appear in connection with meat eating are an impressive example of the fact that, at the end of the eighteenth century, instrumental interaction with nature was felt to be repulsive, a violation of moral and aesthetic sentiments. Thomas views that as the problem of how the material requirements of a society can be brought into harmony with the new feelings and values that society has produced (Thomas 1983: 301). The ambivalence of the modern relationship to animals thus moves into the centre of a reconstruction of modernity which attempts to reveal both the good side and the bad side of the modern relationship to nature. Animals are both eaten and raised. Animals are both abused and pampered. There is no aspect in which the ambivalence of the modern relationship to nature is manifested so much as in the interaction with animals. Those movements that raise the issue of eating animals draw attention to the ambivalence in the modern relationship to nature. The vegetarian movement, the natural foods movement and other nineteenth century movements relating to health, embody this countercultural relationship to nature for the first time with an intentional critique of modernity. These movements took on the attempt to resolve the ambivalence of nature and create an 'unequivocal' relationship to nature. In the process, they were compelled to struggle against the prevailing model of a technical and instrumental relationship to nature.

The dual process of modernization revealed in this contradictory movement will be presented below on the basis of the development of food culture. The starting point is the question of how much the search for healthy food as the foundation of a healthy life is an aspect of cultural modernization which shares fundamental principles of modernity and at the same time transcends them.

Eating as culture in action

Two modern food cultures

The sociological view of modern food culture is that it is class-specific.[21] The difference between haute cuisine and popular cooking is seen as a cultural

---

20 Hardt (1987) pointed out that a change in literary representations from depicting eating as the representation of desire to presenting it as the representation of death occurred at the turn of this century. Even in modern times, eating obviously retains an enhanced version of the symbolic function which characterized the Greek sacrificial meal. Cf. Chapter 4 in this volume.

21 Such social-structural analyses are found, for instance, in Goody (1982). They show that such an analysis must be preceded by the analysis of the shared culture(s), if one wishes to understand the social function of stratum-specific eating cultures appropriately.

expression of the class structure of modern societies. This difference is gaining in importance as modern society shifts the reproduction of social inequality to the cultural level. The ambivalence of modern food culture, however, crosses this social difference. It is based on a symbolic difference: the difference between a carnivorous and a vegetarian relationship to nature. Cultural theory holds that this symbolic difference is more fundamental than the class difference.

The thesis is: the dominant modern culinary culture is carnivorous. Carnivorous culture, as the prevailing culture in modern society, appears cruel reproduced by the lower strata. This carnivorous model appears decent and refined when the upper strata reproduce it. It is bloody in both cases. This carnivorous culture has not gone undisputed. It has been called into question by a vegetarian cultural tradition since the beginning of bourgeois society.[22] This form of social criticism of the prevailing carnivorous culture will be examined below from the perspective of how much it has determined the relationship of modern society to nature or, alternatively, remained marginal.

The double structure of modern culture is articulated in exemplary fashion in the double structure of the culinary culture in modern bourgeois society. In culinary culture, the symbolic foundations of the dominant and countercultural movements in modernity become tangible.

The carnivorous culture of modernity

Bourgeois food culture is primarily carnivorous culture. Bourgeois food culture is the democratized form of the Greek sacrificial feast – that is the central cultural-theoretical assumption here.[23] The Greek sacrificial feast makes the shedding of blood and the eating of flesh the constitutive symbolic act of the polis. The symbolic foundations of the polis as confirmed again and again in this ritual also determine the tradition of modern Europe. They explain the primacy of meat.

One can divide the history of the democratization of carnivorous food culture into four cumulative steps and define them as follows:

1 Bourgeoisification of food culture.
2 Adaptation of proletarian food customs to bourgeois food culture.
3 Standardization of food culture, which finds its characteristic symbol in the hamburger.
4 Transformation of the Third World by European food culture.

This democratization of modern food culture is subject to the following premise: the further democratization progresses, the greater the meat

---

22 Modern vegetarianism thus receives an evolutionary significance which is by no means reflected in its quantitative significance.

23 The Greek sacrificial meal and the Pythagorean groups protesting against this ritual are described in Detienne (1979).

consumption. The symbolic significance of meat, which has its origin in the Greek sacrificial feast, regulates the development of modern food customs. Through the democratization of food culture, the carnivorous element is anchored even in the lower strata. The ethos of meat consumption is generalized over all social classes.[24] The symbolic element of bourgeois culture makes it understandable why bourgeois culture had to contradict itself eventually. That culture's claim to institutionalize the idea of a free and egalitarian communication cannot be brought into harmony with its own symbolic presuppositions. Because of its carnivorous symbolic basis, it systematically contradicts its ideals and, depending on the historical situation, bourgeois culture has been capable of living out this contradiction in different ways.

The 'high-cultural' form of food culture has the function of legitimating one food culture as a 'valid' culture. This culture has found such a form in the aristocratic 'haute cuisine' in Paris (Revel 1982; Mennell 1985). Other than in Paris, this type of haute cuisine existed only in Hangchow.[25] Both food cultures had a style-forming effect and set cultural standards. French food culture even dreamed of the culinary conquest of the world (Aron 1973: 166). Hangchow and Paris are among those cities that were obsessed with food. The condition for this obsession with food in both cases is the presence of a numerically large middle class. Such a middle class arose in Paris after the Revolution (Aron 1973). Marco Polo reports an analogous phenomenon in Hangchow before 1276. Rich rural environs are an additional condition that is also present in both cases. The transformation of a 'haute cuisine' into the 'grande cuisine' of Paris and Hangchow can be explained as a result of a bourgeoisification, which relies on wealthy middle classes.

Yet the development of modern culinary culture did not stop here. The establishment of the 'grande cuisine' brings with it the adaptation of proletarian food customs to bourgeois food culture ('good home cooking'). That too is only an intermediate step on the way to a standardization of food culture transcending all classes and finding its characteristic symbol in the

---

24 The historical investigations of the food supply show that meat consumption was relatively high until the late Middle Ages. In the succeeding centuries until the early nineteenth century, consumption of meat declined for objective reasons. The economist Rocher called this elimination of meat from the diet the 'stage of depecoration'. Teuteberg & Wiegelmann (1972) take off from that point. These studies exhibit, to the extent they interpret the data at all, a peculiar mythology. They accept the modern 'protein mythology', which grants meat a nutritional value superior to all other foods and even associates this with a higher cultural stage. The antithetical concept is known as 'nuts and berries'. These patterns of cultural interpretation (or perhaps prejudices?) consistently mark the interpretation of the available statistical materials on the history of the nutritional situation of various population strata. A good source on this matter is Teuteberg (1992).

25 Cf. Rothschild (1980: 4f.). This comparison also points out that a theory of a single-line evolution of eating culture has little explanatory power.

hamburger.[26] Here carnivorous food culture finds its most succinct expression. This is increasingly accompanied by the internationalization of food culture, culminating in the transformation of the food culture of the Third World by European carnivorous culture.[27]

The democratization of carnivorous culture does more than just legitimize carnivorous food culture. Precisely in the form of 'grande cuisine' it also supplies the possibility of civilizing the oppositional movements against this culture. The form of 'grand cuisine' is also transforming vegetarian culture today and attempting to integrate it into the new high culinary culture. The new natural luxury foods, the three-star natural foods restaurant and international vegetarian cuisine (the 'Keyno' restaurants, for instance) are absorbing the modern culinary counterculture and thereby turning it into a class culture. It is becoming a ruling culture which differentiates itself from the ruled culture by absorbing countercultural elements. Whether that implies the dismemberment of the anticarnivorous culture or promotes the process of incorporating countercultural elements into society remains an open question. It can be answered only when we have more precise knowledge of the logic and dynamics of this modern counterculture.

The anticarnivorous culture of modernity

Culinary culture is a mechanism for reproducing the dominant culture of the modern age. Even the culture of the lower strata cannot be considered a culinary counterculture. It is only the deprived culinary complement to the dominant culinary culture. The carnivorous structural elements of the dominant culture are reproduced in this deprived culture just as much as in high culinary culture. It is proper to speak of an anticarnivorous culture only in the sense of a counterculture opposing the culinary culture of both the upper and the lower strata (bourgeois or petit bourgeois culture as well as proletarian or plebeian culture). Characteristic of the relationship of the dominating culinary culture to the marginalized vegetarian culture are derogatory names, which have only existed since the first half of the nineteenth century, such as 'the nuts among the berries' or 'food faddists'. These derogatory labels arose with the first beginnings of the formation of a bourgeois culture in Germany (Hepp 1987).

The increasing industrialization since the 1870s strengthened this counterculture. It produced both a broader spectrum of countercultural activities (the various bourgeois escape movements) and, increasingly, intellectual justifications for an anticarnivorous culture. That which is collectively referred to today as the 'natural reform' [*Lebensreform*] movement[28]

---

26 The Frankfurt or Viennese sausages are provincial precursors of the cosmopolitan hamburger!

27 Goody particularly emphasizes this aspect. Cf. Goody (1982: 154ff., 175ff.).

28 For the literature of these opposing movements cf. Krabbe (1974). For more recent literature (especially covering the period from 1890 to 1930) cf. Linse (1983a, 1983b).

includes very diverse groupings with very diverse reformist activities and world-views. First, it includes the natural healing movement, which subscribed to the views of Hufeland, Preißnitz and Kneipp, and trusted in natural remedies and natural healing practices. Then comes the vegetarian movement, which forswore meat consumption and thus the killing of animals for ethical reasons. The anti-alcohol movement, which warned against the consequences of excessive consumption of alcohol, also belongs in this category. Finally, it includes the German Youth Movement of the early decades of this century, which strove for freedom from narrow-minded conventions (leading among other things, to the abolition of the stiff collar and the whalebone corset!).

These movements created a demand for alternatives to the products available in those days, and this demand was satisfied by the health food shops [Reformhäuser]. The natural healers needed natural remedies (herbs and teas), the vegetarians substitutes for meat, the opponents of alcohol non-alcoholic beverages and the members of the Wandervögel 'natural' clothing. The 'vegetal' became the quintessence of an alternative to the prevailing food culture. If thought out with sufficient consistency, emphasizing the 'vegetal' leads to a rejection of the 'animal'. This contrast with the culinary culture of bourgeois society was radicalized among the reform-minded vegetarian groups (Krabbe 1974: 50ff.; Sprondel 1986).[29] The supporters of the vegetarian movement were the lower middle and middle classes. Merchants and teachers, civil servants and white-collar workers, craftsmen and skilled workers were among the most frequently mentioned occupations of the members of organized vegetarian movements (Krabbe 1974: 140). This anticarnivorous culture was also a petty bourgeois movement which strove to implement an 'alternative' relationship to nature in reaction to bourgeois modernity.

The natural reformers experienced further growth after the turn of the century. They moved to the country as settlers to till the soil and became refugees from the city. They founded lifestyle or philosophical communes which organized around a certain idea or leader. The most famous of these was the Eden Vegetarian Orchardists' Colony, founded in 1893 (Linse 1983b: 37ff.). The proximity of vegetarian motifs to cooperative organizational forms is characteristic. Accordingly, the objective of the Eden Vegetarian Orchardists' Colony was to connect the vegetarian lifestyle and common ownership of land in a new garden of paradise. This cultural movement experienced its zenith in the inflationary times of the 1920s and early 1930s (Linse 1983a). The 'inflation saints' radicalized the countercultural movements and strengthened their affinities to 'folkish' ideas.[30]

---

29 The following analyses are more than anything else a chapter of German cultural history. For a current view, see Hepp (1987).

30 Susceptibility to political seduction was increasing at the same time. Even this chapter of German cultural history does not escape the pathogenesis that characterized the German history of modernization. See Eder (1985).

The tradition of anticulinary culture is being continued in the contemporary natural foods movement, which has gained importance since the 1970s.[31] This natural foods movement shares many traits with the natural reform movement of the nineteenth century. Its social-structural prerequisites should be sought in the expansion of the middle classes, which even in the nineteenth century supported the model of cultural opposition to bourgeois culture. Currently, it is above all the so-called 'new petty bourgeoisie',[32] the new service professions, particularly in social services, which support this movement and thus continue the countercultural tradition. This movement takes on a new 'quality' in the sense that it focuses on the ecological crises in contemporary industrial societies.[33] It is becoming the cultural producer of the topos of an 'ecological crisis'. It provides new perceptions of problems which can then enter into social conflicts. It formulates a model of social development that sides with nature and against industrial civilization.

This attempt remains ambivalent. On the one hand, this model points towards an economically more rational interaction with nature, known as 'ecological interaction with nature'. On the other hand, this is a model which itself calls the rationality of an 'ecological interaction' with nature into question and demands a non-economic, namely a social, interaction with nature. This thesis of the ambivalence of modern natural reform movements will be illustrated and supported by a sketch of the modern natural foods movement.[34]

The natural foods movement

The topic: healthy eating

Like all other cultures, modern culture distinguishes between that which is good to eat and that which is not. Unlike other cultures, however, that which is not supposed to be eaten is no longer explicitly tabooed and given religious justifications and regulations. Instead, 'rational' recommendations are given that one should not eat this or that. And yet this overstates the difference:

---

31 The literature on the modern natural foods movement tends to be found in personal descriptions and instructional books for practical action: alternative cookbooks, for instance. A good analysis is Kandel & Pelto (1980) and Ameta & Partridge (1989). An informative essay with interviews of vegetarians is found in Graf (1986).

32 On the connection between petty bourgeoisie and new social movements cf. Eder (1993b). On the petty bourgeoisie in general cf. Bourdieu's analysis of French society (Bourdieu 1984b), which also emphasizes the connection between new petty bourgeoisie and counterculture movements.

33 The environmental crisis is also a cultural construct. Whether problems can be perceived as a crisis or not depends on cultural symbolization efforts. Cf. Douglas & Wildavsky (1982).

34 Sketch means that materials are collected together which can be the basis for a research programme. A systematic elaboration is not intended. Some recent environmental cookbooks and scattered environmental 'tracts' served as materials for this sketch.

traditional taboos were also rational, and meaning-creating interpretations are also part of the modern discourse on what to eat. In a specific sense, this discourse is just as religious as its forebears.

Fear of industrialized nature[35] is a central motive of this discourse: 'we are all afraid. This is understandable enough when poison melts in our mouth, and when we can no longer distinguish what looks natural from what is natural' (Nöcker 1983: 12). This motive becomes more consequential the more food is treated as a moral and aesthetic issue. Rudolf Steiner, the founder of the anthroposophical movement, summed up this attitude in the motto: 'You are what you eat!'

The distinction between pure and impure substances is a central topos of the natural foods movement. This topos is radicalized in the idea of vegetarianism as a form of natural harmony, the harmony of body and soul (Sprondel 1986: 322). Purity results naturally for vegetarians because they do not ingest any impure substances. Fear of the impure is combated with a conception of purity that refers to non-scientific attitudinal elements. One such element is the association of grains and shoots with life. To appropriate this type of nature is to appropriate life. The opposite is meat and slaughtering. They stand for death. The appropriation of that kind of nature is the appropriation of death.[36]

The theory underlying vegetarianism is based on the idea of a harmony with nature. Ethical vegetarianism is part of a counter-religious culture in the modern religious tradition. The key to ethical vegetarianism is the religious notion of a salvation that includes animals as part of 'creation'. That also ties in with fear, for all of creation lives with fear and hopes for salvation. As Paul puts it in the Epistle to the Romans (8: 19–23): 'because the creature itself shall also be delivered from the bondage of corruption into the glorious liberty of the children of God. For we know that the whole creation groaneth and travaileth in pain together until now. And not only they, but ourselves also, which have the firstfruits of the Spirit, even we ourselves groan within ourselves, waiting for the adoption, to wit, the redemption of our body.'[37]

This religious motive alone, however, is no longer sufficient. It is joined by motives which conceive of themselves a 'better judgement'. The phrase 'health through whole foods' signals a dietetic knowledge that conceives of itself as the alternative to prevailing dietetics. This practical everyday knowledge increasingly seems to overshadow the religious motives. Talk of 'nutritional awareness' challenges us to subject that which is offered for consumption to a practical test. Nutrition thus becomes an aid to strengthen

---

35 Fear is the common ground the natural foods movement shares with the environmental movement. Cf. Eder (1986c). Fear is the motive that supported, say, the protest against the planned nuclear dump at Gorleben. Cf. Bahr et al. (1981: 50f.).

36 As Tolstoy put it: 'So long as there are slaughterhouses, there will be battlefields'.

37 Cf. the sermon by Hans-Eckehard Bahr (Bahr et al. 1981: 33) entitled 'Hört ihr die Tiere weinen?' (Do you hear the animals weeping?).

people's feeling of responsibility to themselves and to nature. Dietary awareness is ultimately supposed to make it possible 'to view the world through food' (Moore-Lappé 1978: 10). This conception follows a practical logic: if we understand our eating habits, we will understand the morality on which our actions are based. This draws our attention to the morality or, rather, immorality of our practical actions.[38] This practical awareness also has consequences for a rationally based modification of our eating habits. There are both economic as well as physiological justifications for this. The physiological justification goes like this: it is better to get at least half of our daily protein requirements from eggs and dairy products rather than from meat. The economic justification is: the protein waste of our culinary culture, based on meat, is destroying the ecological foundations of the natural environment.[39]

There is a symbolic significance transcending such practical everyday considerations in the recent rejection of pork, which is disseminating through the vegetarian movement: 'The disastrous aspect of pork is that its metabolites cannot be consumed in the normal way within the organism, but only through 'pathological' elimination processes in the form of boils, eczema, *fluor albus* (leucorrhea) and so on' (quoted from Schwarz 1978: 10). This repeats the arguments of Maimonides in a modernized version. That does not exhaustively explain the dislike of pork. It lies deeper, in the negation of pork as the central symbol of the modern carnivorous food culture. There are also hedonistic variants of vegetarianism now disseminating, which contribute towards levelling out the differences between carnivorous and vegetarian culture. The simple argument that 'green foods taste good' is disarming. It hints at sensory experiences that have been lost or suppressed in the wake of the industrialization of food. This 'pure' nature is conceived instrumentally, but it does not exclude meat.

In order to understand the significance of such natural reformist movements for the social learning processes in modernity and locate them systematically in a more appropriate way, the 'opponent' against whom these arguments are directed will be analysed next. Only that can clarify the 'objective significance' of the practices supported by these movements.

The opponent: industrial food

The opponent of the natural foods movement is the industrial exploitation of nature. Industrial goods production changes the production of foodstuffs as well.[40] The industrialization of food production has given this movement

---

38 A characteristic quotation: 'Because our eating habits are so personal and the need for nutrition is so general, food presents the unique opportunity of capturing our interest and also teaching us.' (Moore-Lappé 1978: 10).

39 Cf. as well the explanations for food taboos, which the modern theoretical discourse prefers. See Chapter 3 on 'Culinary Morality' in this volume.

40 Cf. Mintz (1985) on the cultural history of sugar.

more than sufficient concrete evidence. Goody (1982) has pointed out that the problem of adulterated foods has existed ever since the beginning of industrialization. Typical examples are bread made from flour mixed with sawdust, or sausage adulterated with non-meat additives. Those practices still had a directly health-threatening significance. But in combating them a motif slipped in, to a greater extent for the middle classes than for the lower ones, which extends beyond mere assurance of survival. Health becomes a concept whose symbolic component grows to the same extent the industrialization of food production advances.

Current opponents of natural reform movements are distinguished by anticipating the protest and adjusting the range of products offered to it. There is a type of research for improving bread and grain production which is only 'cosmetic improvement' (Thomas, B. 1986). The industrial production of food accommodates the requirements of taste (Barlösius 1987). 'Sensory analysis', a scientific technique for testing sensory qualities, has been statistically standardized and adapted over and over again to changing tastes. This provokes a search for true, non-standardized tasting and smelling, for an authentic sensibility in tasting and smelling the natural environment. Modern natural reformist protest targets the 'regimentation of taste' by industry. It searches for the true nature, which has got lost in the process of industrializing and technifying sensory impressions. This thesis of the 'waning of the senses' (Kamper & Wulf 1984) applies particularly well to mass culture, which relies on the separation of a differentiated aroma production and an undifferentiated culture of perception and taste (which oddly enough ensures the acceptance of such food!) (Barlösius 1987: 374f.).

Another opponent is industry, which 'chemically' contaminates 'natural' foods. In this case, the enemy is the contamination of the natural rather than the regimentation of taste. Nature is opposed to the artificial, 'chemical' to 'organic'. Studies of the chemistry of foodstuffs (Katalyse e.V. 1986) single out the opponent and provide orientation for the search for the 'organic', for nature in everyday life. This down-to-earth, practical critique is increasingly allied with a critique of the food ideology of advanced industrial societies. Industrial provision of 'high-protein' food is criticized as a 'protein mythology' (Moore-Lappé 1978: 55ff.). In that view, 'high-protein' is simply equated with animal food. According to this mythology, only animal protein can fulfil human protein requirements.[41] This mythology reproduces the carnivorous culture of modernity. The hamburger has become its quintessence. It shows the connection between carnivorous culture and modern culture: the hamburger provides the ideologically prized protein nutrition and is simultaneously the expression of the fast-food ideology. Here the relationship between natural food motifs and industrial food production

41 Over and over one sees the attempt to justify the counterculture in utilitarian terms. This is nothing other than an attempt to make the counterculture unrecognizable in the prevailing culture.

finds its most succinct expression. The hamburger becomes the symbol of unchecked beef production in the Third World and the guarantor of a democratized carnivorous culture.[42]

These symbolic ambiguities also reflect back on the modern natural foods movement. They turn it into a constantly changing phenomenon, reaching from sectarian radicalism to mass hysteria. Countercultural motifs are articulated in all these reactions to the dominant culinary culture. This raises the question of how it can be possible, in this confusing image, to determine the social expressions of the modern natural foods movement as a movement.

The formation of the natural foods movement

The modern natural foods movement is based on small-scale associative group formation linked together through 'networks'.[43] This networking (often with a high loading on aspects of economizing consumption) does not touch the anti-organizational attitude of this movement. This attitude is supported by the idea of a community characteristic for anti-modern movements which see living in a community of 'networks' as being closer to nature than living in town or in a metropolis.

This cultural opposition movement is falling increasingly under the sway of the environmental movement which forces it to enter into competition with the political and social streams of thought equally effective in this movement. It is becoming the 'third arm' of the environmental movement. Its first arm appeals to the political tradition of civil rights, insisting on the right to a decent private sphere and to a self-controlled community. Citizens' initiative movements and conservationist movements make up this first arm of the environmental movement. The second arm appeals more to the tradition of the workers' movement which demands participatory and social rights. The Green movement and the political ecology movement, which engage in political struggles for power and influence on decisions with socially vital consequences, make up this second arm. Collective action becomes less moral and more strategic and legalistic. The third arm is fed on reactions to the challenges of modern culture, on countermodernist motifs defending and attempting to put into practice the ideals of the natural reform movement, or, as these are known today, alternative lifestyles. In this context, the natural foods movement appears to be the type of alternative movement that can at least respond to the down-to-earth practical needs of large parts of the populace.

---

42 Cf. Grefe, Heller, Herbst & Pater (1985) as an example for such debates, as well as the article in the journal *Natur* (No. 10/1985: 30ff.).

43 Associative group formation points to the ideal of bourgeois social self-construction, which in different national contexts is 'distorted' in various ways: either privatized (Germany), bureaucratized (France), or commercialized and cast in political/ethnic class structures (England/USA).

The combination of the first 'two arms' with the third one constitutes the equivocality which characterizes the project and the organizational form of the modern environmental movement. On the one hand, it claims a historical project in its self-understanding as a movement which replaces the movements that have so far shaped modern society. Organizationally, it is also up to the challenges of mass-media communication as phenomena such as Greenpeace or the WWF (World Wildlife Fund) demonstrate (Hansen 1991; Statham 1995). On the other hand, this movement is also a cultural movement anchored in the everyday life-world and trying to escape from organizational forms and historical missions. This gives rise to the 'fluidity' (Gusfield 1981a) and to the 'narcissism' which have been characteristic of modern opposition movements. This equivocality amounts to a paradox: the more the environmental movement attempts to organize itself, the more it will foster attempts at demarcation that in turn intensify the 'fluid' and narcissistic character of the cultural opposition movement within the environmental movement.

Thus ambivalence is the first connecting link between the environmental movement and the cultural opposition movement developing within it. The ambivalence of modernity is reproduced in this movement. The natural foods movement is just a case of this ambivalence of modernity insofar as it contributes to the counterculture tradition in the environmental movement and exhibits simultaneously the tendency to formal organization through creating ever more complex networks of groups.

This equivocality is compensated by a cultural form which is based not on a shared ideology but on a shared emotion. What unites the arms of the environmental movement, beyond their entanglement in the ambivalence of modernity, is basically fear. It unifies the natural foods movement with the environmental movement, even if the rational bases of the fear have different roots. The environmental movement is afraid of the ecological disaster that is now at hand, because of the uncontrolled and irrational use of the resources of this world. The natural foods movement is afraid of the impurity that is intensified by the technification of the industrial food culture. This is the encounter, then, of a rationalistic and a symbolic concept of fear. It both unites and divides the environmental movement. It unites it on the level of social protest against the world of advanced industrial societies. It divides it on the level of the cultural traditions the movement embodies. The characteristic feature of the ecological movement is to be both a pressure group and a moral crusade (Eder 1993c: 141ff.).

The public resonance to the natural foods movement tied into the environmental movement should not mislead us, however, into viewing these embodiments of countercultural forces as already being the key to a new type of reason, much less the assurance of such a new type of reason. It should not mislead us into making the tradition of modern countercultural movements the starting point for a salvation or redemption myth of modernity or the world. Rather, the history of such opposition movements has shown that they are politically ambivalent and tend to be radicalized politically in times of crisis. And nothing provides us with any guarantee that this would be different today. Neither should it mislead us, however, to deny this countercultural tradition. Instead, the countercultural tradition must always be examined as a latent foundation of modern sensory experience, if we wish to capture the ambivalent symbolic foundations of the modern relationship to nature by reflection and to control it in practical terms.

A new state of nature?

Especially in Europe, the development towards modernity has created that specific contradictoriness and ambivalence which have determined the political and social conflicts over nature. This European cultural tradition is becoming increasingly explosive the more modern society needs nature in order to reproduce its material foundations. This raises the issue of the social state of nature that is now beginning to become visible. And it raises the issue of the development paths that open up from this state of nature.

The development of the modern state of nature is characterized first of all by the fact that modern society must exploit nature increasingly in order simply to survive as modern society. It culminates in what Moscovici called the 'cybernetic state of nature'. This state of nature produces a systematic connection, controlled by science and technology, between the needs of people and the possibilities of nature. This is a positive modification of the 'iron shell' in which, as Max Weber predicted, modern people will entrap themselves. Yet this idea underestimates the internal dynamism of modern culture and its symbolic elements, because this development has also led to a new sensibility toward nature. A sentimental relationship to nature has become possible precisely through the distance from nature made possible by modern knowledge of it. This sentimental relationship shows and expresses the ambivalence and pathological potentiality of the symbolic foundations of modern culture. One of the objectives of these reflections has been to work out the implicit rationality of such potentials. It contradicts the rationality of the cybernetic state of nature. It is practical reason transcending instrumental ecological reason that industrialism preaches today. Seeking more than a responsible interaction with nature, it draws attention to the logic of the sentiments and feelings that determine our actions and interaction with nature prior to any ethics of responsibility.

It is impossible to predict how modern society will resolve this contradiction in its culture.[44] That it must solve it, however, is scarcely subject to doubt. Whether this will take place within the logic of the cybernetic state of nature or within a 'romantic' or 'savage' relationship to nature is a question of the conditions of social and political struggles in advanced industrial

---

44 As an optimistic variant of the assertion of a new relationship with nature in late modernity cf. Dreitzel (1981: 221ff.).

societies.[45] Thus the new state of nature becomes increasingly a question of politics. The spirit of environmentalism turns political. It engenders a new politics which is the modern politics of nature. Nature becomes the medium of a new politics in modern societies, a process in which the very foundations of democratic politics in modern societies are redefined. The merging of counterculture with dominant culture produces an effect which transcends the question of nature as an environmental issue: this issue is turned into an issue thematizing the legitimacy of a modern political and social order.[46]

---

45 The logic of the cybernetic state of nature can either follow the logic of the free market (Anderson & Leal 1991; Elkington & Burke 1989; Fischer & Schot 1993) or the logic of political regulation (Liberatore 1991; Lowe 1990; O'Riordan & Wynne 1987). The opposed logic of deep ecology has been described in Sessions (1987) and Nash (1989). Nicholson (1970, 1987) finally represents a modernized version of conservationism. They all are interesting cases of a fusion of both logics which brings back politics into environmentalism.

46 This thesis has already been forcefully put forward by Beck (1992, 1993). This topic will be elaborated in Part III of this volume.

PART III

THE MODERN POLITICS OF NATURE

6

FRAMING AND COMMUNICATING NATURE: THE POLITICAL TRANSFORMATION OF MODERN ENVIRONMENTALISM

The evolution of the spirit of environmentalism

Environmentalism and modernity

In this chapter the question is addressed as to whether environmentalism is changing modern culture. Our thesis is that environmentalism is a test of the capacity of modern societies to develop institutions that are capable of providing rules of fairness in the provision of collective goods. One example of such a collective good would be a natural environment which can be enjoyed and used by everybody. Furthermore, environmentalism has led to a crystallization of new cultural patterns. This indicates that what is at stake in environmentalism is not the survival of mankind, but the cultural foundations of the social order of modern societies. The argument is that modern environmentalism entails a dramatization of the relationship between man and nature in modern culture. The theoretical basis for this argument is that the relationship between man and nature refers to the binary code of culture versus nature which is a constitutive element in the cultural code of a society.[1]

---

1 This proposition is taken from Lévi-Strauss (1964c). The role of nature in the self-understanding of modern culture has been central to the modern history of ideas since Rousseau. It continues to feed the self-critique and self-reflexivity of modern thinking in authors as different as Bateson (1972) or Rorty (1979). The theory of culture which offers an analytical understanding of this relationship is found in the modern sociological theory of culture (Alexander 1989b, 1990).

Modern environmentalism thematizes a cultural code which is linked to European cultural history. This culture is a mixture: domination of nature being the primary relationship with nature; and sensibility towards nature being its inferior counterpart.[2] The empirical question that arises is to what extent this European cultural tradition is reproduced and may eventually be transformed by modern environmentalism. I claim that contemporary environmentalism is a turning point in the cultural evolution of modernity insofar as it provides a new cultural orientation by substituting ecology for industrialism as the basic cultural model for modernization. Moreover, it changes the nature of politics by inventing the politics of nature. Modern environmentalism leads to a new phase in the institutionalization of political agency which is part of the making of modern society. This new phase I shall call the age of 'post-environmentalism'.

The history of *modern* environmentalism[3] starts in the late 1960s. It can be divided into three phases: a first phase when the incompatibility of ecology and economy characterized environmental problems; a second phase when regulatory approaches dominated environmental action and discourse, with sustainable development as the latest manifestation; and a third phase which emerges today, that is, the cultural normalization of environmental concerns and their integration with established patterns of ideological thought. Most interpretations of the recent history of environmentalism advocate a unidimensional and continuous learning process in this development, claiming that there is more environmental consciousness, more political energy spent on it, and a deeper understanding of ecosystemic processes.[4]

This understanding of the history of modern environmentalism ought to be relativized by reference to cyclical patterns and cultural differences.[5] First, environmentalism is linked to cyclical waves of social protest. The last stage of the history described above is probably an instance of the end of a protest cycle. Secondly, rather than an evolution of environmentalism toward some kind of universal environmental ethics, there is an evolution of different worlds of environmentalism which are cultural responses to specific social conditions. The project of environmentalism is a series of 'green particularisms' rather than a collective project.[6]

---

2 This has been discussed in Part II of this volume. See also the discussion in Eder (1990b, 1994).

3 In addition to the materials presented above, an analysis of the prehistory of modern environmentalism (from more historical-descriptive points of view and with different intentions) can be found in Bramwell (1989), Brüggemeier & Rommelspacher (1987), Deléage (1991), Nash (1982), Pepper (1984), Trepl (1987) and Worster (1987).

4 For an analysis of this recent history see Brand (1993).

5 The idea of cyclical waves is a theoretical reaction to the progressivist ideas of development that have dominated sociological theories of modernity and modernization. A critique of these assumptions can be found in Alexander (1989a) and Eder (1990b).

6 An interesting analysis of the cyclical waves of environmentalism is found in Brand (1990). For an empirical approach which aims at analysing this phenomenon, see Eder (1992b).

Given these caveats it is still possible to assess the net outcome of the history of modern environmentalism. It is our basic assumption that underlying the social and cultural differences that have both fostered and blocked the evolution of modern environmentalism a public discourse emerges which presents concern for the environment as a coherent project. The net result is a discursive space with a universal frame of reference based on a particular way of relating man to nature. This project differs from the universalism of the Enlightenment which derived a universal frame of reference from social relations. The association of free and equal human beings, coordinating and regulating their activities through discursive procedures has been the basis of universalism in modern culture. This universalism is based on the idea that principles of social action can be universalized, that is, they can in principle be agreed upon by all the participants in a social situation.[7] This universalism can be naturalized in two ways. It is either turned into a metaphor as soon as nature becomes a part of the interaction situation. This is done by reifying nature as an actor capable of following rules that can be submitted to the test of universalizability. Or nature becomes the context of social interaction by naturalizing the logic by which interacting people relate to each other. This naturalization of the universalism which is inherited from the Enlightenment[8] turns into a fictitious universalism. This opens the door to a specifically modern anti-universalism. Nature becomes the starting point for a romantic backlash, for naturalizing social life, for a new Darwinism and the return of ascriptivism as a principle of social order.[9]

However, there is another universalist side to environmentalism. This other side has to do with two factors. The first is that environmentalism is based on systematically generated knowledge insofar as knowledge about the state of the environment is based necessarily on scientific evidence. Ozone holes are phenomena which do not lead to immediate concrete perception. They are scientific constructions. The second is that environmentalism is based on the idea of a collective will to provide collective goods and guarantee the fair distribution of these goods so that everybody can enjoy them equally. The fair *distribution* of such collective goods is thus secondary to the fair *contribution* of everybody to the production or securing of them. Modern environmentalism is an element of modern culture which

---

7 This is the classic notion of modernity which has been emphatically developed by Habermas (1984, 1987, 1992). See also my analysis of the principles of modernity in politics (Eder 1985).

8 The new emphasis on ascriptive elements in the construction of a social order – such as ethnicity, gender, age – points to a new naturalization of society. The critique of this naturalization has been developed in Chapter 1 in this volume.

9 A troublesome feature of modern environmentalism is that it can be linked to nearly any kind of belief, to Kantian ethics as well as to biological Darwinism. This property has led diverse attempts to integrate environmentalism into different ideological streams. An example is the attempt to connect environmentalism to liberal political theory (Dobson & Lucardie 1993). These discussions show clearly that such a connection is not exclusive.

extends the principle of universalization beyond the fairness of distribution of a common good and towards the fairness of contribution to a common good.

This double character of modern environmentalism prohibits explanations of environmentalism which see it as a step in the continuous unfolding of modernity. It also refutes the notion of environmentalism as a mere remnant of old but revived particularist traditions. It is a more complicated phenomenon that has to be seen in its political context. Environmentalism is a test on the capacity of modern society to keep up with its own universalist premises. It is a test of modern culture to reconstruct in a reflexive way the traditions from which it stems. Modern culture might often fail this test. But it can also pass the test. In this sense environmentalism is a key to the prospects of modern culture.

From environmentalism to ecological discourse

Modern environmentalism has fed the protest discourse of the last two decades in Western societies. However, the modern environmental movement, once the carrier of a new relationship of modern society with nature, no longer dominates the public discourse on the environment. During the 1980s, environmental protest groups put the environment on the public agenda. In the meantime its opponents have also appropriated the issue. Indeed, the environmental movements no longer have to struggle to voice their concerns; they have actually become topical. Ironically, there are now so many voices that it is difficult to be heard. Environmentalism is a voice that has to struggle for survival in the marketplace. This raises a first question: what happens to environmentalism when it is exposed to public discourse? The answer is that an ecological discourse emerges which transforms environmentalism into a political ideology, thus competing with the ones inherited from the nineteenth century. It becomes a medium of political conflicts and public debate which changes the political culture of modern societies. This leads to a second question: can environmental movements survive the marketplace of public discourse on the environment? The answer is that they do, while transforming themselves into well-organized public interest groups. Environmentalist groups become part of a system of ecological communication which makes environmental problems a common currency in public debate. The public debate on environmentalism also changes the institutional infrastructure of modern society. This raises a third question: do these two processes lead to more democracy or are we simply entering a new technocratic age in the name of environmental protection?

The answer to such questions requires an analysis of the logic and dynamics of public discourse on the environment, because public discourse is the arena where environmental concerns are tested for their power and legitimacy. Environmental protest actors are forced by this situation to defend their part in the public discourse on the environment which they once launched themselves. In order to survive the marketplace of public discourse, they must defend their public image. This public image can no longer be anchored in presenting oneself as being the only one who sensitizes environmental concerns. This 'monopoly' situation is increasingly replaced by one in which competitors emerge in the market of producing and communicating 'green' images. Keeping a public image is bound to a discourse where interactive strategic moves of competing actors begin to define the discursive field. Environmentalism is emerging from and integrated into what I shall refer to as 'ecological communication'. This development transforms the environmental movement into 'cultural pressure groups' (Statham 1992) and forces industrial actors to present themselves as public interest groups. Public discourse is, therefore, a key to the understanding of the transformation of environmentalism into an ecological discourse that is open to the whole of society. Furthermore, this extension of discourse in modern society changes the methodological foundations for the analysis: it forces us to go from the critique of ideology as a methodology to the methodology of discourse analysis.

A methodology for public discourse analysis

The methodological starting point for the analysis and explanation of the dynamics and logic of ecological communication is *frame analysis* (Gamson & Modigliani 1989; Gamson 1992; Snow, Rochford, Worden & Benford 1986; Snow & Benford 1988, 1992). Frames refer to stable patterns of experiencing and perceiving events in the world which structure social reality. An example is reading a newspaper, where frames allow us easily to identify what is written and to locate where things are written. We use and apply frames in order to sort the world, thus reducing the continuous stream of events to a limited number of significant events. Frames give to these selected events an objective meaning, thus disregarding subjective differences and idiosyncrasies ascribed to individual persons. Discourse analysis looks at the medium in and through which frames are constructed and reconstructed. Frames and discourse are therefore complementary phenomena. From a methodological point of view, frames are the micro-units of a discourse analysis.[10]

---

10 Discourse analysis can mean very different things ranging from philosophy to conversational analysis. We use the term in the sense that Van Dijk (1985, 1988) has given to it. Discourse analysis is simultaneously the analysis of the semantics of texts and the analysis of discursive strategies of actors. This duality of discourse analysis is the most interesting aspect for sociological analysis, because it allows us to relate textual representations of social reality to the social processes generating them. For such uses of discourse analysis see Bennett (1980), Cicourel (1980), Corsaro (1981). Further explications of discourse analysis as sociological method are found in Brown & Yule (1983), Fairclough (1989, 1992), Potter & Wetherell (1987), Wetherell & Potter (1988) with different emphases on linguistic, social-psychological or sociological perspectives. For a sociological application of discourse analysis see Donati (1992) and Gamson (1992).

The methodology for a discourse analysis of ecological communication presented here follows three steps. The first step involves identifying the cognitive devices for constructing frames; the second, analysing this construction of frames as a process of symbolic packaging; and the third, identifying the masterframe which emerges from competing framing strategies in public discourse. The emergent masterframe is to be specified by analysing the new ethical and identity frames in ecological discourse.

The first step in the discourse analysis of ecological communication is to identify cognitive framing devices in environmental discourse. Three basic cognitive framing devices can be distinguished in the universe of discourse of modern societies. These are the framing devices of *moral responsibility*, of *empirical objectivity*, and of *aesthetic judgement*.[11] These three framing devices can be seen as relating to different worlds: the social, factual and subjective world. Given that modernity is a culture which has differentiated these three dimensions, an analysis of frames has to be based upon the systematic distinction between three cognitive orders: the world of social norms, of empirical facts, and of aesthetic judgements.[12] Furthermore, this classification of framing devices defines the cognitive sources on which social actors draw in order to create an identity as a 'collective actor' (Eder 1993c).

The 'voice' we hear in public discourse is the voice of a collective actor who is capable of mobilizing communicative resources in order to enter the realm of public discourse. The analysis of this voice is the task of the second step of the proposed discourse analysis. This involves identifying the symbolic forms which organize the framing devices into communicable

---

11 Eyerman & Jamison (1991) make a similar distinction between what they call 'knowledge interests'. They distinguish between cosmological, technological and organizational interests. We prefer the term framing devices to knowledge interests because it allows a closer relation to empirical indicators. Knowledge interests are first of all philosophical terms (introduced by Habermas in 1968b) that are tied to a rational discourse and therefore have a normative implication. When distinguishing framing devices, the distinction of knowledge interests helps us to classify them. The normative model of knowledge interests serves only as a critical guide to framing processes, but not as a means for analysing reality.

12 The tripartite distinction is based on conceptions that we use while sitting on the shoulders of philosophical giants: it is a modest replication of the Kantian distinction between 'praktischer Vernunft', 'theoretischer Vernunft' and 'Urteilskraft'. It is also reproduced in the Habermasian distinction of validity claims: the practical, the theoretical and the aesthetic claim of validity (Habermas 1984). Gamson does not provide a systematic ground for distinguishing different frames. Given this, recourse is made to this theory of modernity that derives its sociological aspect from classic Weberian notions of a differentiation of 'values spheres' as constitutive for modern rationality. This systematic treatment will be the analytical starting point of the proposed discourse analysis.

frames.[13] Framing devices are used by social actors for either generating a moral sense of themselves or for furthering their rational interests. For both purposes, framing devices have to be embedded in collectively shared symbolic forms. Through symbolic packaging framing devices are 'attached' to the social world, to social situations and to social actors. To identify frames, it is therefore necessary to include the social context of framing devices, that is, empirical social situations with real actors. I refer to this phenomenon as 'symbolic packaging'.[14] The frames in action-contexts cannot be understood outside the specific symbolic package that gives them consistency, coherence and validity. Thus the second step of discourse analysis involves a move from the level of the analysis of cognitive structures to the level of *narrative* structures.[15] Narrative consistency and coherence, which are determined by symbolic packages, are the key to an explanation of the framing and communicating of environmental issues.[16]

Symbolic packages are the means of *framing strategies* of collective actors. In ecological communication these collective actors include movement actors (environmentalists), industrial actors, political actors, experts or media actors. Collective actors not only seek to communicate frames, but they also generate 'alternative' packages for environmental problems. This enables them to distinguish themselves from other collective actors. Movement actors thus package their framing devices in an oppositional symbolism. That this opposition is intentional may be made public by using words such as 'alternative', 'counter' and 'critical'. Movement-based discourses are 'counterdiscourses' to a dominant discourse.[17] The symbolic

---

13 The role of symbols has been a prominent topic in cultural anthropology. A theoretically interesting reading of the role of symbols in the reproduction of social life is found in Leach (1976) and Van Baal (1971). Symbols are what is processed between social actors, whereas framing devices are what is processed within the mind of social actors. The special relationship of symbols to what they communicate is another theoretically interesting question. There is an obvious connection between aesthetic framing devices and symbolic communication. A promising way to approach this connection is through what has been called 'mimesis', a reflexive sensual experience of the world (Gebauer & Wulf 1992). But also moral and empirical framing devices are dependent upon symbols for their communication which implies a systematic restriction for a purely cognitivistic approach even with regard to the framing device of empirical objectivity.

14 We take this expression from Gamson who distinguishes between reasoning devices and symbolic devices (Gamson & Modigliani 1987), but we give it a more central place in frame analysis.

15 There is a growing social-science literature on the role of narratives in understanding and explaining social action. For a systematic differentiation of cognitive and narrative forms of discourse, see Fisher (1984). For recent attempts see Abell (1987).

16 In the sociology of culture there is a general move from meaning as contained in text to meaning as communicated through text. A programmatic text has been that of Swidler (1986) coining the formula of 'culture in action'. For the further development of this discussion see Wuthnow (1987). See also Eder (1992c) for a further discussion of these ideas.

17 The term 'counterdiscourse' has been used by Terdiman (1985) to analyse forms of symbolic resistance in nineteenth-century France. This is an excellent piece of research applying productively a discourse analysis to historical events.

package of industrial actors, on the other hand, is related to a world where actors are engaged in learning to create a better and 'sustainable' world and desperately trying to convince society of their progressive ideas. This is the concern of industrial actors for moral and scientific progress and for an environment that allows for the economic well-being of people. Political actors, finally, try to define environmental problems by packages which are capable of conveying ideological consent, political responsibility and responsiveness to the concerns of the people. In each of these examples cognitive framing devices are used to validate the packages. A symbolic package that resonates in public discourse is then a fully fledged 'frame'.[18]

A third step for a discourse analysis of environmentalism emerges from looking at the way in which frames are communicated to the public and exposed to public discourse. This is the analysis of how actors compete for the control of frames in a given discursive field and push their particular framing of issues. It constitutes the level of 'public' discourse analysis. Frames create the identity of a collective actor and the collective actor's sources of legitimation in the public arena. The public communication of frames has an emergent effect: as soon as frames are communicated, they become the medium of exchange in a discourse. The more collective actors emerge in a society, the more communication increases. Whereas frames are the intentional products of collective actors (this is obvious in the case of advertisements and PR activities), discourses are unintentional phenomena. They emerge as a result of framing strategies of competing actors. Frames which are produced by actors and communicated to other actors do not coexist peacefully in public discourse, they function like a 'capital' in public discourse.[19] Accumulating *frame capital* in order to control the use of frames is the basic mechanism that constitutes public discourse. An understanding of frame competition leads us from the analysis of collective actors to an analysis of the way in which frames mediate between collective actors. The

---

18 The difference between framing devices and frames is thus the difference between the *modus operandi* and the *opus operatum*: framing devices are the means for constructing frames, and symbolic packages provide the means for communicating such constructions. Frames are the output of these constructive processes: a complex symbolic form that resonates in public discourse. This conceptualization tries to propose a more rigorous way of analysing frames. The existing literature is still rather lax on this point.

19 This economic metaphor could be extended. When frames are seen as capital, then framing devices are the currency (here we have to do with three important currencies). Inflationary use is eventually made in framing strategies which then devalues environmental problems and revalues competing social problems. This is a possible explanation of cycles of attention for environmental issues.

emphasis thus shifts to the 'media' of communication.[20] Frames are the 'input' into what I call emphatically a 'public discourse'.[21]

In public discourses frames are selected and stabilized. In this step of discourse analysis, the dynamics of the media for verbal communication become the centre of analysis. By dealing with public communication, the mass media have increasingly become the key to the production of the public discourse on the environment. Not only have social movements become dependent on media coverage (which on the other hand has made media coverage a resource for movement organization), but industrial actors have also begun to invest in a positive image through PR activities. Electoral campaigning, the traditional hegemonic mode of public communication, gradually decreases in importance given the fact that political parties tend to agree on what are the basic issues.[22]

The output of public discourse is a masterframe which is collectively accepted and used as a reference in the communication of environmental issues.[23] Masterframes are part of a reality beyond the reach of the intentional action of collective actors. No collective actor knows for sure whether its framing of issues will resonate and how it will resonate. They often delude themselves. A situation develops where there are competing collective actors trying to appropriate or reappropriate the definition of

---

20 The sociological analysis of 'media of communication' in the tradition of Parsons and its reformulation by Habermas (1984, 1987) and Luhmann (1984) has ended in the opposition of approaches which treat media of communication according to an instrumentalist model of language and generalize it to money, power and love (Luhmann), or according to a normative model of language that claims that media of communication 'ultimately' are bound to validity claims built into human language competence. These views are not incompatible. Money and power are media that also use language. The differences lie in the way of how language is used. We propose to distinguish between media of communication with respect to whether they are text-based or not. Those media that have to do with texts comprise those that allow for communication of oral or written information such as books, news, popular sayings, proverbs, theories. Their institutional carriers are mass media, libraries, personal talk encounters, etc. Money and love are different in that they are a non-textual symbolic device for communication. Power on the contrary is a symbolic device that is constituted on text-based communication: any command and any understanding of it are textual phenomena. Power is a language-based medium of communication *par excellence*.

21 By 'emphatic' I mean that public discourse approaches the model of the reasoning public that has been formulated in the social construction of political modernity by Enlightenment philosophers and thinkers. See the classic study by Habermas published first in 1962 (Habermas 1989). An attempt to continue along these lines can be found in Eder (1985).

22 A good example is the role of green parties in political life. The literature on their importance cedes from an exaggerated to a more realistic view. The traditional manner of equating environmental social movements with green parties and using the success of green parties as an 'indicator' of the strength of environmental movements has never been an adequate method of analysis. It becomes less so the more movement organizations and business organizations engage directly in the public discourse on the institutional regulation of the problem of nature.

23 We would prefer the expression macro-frames because they exist as a macro-phenomenon in discourse. However, the term masterframe has already been established and is, therefore, kept.

issues (or social problems). From competition over the control of frames emerges a discourse which defines the *collective* validity of frames of reality. Frames with this property are masterframes: they determine the resonance of the public discourse to what social actors are trying to communicate in public debate. This methodology for analysing a discursive field as the context of collective action guides the following analysis of modern environmentalism.

Framing devices in modern environmentalism

The cognitive construction of nature

Three cognitive framing devices were distinguished above: moral responsibility, empirical objectivity and aesthetic judgement. Moral framing devices tell us how, and according to which principles, to behave in this world. They differ from objectifying framing devices in that the latter rely upon empirical knowledge of the world. The framing device of aesthetic judgement is constitutive for organizing the subjective experience and perception of the world. These cognitive framing devices can be seen as organizing principles of a modern discourse. Within the discourse on nature these cognitive framing devices conceptualize the 'problem of nature'[24] and give it cognitive consistency and coherence. The first framing device generates a form of moral responsibility of man toward nature. The second organizes the empirical observation of nature and the scientific mode by which it is 'objectified'. The third refers to the qualities inherent in humankind's expressive relationship with nature.

In the discourse on nature these three framing devices are all present. However, the more these framing devices are combined, the more the model of functionally differentiated cultural spheres – within which specialized framing devices regulate the discourse on nature – is put into question. The modern discourse on nature, therefore, requires a model for the recombination of differentiated moral, factual and aesthetic framing devices.[25] The functional specialization of institutions for framing nature no longer conveys legitimacy. Thus the scientific community, as the institution controlling the definition of nature, has lost credibility (Wynne 1988a). Political institutions have to share power in defining what the relevant issues should be with actors outside the realm of institutional politics. Also the definitions of the expressive value of nature are no longer the privileged object of an autonomous sphere of artistic production. Pop art and musical

---

24 I will use the term 'problem of nature' to denote any cultural element that relates to problems arising out of the relationship of society and nature. Also see Eder (1990b).

25 That frame competition leads in some cases to dedifferentiation can be observed in some of the deep-ecology discourses that have developed over the last two decades.

campaigning (like any 'post-modern' cultural asset) have dissolved the autonomy of 'high culture'. Artistic culture has become a commodity and a political resource for mobilizing power. This is not dedifferentiation in the sense of a regressive development, but the introduction of these cultural spheres into the public sphere. There is a double process underlying this process: the immersion of culture into the marketplace, its becoming a commodity that is exchanged; and its immersion into public communication, its becoming an ordinary element in public discourse.

As it is in environmentalism that these developments crystallize, environmentalism becomes a key to the analysis of 'advanced' modern society. Environmentalism not only thematizes problems of the environment, but it has become an exemplary case for the reconstitution of society after the failure of systemic steering, in both the capitalist and socialist variants. Environmentalism is a case where the self-understanding of modern society is redefined as an order which constitutes collective action for solving collective problems.[26] The framing devices used in environmentalism are, therefore, the micro-units in the understanding and explanation of environmentalism as a cultural force.

Three framing devices

One way of understanding environmentalism is within the framing device of man's moral responsibility toward nature. This moral framing device can be traced back to ideas of a paradisiac nature where humans and nature were living together in harmony. This idea has been – after paradise was lost forever – transformed into a responsibility toward nature which has gained two ways of expression, the first being a type of responsibility that cares for nature because of its utility for mankind, the second being a type of responsibility that cares for nature because of general principles that apply to both humankind and nature. In modern culture the ethical traditions have developed along these lines, leading to two primary ways of framing moral responsibility for nature: the utilitarian and the deontological traditions.[27]

Historically, the utilitarian tradition has developed a much more positive attitude towards nature than the deontological tradition. The deontological tradition perceives nature from the point of view of its specific rationality.

---

26 This argument is further developed by Donati (1995, 1996). He shows how the structure of environmentalist thinking is a central element in the explanation of collective action and institution-building in advanced modern societies.

27 Alongside these two traditions (the utilitarian one that goes back to Bentham, the deontological one going back to Kant), traditionalistic frames have survived and been mixed in different ways with these two traditions. Communitarian approaches, for example, have developed close connections with deontological approaches, whereas utilitarian philosophies have been combined with the 'intuitive' notion of the just and the good. We do not want to go into the analysis of these philosophical positions, but they can give us some indicators for the specific cognitive frame underlying moral arguments in man's relationship with nature.

Typical discussions of this kind are questions such as 'Are animals reasonable beings?', which asks for principles that can be applied to animals and thus defines the applicability of moral principles to the interaction of mankind and nature.[28] This implies from the outset a conception of nature that is subject to the reason of man. Nature is running (more or less) short of reason. To what extent this allows for an instrumental relationship toward nature depends on the way in which nature is conceived. This conception ranges from romantic idealism to 'possessive individualism'. The utilitarian tradition, on the other hand, has developed a different point of view, asking to what degree animals are capable of feeling. The answer to this question determines the degree of moral responsibility that is attributed toward these animals. It motivates animal liberators who see the equal treatment of all beings as the fundamental premise of human moral action, a premise characteristic of the utilitarian ethics of animal liberation (Singer 1976). It also motivates policy making, regulating the killing of animals by minimizing the amount of suffering necessary for those animals used for human production and consumption.[29]

From a sociological perspective[30] there is a common cognitive basis to both moral positions: nature is – given a basic definition of its inherent 'rationality' – something to which moral sentiments or moral principles can be applied. Moral concern with nature links the question of nature to basic cognitive structures of modernity. This link goes beyond the 'old' concern of the just distribution of goods that has dominated modern society so far. The framing device of moral responsibility toward nature opens up the symbolic space of modern society for a moral frame that has to do with an idea of a good life beyond the principles inherent to the idea of justice. Environmentalism turns out to be a key mechanism in reorganizing the relationship between the principles of justice and good life, a relationship that feeds present-day philosophical discussions.

The second framing device underlying environmentalism refers to empirical objectivity. This framing device is linked to the mechanistic conception of nature that has caused scientific progress in modern societies. The modern claim of empirical objectivity was based upon the obvious

---

28 An interesting collection of classical philosophical answers to this question can be found in Schütt (1990a). An excellent discussion of the history of the philosophical discussions on how to treat animals is found in Passmore (1975).

29 For a discussion of internal philosophical differentiations within environmentally motivated ethical discussions see Callicott (1992). He sets off animal welfare ethics from environmental ethics thus confronting an individualist utilitarian position with a collectivist holistic position. Since the anchorage in Kantian philosophy is avoided, this philosophy tends toward a radical naturalism.

30 Sociologists are not so much interested in the subtle differentiation of cognitive positions in philosophical discourses, as in the way in which moral arguments are used. They do not judge moral positions according to philosophical discourse standards, but try to figure out in which way moral arguments allow to give good reasons to social actions and the communication of their meaning.

success of this mechanistic model of nature. However, the modern and especially ecological critique of science has led to an ambivalent relationship. The critique of science and an increasing dependence upon science turn out to be intertwined. With the rise of modern environmentalism, it has become obvious that science no longer controls the vision of the world. Experts have to tell us what the facts are, yet they produce contradictory evidence. Objective knowledge no longer offers the certainty that is the basis of its cognitive authority. A good indicator for the way in which this problem is dealt with is the scientific discussion on *risk*.[31] Risks are things we do not know exactly about; they are possible events in the world. As long as we can base our judgement on the possible risks of past events, this problem can be handled within terms of probability. As soon as it is necessary to define the possible event, the problem of scientific certainty demands a more refined notion of the framing device of empirical objectivity.

The framing device of empirical objectivity in ecological communication is based on a paradoxical structure: it generates 'hard facts' about nature, such as objective damages to the natural environment, and it can no longer claim the authority of expert knowledge.[32] There is nothing more 'factual' than environmental problems, yet the framing device of empirical objectivity has lost its hegemonic role in modern culture. The increase in scientific expertise related to describing and mobilizing environmental issues[33] creates the paradox of a reliance on the framing device of empirical objectivity and simultaneous loss of scientific authority on objectivity. Environmentalism has put into question the procedures through which facts about nature are objectified and represented as empirically valid.

The cultural theory of science (Wynne 1988b) offers a possibility to reconsider the role of the framing device of empirical objectivity in ecological communication. Its conception of the role of science in social life permits a reassessment of the notion of facts. The scientific assumptions about facts are seen as a social construction. The framing device of empirical objectivity is thus explicated as a culturally mediated one. This cultural

---

31 Among the important contributions to this discussion of the culturalist approach see Douglas & Wildavsky (1982), Douglas (1986a, 1988) and Thompson, Ellis & Wildavsky (1990). See also Krimsky & Plough (1988) for a communication approach to risk. For an overview of the vast literature see Conrad (1983, 1987).

32 This undermining has taken place in academic as well as in public discourse. Constructivist perspectives and sociology-of-knowledge arguments flourish in academic discourses, affecting basic methodological principles of this discourse. In public discourse, distance to expert knowledge and a renaissance of experiential knowledge describe recent tendencies in the relation of science and its public. See as an excellent discussion, using the Windscale case, Wynne (1991). The general theoretical point is discussed in Wynne (1988b). A similar point is made by Shrader-Frechette (1991).

33 An interesting indicator is the role that environmental issues play in the media, specifically in those sections which report on science news. The section itself is often named 'Science and Environment', which shows the close relationship environmental discussions have established with scientific knowledge.

theory allows for the assumption of contradictory certainties or even 'plural rationalities' (Thompson 1991). The framing device of empirical objectivity remains central for ecological communication, but it can no longer claim undisputed cognitive authority; rather it becomes a medium of clashing claims. This means that it becomes even more important than ever, because it provokes the increase of communication of empirical facts. The critique of 'hard facts' (Thompson 1984; Eder 1994) in ecological communication thus manifests what has been called the 'reflexivity' of modernity.[34]

The third framing device closely tied to the way modern societies perceive nature as a relevant context of their reproduction refers to the aesthetic aspect of the relationship of man with nature. In modern environmentalism nature is also seen as the locus of an expressive relationship. The history of the European relationship with nature is characterized by the fact that nature is seen not only as something to be dominated, but also as something to be cared for, as an object of *sensibility*. The expulsion from paradise (which is original nature) – the central myth of Western culture – has been linked with the necessity to dominate nature, to make it man's servant. But paradise has never lost its appeal: the paradisiac nature still serves as a model of a better life.[35] This idea of a paradisiac stage is generalized into a frame of an unpolluted nature. From this conception of nature neither practical guidelines for using nature nor insights into the working of nature can be derived. It constitutes a third way of relating man to nature, as being subject to aesthetic judgement.

Such a relationship is central to the romantic attitude to nature which developed alongside the progressivist idea of the Enlightenment where nature is made an object of scientific investigation. Art has been the medium of communicating the expressive aspect of man's relation to nature, both in popular and high culture variants (Brinkmann 1978, Brunschwig 1975, Shewder 1984, Weiß 1986). The aesthetic use of nature and the communication of aesthetic judgements of man's relationship with nature have become a central feature in environmentalism. It has also been used both for mobilizing people for environmental concerns and for green advertising. Thus the frame of aesthetic judgement gains in importance the more public communication on nature increases.

This aesthetic relationship between man and nature is no longer a privilege of literary circles or of art as an avant-garde institution. Rather, its effects recouple art with the everyday social world. A sociological theory of artistic production is the theoretical tool for explaining the aesthetic dimension of environmentalism.[36] It shows how pervasive aspects of

---

34 Reflexivity is a central notion in Beck's concept of modernity. See Beck (1992). The link between reflexivity and science is discussed in Ashmore (1989) and Potter (1989). See also the contributions in Woolgar (1988).

35 Cf. Chapters 3 and 4 in this volume. See also Eder (1994).

36 For such a theoretical strategy Bourdieu (1984b) and, building on him, DiMaggio (1988) are pertinent.

aesthetic judgements are in everyday social life, which avoids the restriction of aesthetic criteria solely to high artistic production.[37]

The symbolic packages of modern environmentalism

Framing environmental concerns

Environmentalism is based on a cultural form within which moral, factual and aesthetic framing devices provide the cognitive basis for framing the relationship of man with nature. These moral, empirical and aesthetic framing devices in environmentalism are the elements that are used in ecological communication by environmentalists to create a specific image of themselves. This process is called *symbolic packaging*. Symbolic packaging enables the attribution of framing devices to protest actors and their issues. This attribution is an important mechanism in the constitution of a collective protest actor. Without a frame that is recognizable by others as distinctive, a collective protest actor cannot constitute himself as a collective actor (Snow, Rochford, Worden & Benford 1986; Snow & Benford 1988). The symbolic construction of a protest frame is, therefore, the key to explaining the rise of environmentalism in advanced modern societies.[38]

Three packages of framing devices by which protest actors constitute themselves as a collective actor will be distinguished: conservationist, ecological and fundamentalist. All three packages create collective images of environmental actors, actions and events. They are the medium through which cognitive framing devices are reproduced in environmentalism.[39] I call this process of symbolic packaging a *framing strategy*. The social construction of a protest discourse through framing strategies is based on two mechanisms: that collective protest actors must find a coherent conception of what they do that is acceptable to their constituency and that they must distinguish themselves from other non-protest collective actors.[40]

---

37 Today, proof of this is found in the link of advertising culture with environmental concerns. A good example is the special issue of *Advertising Age* of January 29, 1991, dealing with the Green Marketing Revolution.

38 This proposition underlies the work of Snow et al. (1986, 1988, 1992) on frame alignment in social movements. However, there are also other actors, mainly business organizations and policy makers, who have started to use the framing devices of modern environmentalism to create their own symbolic constructions of environmental problems. Only before the mid-1980s has packaging the environmental issue been a specialty of protest actors. Their packages have, in the meantime, been taken over by their opponents and assimilated to their interests. This will be an important point later on in the analysis of emerging masterframes in public discourse.

39 This argument emphasizes that the medium is different from the outcome and that the medium implies an agency perspective whereas the outcome can be analysed in terms of structural arrangements and rearrangements of texts. The theoretical discussion on this point (especially that of Giddens 1984) so far has been quite confusing.

40 For an empirical analysis of a cultural form of environmentalism see Donati (1995).

The three symbolic packages each represent a structurally distinct version of linking nature and society. The conservationist package is separating nature and society, reserving for each a part of the world. The political ecology package, contrary to the first, is integrating nature and society. The fundamentalist package is fusing nature and society: nature becomes a fellow creature. These different ways of linking nature and society are *frames* of collective action, which give both meaning and purpose to it. These frames then are the material with which public discourses on nature are constructed. Thus the analysis of symbolic packages and the corresponding framing strategies on environmentalist protest actors is a necessary second step in the discourse analysis of environmentalism.

Three symbolic packages in contemporary environmentalist culture

A first package which offers a frame of collective action is the conservationist package. It uses symbols and imageries of nature that must be kept intact against civilization. This package has deep historical roots and can be traced back to the dichotomy of nature and culture since early modern times. Historical research undertaken by Thomas (1983) summarizes the alternatives of the relationship between man and nature in modern society in the following three dichotomies: *town and country*, *cultivation and wilderness*, and finally *conquest and conservation* (Thomas 1983: 242ff.). After the experience of the great urban epidemics, the country became sentimentally the locus of a better life, a life closer to nature. The wilderness was where the ancient virtues of mankind, his or her natural forces, were still useful and, even, necessary. Conservation principles developed as an attempt to save the natural world from the destructive effects of civilization. These ideas lay at the base of cultural movements that have emerged from the eighteenth century onwards. They idealize country life, seek a better life in the wilderness and call for the conservation of nature and a right to life for threatened creatures.

The conservationist package, based on the metaphor of a self-regulating nature that has been disturbed by human intervention, has its roots in the idea of a divine order which exists independently of human action. Aesthetic framing devices serve as a hidden agenda in this package. By giving nature a value of its own and making it the source of subjective experience, this package draws upon a long tradition of aesthetic judgements of nature. Combining this romantic idea of nature with a scientific notion of nature enabled the development of a frame in which nature is distinct from society. Such combined framing devices have gained prominence in so far as *biological metaphors* have contributed to a large extent to the conservationist idea that nature has a value of itself. The idea of a divine order can easily be assimilated to biological notions of a self-organization of nature.

Based on the strict separation of nature and non-nature (culture and society) the relationship between the two becomes the central problem of the conservationist package.[41] This is why moral framing devices ultimately become the organizing principle of this package – simply because they argue for a fair distribution of shares in a nature that has been excluded from man's intervention. By ascribing morality to nature (and natural relations between the elements of nature) and to human social relations, nature not only has a morality in itself which man cannot alter, but it also shares a moral world with the human world. The religious world-view of *creation* is, therefore, the germane cultural tradition from which this symbolic package historically derives. This is also the reason why the conservationist package has been considered as a basically conservative one.[42]

A second package of environmentalism, the political ecology package, refers to the attempt to see nature primarily as a political question. The political ecology package gives social actors a constructive role in the relationship between man and nature. This symbolic package is 'realism in green politics' (Wiesenthal 1993) and the position it represents has been called 'political ecology' (Lowe & Rüdig 1986). Its basic assumption is that the environment is a field of political struggles and as such is open to human (political) intervention. The conservationist idea of a nature that has to be maintained (for whatever reasons) is replaced by an idea of the political making of a 'better' nature. Thus nature has no longer any intrinsic values. This symbolic package is therefore primarily political, and the boundary drawn by this package separates green politics and conservationist environ-mentalism.[43] This symbolic package cuts across the traditional ideologies while remaining in the Enlightenment tradition and carries with it all the different ideological currents that have characterized modern political thought. Thus conservative, liberal and socialist ideologies all provide legitimation for human agency on the environment.

Political ecology is highly loaded on the objectivity device[44]. A permanent observation of the state of the environment is a basic asset of the communication on actions taken by political ecology groups. Its moral

---

41 These symbolic packages are used above all in the communication campaigns of organizations such as WWF and Greenpeace.

42 See, as the most informative contribution on the conservationist position, Nicholson (1987). The assertion of conservatism is historically grounded: conservation groups have normally situated themselves on the right of the spectrum of political ideologies. However, this is changing in the transformation of environmentalism into ecological discourse. For a case study of this process on an American example, see Hays (1958, 1987).

43 Jonathon Porritt has made a most effective attempt to promote this type of package. See Porritt (1984) and Porritt & Winner (1988). The conceptualization of this difference varies in the different countries. In France the distinction is between 'écologistes' and 'environnemen-talistes'. For the French case see Allan-Michaud (1990). In Germany this difference is close to the one between 'Umweltschützer' or 'Naturschützer' and 'die Grünen'; the latter are again divided between the 'Realos' (the realists) and the 'Fundis' (the fundamentalists). In any case the wordings of the difference are not very consistent. Our distinction between conservationism and political ecology is defined analytically.

44 The special characteristic of this use of science in politics is the formula of 'science for the people'. Measuring environmental pollution makes perfect sense for such a symbolic package.

framing devices are characterized by an agency symbolism that is closely connected to ideas of an ethics of responsibility. This type of an environmental ethic provides principles that are either of a utilitarian or a deontological nature. Its aesthetic framing device is based upon an emphatic notion of the 'individual' and his or her needs. But the aesthetic framing device is subordinated to the other two framing devices. Hence the political ecology package can be considered as one that continues and reproduces the type of modernity that is associated with the Enlightenment tradition.[45]

A third package found in the contemporary world of environmentalism is the fundamentalist one. Deep ecology[46] is an attempt to claim an intrinsic value of nature to which man has to be subsumed. Man is seen as part of nature; the metaphors range from biological images to religious images of the creation, of which man is only a small part. The principles of deep ecology, which best represent this symbolic package, are basically rooted in a conception of nature which attributes itself with a value. Within this pakage, moral, cognitive and aesthetic framing devices can easily be fused using a dualistic model of the world which separates the world of man and the world of nature. The metaphor of 'living' is basic to this package (McKibben 1990). It allows one to subsume both man and nature to a symbolic representation that comprises both as equal elements. This explains the strong concern for the rights of animals, the rights of nature as such (that is, anthropomorphic notions of nature) as well as naturalistic accounts of the social world.

The framing devices of moral responsibility and empirical objectivity remain highly ambivalent within this symbolic package. Scientifically based fundamentalism is – after historical experiences with biologistic notions of the social world – no longer a legitimate endeavour. Therefore, a close link to moral principles prevails in fundamentalist accounts of an environmental ethics.[47] Its most interesting effect is a legitimation of the 'naturalistic fallacy' as a mode of moral justification. Within this naturalistic fallacy the meaning attributed to one's action is also meaning that is contained in the empirical world. Thus the fusion of the moral and the empirical transforms the quest for meaning into an objective existence of meaning that is given before any human action. One has only to give him/herself up to nature and, consequently, meaning will be revealed. Thus the fundamentalist package

---

45 This symbolic package is the one that has found a way of linking old modern traditions of critical thought (here above all Marxism) with environmentalism. A good example is the programmatic statement of a political ecology position by Deléage (1992).

46 A review is given in Sessions (1987). See Luke (1988) for a good critique.

47 An account of this fusion can be found in Nash (1989). This book is itself an example of the fusion discussed above: it is at the same time a history of environmental ethics and a defence of a fundamentalist view of such an ethics. Thus scientific objectivity, concern with the 'ultimate condition', and moral discourse are closely connected.

resembles a fusion of the three framing devices distinguished above.[48] It is this fusion which mobilizes fundamentalist movements within the environmental movement. It also makes the fundamentalist package distinct from the 'pluralistic' fusion of cognitive framing devices which is characteristic of political ecology and from the segmentary fusion which is characteristic of the conservationist package.

The significance of the fundamentalist package lies less in its quantity than in its role in public communication.[49] Fundamentalist packages are a favourite target for antagonistic communication. They serve the classic outsider function, for both competing environmentalist groups as well as for anti-environmentalist political and business actors. As long as antagonistic communication on the environment dominates public discourse the qualitative importance of these groups will remain. However, when environmentalism starts to become cooperative, the role of deep ecology will change, eroding the structural basis for this symbolic package of environmentalism.

By analysing the frames of collective action of environmentalists the historical and social starting points for ecological communication in modern society have been defined. What remains is to describe the way in which environmentalism has influenced public discourse on social problems and issues, thereby becoming part of the public discourse itself. Two hypotheses will guide the following discussion. The first is that in the process of the symbolic packaging of a 'green agenda' a consensus is emerging which defines a new ideological reference for public discourse: *ecological discourse* is becoming a 'dominant ideology'. I will show how a new ideological masterframe is established in public discourse through symbolic packaging. The second hypothesis is that ecological discourse undermines the cultural basis of protest movements. The collective consensus on a green agenda that was previously set by environmentalists is the beginning of what can be called a 'post-environmentalist' age (Young 1990).

From environmentalism to ecological discourse

Ecology as ideology

In the last decade the symbolic packages of environmentalism have entered public discourse and received widespread resonance. They have become a

---

48 Bookchin's attack on deep ecology in favour of what he calls 'social ecology' (Bookchin 1980, 1982) shows a total fusion of framing devices. Social ecology emphasizes the role and responsibility of society in creating the environment. The adjective 'social' is nothing but an attempt to integrate the political ecology package into the deep-ecology package.

49 In private communication these fundamentalist packages seem to be much more widespread than the public discourse indicates. An analysis of the number of books with a deep-ecology perspective would probably produce surprising results. Deep ecology is a best-selling topic, not conservationism or even political ecology, the latter having the lowest resonance in the mass public.

shared ideological knowledge. This has had the effect that the symbolic packages which are communicated by environmentalists have to struggle for survival in the marketplace of public discourse. Environmentalists have to compete with opposing collective actors for control of the symbolic packages. Such competition leads to varying discourse coalitions with other collective actors, which in turn are shaped by the opportunity structure of given institutional contexts.[50] In such processes dominant frames emerge that make symbolic packages independent of their carriers and transform them into elements of public discourse. Dominant frames are defined as those elements of a discourse which are beyond the control of the actors who initially invented them as symbolic packages. In the ongoing public discourse on the environment, existing frames are reorganized and reconstituted with new meanings over time or new frames emerge for old problems. Such emergent frames in public discourse are called 'masterframes'.[51] Masterframes are the organizing principles of what has traditionally been called 'ideology'. An ideology is defined as a dominant form of framing social reality. This makes the theory of ideology itself a special case of framing social reality.[52]

Environmentalism has been very creative in the construction of symbolic packages where moral, empirical and aesthetic concerns are combined. This creativity has been made possible by the property of mutual substitutability which is a characteristic of cognitive framing devices. This creativity has been realized in waves of collective mobilization, that is, by the capacity for collective agency. A self-propelling process has been set in motion in which collective action has increased communication on the environment in modern societies which subsequently has reinforced the capacity of collective action. The end of this self-propelling process is reached when ecological communication has become a principal mode of public communication in modern societies.[53] For it then turns into an ideology, a collectively shared masterframe of social reality. The effectiveness of environmentalist

---

50 In other words, they are socially 'embedded'. This expression is taken from Granovetter (1985), who argues in a similar way with regard to economic action. In perceiving symbolic packages as strategies for communicating one's ideas and interests, this model can easily be adapted to suit our purposes.

51 This term has been introduced in social movement research. Cf. Snow & Benford (1992).

52 The language of 'ideology' is also used by Van Parijs (1991a) who speaks of political ecology as a complement to the other ideological currents such as liberalism and socialism. In our language ideology is an ethical derivative of a masterframe (e.g. socialism as an ideological derivative of the masterframe of industrialism or liberalism as an ideological derivative of Enlightenment).

53 This is the main point of Luhmann's essay on 'ecological communication' (Luhmann 1989). Ecological communication, he declares, creates noise, sometimes even too much with the effect that people no longer want to listen. Although the latter argument may be idiosyncratic, it nevertheless points out that ecological communication has significantly increased communication in modern societies.

packages on public discourse can be measured by their resonance in public discourse, namely by their capacity for *public agenda-setting*.

Public agenda-setting is the main variable explaining the rise and fall of public discourses.[54] The more information on environmental issues is dependent on media communication, the more media agenda-setting becomes the determinant of public discourse.[55] This implies that personal experiences and personal knowledge and wisdom do not play a primary role in the setting of a public issue agenda. It is the media who take over the role personal experience once had in political issue-making and conflict.[56] The media is probably the most important link between frame packages and the public agenda that enters public discourse. Moreover, this variable brings in the public itself. Public agenda-setting is not only determined by the input into public discourse, but also by the effects its output has on people. The public as such, the 'people', react to the output, making sense of it and adjusting their behaviour and action according to the way they have interpreted it. They react as consumers adjusting their consumer preferences; they react as voters adjusting their electoral preferences; and they react as 'political animals' adjusting their preferences of engagement in public life. All these reactions in turn influence the collective actors who package frames in order to make them communicable. This links the input to the output. The processes which generate this feedback link are still only partially known (except for voter preferences which in any case are losing importance in shaping the policy outcomes that determine the course of social development). Studies undertaken on green consumption and on interpersonal modes of making sense of politics will, in time, add to our knowledge and provide a more adequate model of how public discourses work in producing and reproducing a public space.

To what extent do the three symbolic packages distinguished above, namely conservationism, political ecology and deep ecology, resonate in public discourse? This is first of all a historical question. Although these packages have shaped the discourse on the environment over the last two

---

54 Here reference is made to the well-defined corpus of literature on agenda-setting. The classics are McCombs & Shaw (1972, 1977a,b) and McCombs (1981). Further important contributions are found in Erbring, Goldenberg & Miller (1980), Cook, Taylor, Goetz, Gordon, Protess, Leff & Molotch (1983) and Brosius & Kepplinger (1990). Overviews of the literature are found in Rogers & Dearing (1988) and Reese (1991). An interesting piece of research which shows the importance of print media for the attraction of public attention to environmental issues is Atwater, Salwen & Anderson (1985).

55 Frames have to fit into the format of public communication, especially – as it is the most widespread – the news format. The news format is the object of a substantial amount of literature. Most useful, especially from a methodological point of view, is Van Dijk (1988).

56 An excellent theoretical and empirical discussion can be found in Lahusen (1994). He uses theories of rituals and neoinstitutional theories to explain the use of public discourse by social movement organizations. The 'mediated' personal experience becomes the key to the role of these organizations. An attempt at rehabilitation of personal experience is found in Gamson (1992).

decades, making environmentalism into a genuine protest frame, today they are struggling for survival in the public discourse. In the course of the 'greening' of advanced modern societies the symbolic packages of environmentalism lose their distinctiveness. What is left is a new masterframe that creates a new ideological consensus: the new consensus is ecology as non-controversial collective concern. Environmental discourses are increasingly conceptualized as ecological discourses which are even accompanied by dictionaries of 'ecological thinking' (De Roose & Van Parijs 1991). Ecology has become a catchword for the basic functions of public discourse: to raise ethical questions of a legitimate social order and to raise the question of a collective identity. Moreover, the emergence of ecology as a masterframe in modern culture has given a privileged role to political ecology within the diverse environmentalist positions. My thesis is that the increasing dominance of ecology in public discourse leads not only to a change in importance that is attributed to the environmentalist package of political ecology, but also to a change of the *masterframe* in the ideology of advanced modern societies, namely from the industrial to a post-industrial paradigm.

This new 'post-industrial' masterframe in public discourse can be analysed at two levels. The first concerns *ethical frames* that emerge in the process of the institutionalization of the discourse on the environment. The second has to do with the emergence of *collective identity frames* in this discourse. This analysis is based on two assumptions. First, ethical theories and fora of ethical debate have become central for legitimating the relation of modern political institutions to environmental issues. Secondly, possessing a 'green identity' has become a central symbolic asset in modern society. This goes against the traditional idea that factual frames, pure information on the state of the environment, are enough. Without packaging information on the environment nothing will be accomplished: neither legitimacy for political institutions, nor rational attitudes or behaviour of the people. Such a claim assumes that ethical frames and identity frames, rather than the stage of deterioration of the environment, explain the centrality of the public discourse on the environment in the reproduction of advanced modern societies.

Legitimating institutions: ethical frames in ecological discourse

Ecological discourse is no longer concerned with the mere 'problem of nature'. It has become an attack on the legitimacy of existing institutions that are dealing with this problem. Environmentalism has led to a legitimation crisis of modern political institutions. However, the production of a new ideological masterframe also provides the possibility for a way out. Legitimating social institutions through environment-related ethical frames is the solution to be considered below.

Present-day ecological discourse is based on a rather pragmatic philosophy that is displaced from academic discussions of environmental ethics and the cleavage between preservationist and conservationist points of view. This ecological discourse has been increasingly decoupled from notions of a substantive ethics and left to competing formulations of an adequate ethics for an ecologically responsible society.[57] This leads to a 'proceduralization' of ethical conceptions (Habermas 1992, Eder 1986b), which means that environmental ethics has to define its substance through procedures of public debate. For example, a procedural ethics underlies the idea of sustainable development. Sustainable development implies different criteria of sustainability regarding the provision for future generations and the distribution among present generations who start with different life chances (Barry 1983). The 'ecological' reformulation is no longer based on substantive notions of the value of nature, but on the notion of a fair distribution of nature's resources. When nature is defined and valued as a *collective good*, moral arguments in ecological discourse will not only serve to preserve this collective good for present and future generations, but also generate the problem of distributing such a collective good. Such moral arguments necessarily relate the problem of nature to the problem of distributive justice (for example, the distribution of rights to pollute). Assuming that there is a consensus on the collective good which is 'nature', the question arises as to who should pay how much for protecting the collective good and preserving nature. This is a special case of the idea of distributive justice. It is special in that it introduces external limits to the distribution of goods which also guarantees the availability of the collective good – that is, 'nature' – for present and future generations.

The difference between the problem of nature and the problem of distributive justice is, therefore, much more complicated than is assumed by the claim that the problem of nature leads beyond the problem of justice.[58] What has changed is the context in which distributional problems are solved. When nature is a scarce good, the use of natural resources has to be regulated by some criteria of distributive justice. The difference then is that scarcity is defined in nature: her resources are limited.[59] It is no longer possible to use nature with scant regard for the effects of our actions upon nature and the repercussions of this on the fair distribution of natural resources.[60]

---

57 There is a growing literature on an environmental ethics. See, among many others, Attfield (1983b), Barbour (1973), Dower (1989), Hargrove (1989), Jonas (1984), Stone (1987). These approaches are empirical proof of moral pluralism in the discourse on an environmental ethics.

58 Such an argument has often been taken as an indicator of culture change, both by the proponents of a postmaterialist value change and by the proponents of the 'newness' of the new social movements.

59 This is controversial. Natural scientists show us how inventive nature is and that the destruction of part of nature is not necessarily a destruction of nature as such. The destruction can, on the contrary, trigger evolutionary processes. This optimistic view has characterized the anti-ecological discourse of the last two decades.

60 The idea of a distributive justice for collective goods can be elucidated by constructing an optimal distribution of collective risks in a society. These topics are the subject of an extensive discussion in economics and philosophy. For further references see Pearce, Markandya and Barbier (1989). An early statement is found in Baumol & Oates (1988 [1975]); a new look within the new ecological paradigm of 'sustainable development' is found in Redclift (1990).

No society engaging in ecological discourse escapes the problem of combining the principle of minimizing environmental damages with the principle of the just distribution of restrictions on the behaviour of people. As this balancing process will not regulate itself, a balancer is needed. Traditionally, the state has been the guarantor of the rationality of such balancing actions. Environmentalism has also changed the role of the state. In environmental matters the state is no longer the collective actor who controls the processes of decision making. Informal networks of collective actors have been challenging the way in which problems of distributing risks have an impact on the environment. It is here where the interesting ethical questions really start; there is a consensus that nature is a collective good, but now the value of this collective good is contested.

This process has attributed environmental ethics with the specific form of an ethics which shapes and legitimates political institutions. The value of nature is thus seen as a political question, to be defended by those who claim that nature has a special value. The state cannot defend the value of nature because of its engagement in social policy matters. Functionally specified as the actor who guarantees social cohesion, defending society against inner and outer violence and against the disruptive consequences of market processes, the state has to take nature as a collective good which comes after taking care of social order. Nature needs an advocate beyond the state and the economy. This advocate is to be found in a social sphere which is neither public nor private, but their negation (Van Parijs 1991a: 139ff.). If there is anything new in the ethical discussions of environmental discourse, it is in the *creation and sustenance* of an autonomous sphere that defends the value of nature as a collective good. Who else could defend this collective good as more than a mere instrumentalist notion other than those who want see nature as a spiritual inspiration, a source of emotional experience, or an object of aesthetic judgement? Thus the needs tied to 'nature' as the collective good play a central role and have to be organized beyond the state and the economy. To politicize such needs they have to be communicated; they have to be made political. The conceptualization and justification of a collective actor anchored outside state and economy[61] therefore makes ecology a political endeavour.

This ethical discussion has also affected *science* as an institution. The ecological influence can be felt in the social sciences and above all in economics. The idea of a green economics (Porritt 1984: 126–44) is not an alternative economics, but is an environmental economics which is a flowering field in economics as a social science. It no longer analyses nature

---

61 Social movements are a possible candidate, but their centrality has been overemphasized in the period of high collective mobilization in Western countries. Attempts at an ethics of collective responsibility can no longer be based solely upon these collective actors. Mobilization is no guarantee of a rationality that will give to nature a value as a collective good. The internal social organization of this collective actor and its organizing principle as a social sphere have to be clarified. The discussion on the classic notion of a 'public sphere' that has started again in recent years points towards the necessary direction.

as a given asset of economic action, but as something in interaction with man and his action upon her. It gives science an ethical dimension. Science's often discussed 'credibility gaps' (Wynne 1988a) lessen to the extent that political ecology generates an idea of a practical science which makes its goals and aims accessible to the personal wisdom and experience of people.[62] The effects go even deeper when considering the basis of science as an institution, namely its reliance on facts. Science has not only an ethical context which limits the range of scientific curiosity, but its construction of facts is also socially constituted (Eder 1994). Ethical perspectives then necessarily enter the construction of scientific facts.

The ecological critique of science has led to a generalization of the factual frame which extends the range of the factual frame to all spheres of life by the process of critique.[63] The ecological attack on the concept of facts has contributed to their rethinking in terms of their social constitution. Measuring problems in environmental sciences has highlighted the problem that the measurement of facts also defines what the facts are.[64] Thus the idea of an interactive relationship between observer and object belongs to the structuring features of ecologically-oriented science. The ecological attack has – and this is implied in the former argument – contributed to a change in the mechanistic conception of nature that is the heritage of early modern science. Systemic forms of thinking are the basic characteristic of the ecological claim of interdisciplinary and boundary crossing approaches to analysing reality (Lovelock 1989). Contrary to the fundamentalist quest for an alternative science or even anti-science,[65] ecology provides an ethical frame for the use of scientific expertise and the communication of scientific certainties in a situation where certainties are rare and expertise fallible.

Creating consent: identity frames in ecological discourse

A further effect of the emergence of ecology as a masterframe is the emergence of identity frames in the protest discourse on the environment. Environmentalism is the search for a human being's place in nature, a quasi-anthropological situation that has served as a medium for posing the question of identity. This quest for identity has traditionally been satisfied by

---

62 The discussion on the finalization of science, the increasing orientation of scientific theorizing and research at social goals, has been an early version of this kind of scientific methodology. See Böhme et al. (1972, 1978). See Van den Daele (1987) as a critical evaluation of this early attempt.

63 An interesting effect of this can be found in the newspaper reporting on ecology which has become identical with reports on science. The rubrics 'science, environment, ecology' have gained – in this or similar combinations – a stable representation in public communication.

64 This is true for natural as well as of social facts. Within the social sciences this phenomenon falls under the heading of 'reflexivity'. It is sufficient to note that one of the most influential books on environmental problems, Beck's *Risk Society* (Beck 1992) relates the notion of an emerging risk society and the notion of societal reflexivity.

65 Van den Daele (1987) speaks of the 'dream of an alternative science' which is necessarily unrealizable.

religious belief systems. Religion contains cognitive, moral and aesthetic framing devices which contain a 'counterfactual' solution to the problem of personal identity.[66] The religious solution to the problem of personal identity also characterizes modern societies. Modern societies had once thought to find personal identity in material equality and in the absence of alienation from work. This is no longer the case. The socialist ideology (from the welfare state version to the 'real' socialist version) has lost all appeal regarding its ability to provide an answer to this problem. It no longer sustains a frame that is capable of defining the problem of personal identity and the ways of resolving it. In the dissolution, new religious ideologies emerge carried by new religious movements (Beckford 1986). These 'new religious movements' are probably a temporary and perhaps even necessary regression in this transition. They manifest free-floating cultural ideas without a centre. The upsurge of religiously based movements has given a final blow to the model of secularization as the basic trend of modernization.[67] This 'return' to religion is not necessarily a regression. It rather indicates a growing need for the grounding of the construction of personal identity in a cognitive frame that is collectively shared.[68]

First, when understood as a generalized concern for nature ecology fulfils the function which has previously been fulfilled by traditional religions: namely, that of giving a coherent account of man's place in the world and providing the basis for a moral conception of society. Secondly, ecology is an ideology that adds scientific certainty to man's place in the world and provides a quasi-objective basis for a moral conception of society. The difference between religion and ideology can be stated as follows: religion relates salvation to the quest of identity, whereas ideology relates salvation to scientific certainty. In religion, certainty is the outcome of identity (the identification with God). In ideology, identity is the outcome of scientific certainty (the belief in scientific laws). Ecology contains both options at the

---

66 This counterfactual solution has been made a factual solution only among the 'religious virtuosi' analysed by Max Weber in his sociology of religion. In Protestantism even these virtuosi no longer succeed in realizing the counterfactual ideal of personal identity. Instead, they were those most terrified about the impossibility of realizing it.

67 The rise of what has been called 'Political Islam' (Ayubi 1991; Salvatore 1994) is pertinent here. Such a phenomenon can be seen as a mere religious movement trying to restore an idealized past. However, this is true only for a fraction of the movements subsumed under this concept. The main role of the movements is rather to serve as a cognitive frame within which people can redefine their personal identity. The collective identity of being part of Islam is therefore basically a cognitive frame that allows a resolution to the problem of personal identity.

68 The problem of which criteria should distinguish between regressive and non-regressive forms of religious revival implies a theory of rationality that is applicable to the idea of identity. Since identity is a concept that has much to do with emotions and affective behaviour, it is unavoidable that a cognitivistic theory would have some difficulties in dealing with this. Cf. Habermas's discussion of a postconventional identity of modern society (Habermas 1979). This discussion has been revived by the upsurge of religious and nationalist conflicts since the late 1980s.

same time. This makes ecology a belief system which can be both religious and ideological.

Ecology has an explicit link to religious ideas in the Christian tradition which has linked the expulsion from paradise with the necessity to dominate nature, to make nature man's servant. This idea serves as a critical reference for the way institutionalized religions have persistently contributed to the loss of paradisiac nature. A comparative look at religious traditions shows that non-Judean and non-Christian traditions (Taoism), in spite of a concern for nature, do not foster environmental concerns. The same holds for Islam (which contains the idea of a paradise where man lives in harmony with nature). Why is there no environmental movement? Weber's answer is that an active relationship with nature is a presupposition for a practical concern with nature. There is a link between activism and environmental concerns. But this relationship can also be explained by the level of economic development between Christian and non-Christian countries. Therefore, there is a need for additional indicators to identify the role of religious traditions. This additional criterion can be found by comparing different Christian cultures. Christianity – divided generally between Catholic and Protestant traditions – implies different ways of activism toward the world. In Catholic traditions man is subject to earth ('Gottesebenbildlichkeit', meaning man being made in a homologous way to God). This implies that man is the lesser god. Activism is thus not imperative for securing good relations with God. There is already a basic relationship with God that can only be lost through human action. In Protestant traditions the human creature is corrupted; non-human nature is 'Mitnatur', that is, nature with other creatures. This means that man has to struggle to establish relations with God. Thus a more active relationship in the relation between man and nature in Protestant countries is expected. This holds true when comparing cases. In traditionally Protestant countries shaped by inner-worldly asceticism the environmental movement flourishes, creating a moralization of nature and environmental concerns. This is in sharp contrast to Catholic countries where the neglect of environmental issues is far more widespread. To create the dynamic of ecological discourse in these countries a second factor has to occur: the ideological dimension of environmentalism. This ideological dimension has to do with the eco-'logical' beliefs it promotes. Ecology is scientific knowledge. Ecological discourse conveys an image of a rationally-constructed and scientifically-based idea system, an 'ideology' (Deléage 1991). Combining the religious references with the scientific references of environmentalism gives rise to a highly specific modern world-view: a secular syncretism beyond traditionalism.[69]

---

69 An interesting discussion on the 'Greening of Religion' is found in Nash (1989: 87ff.). There is evidence of the same paradox with religion as there is with science. The anti-religious feeling is strong, arguing against an incorporation of religion into a green 'philosophy'. The famous attack of Lynn White (1967, 1973) on Christian religion refers to it as the most anthropocentric religion the world has ever seen. The seminal essay of 1967 is also found

The diminishing grip of cultural traditions, due to internal traditionalism and institutional disembedding, has led to a situation where the elements of culture have to be constructed anew. It has been demonstrated that the rearrangement of new belief systems takes place within the context of the media.[70] Environmentalism as a media creation would be too strong a formula, but grasps an important mechanism of the making of a new tradition. Environmentalism is a belief system which is created in public debates around the elementary concerns of human beings such as health, purity and life. It produces specific combinations of cognitive and identitarian concerns, world-views and symbolic practices. This mediated belief system no longer has to rely upon the idea of a religious community of believers. To the extent that religious organization has lost its pervasive force in everyday life, personal identity is no longer the privilege of the believers. The substitute has been the idea of an associational community, where the notion of 'community' is the secularized version of the traditional community of believers. This secular community replaces the traditional religious group. The reference to the associational community among human beings becomes the major force in the cognitive framing of personal identity.[71]

The connection between ecology and identity has been established in recent theoretical discussions on modernity and the idea of the modern self. Ecology appears as a strategy for the reorganization of self and identity in modern society (Beck 1992; Giddens 1991). It gives a coherent interpretation to the emphasis on the expressive side of one's personal existence. Deep ecology is its most radical expression, relating ecological beliefs to meditation groups, personal growth movements, New Age groups and different types of green religiosity. These movements are becoming the target of more 'secularly' minded groups such as the WWF, seeking (as its mission statement says) to develop its 'Fourth Leg' which aims to develop a grasp on the personal ideas and experiences that influence everyday practices (Centre for the Study of Environmental Change 1991). To what extent this transformation of spiritual feelings into more secular beliefs will succeed remains to be seen. It will certainly imply a strong backlash from deep-ecology groups, and cause internal ideological struggles. Deep ecology no longer occupies the terrain of identity and self-realization. It competes with other belief systems in modern ecological discourse. Competitive

---

together with critiques of it in Barbour (1973). Generally, it is not the established Church, but a minority movement within the traditional churches that joins environmentalism. Heterodox traditions in Christian religion have always tended to move toward this kind of philosophy, Saint Francis being only one, but the most famous, example. See also the review of this discussion by Sessions (1987) and my discussion on counterculture movements in Eder (1993c).

70 This is discussed regarding the case of environmentalism in Hansen (1991). See also the contributions to Hansen (1993b).

71 The return of the community is not only confined to philosophical discourse (MacIntyre 1985, 1988), but also in real life as the return of the quest for ethnic and national identity.

games in the field of identity construction are deadly for the beliefs of deep ecology, for they cannot coexist with other gods. The new god is ecology. Ecology is a new belief system for grounding identity.

Towards post-environmentalism?

Is the age of environmentalism vanishing? The increasing communication of environmental issues has caught the environmental movement in a paradox: the movement that created the green public agenda can no longer be sure to be present on the media agenda. Its existence is bound to this public agenda, which in turn is bound to the symbols of environmental dangers that once resonated deeply and created the culture of environmentalism. On the other hand, the media agenda which increasingly influences the policy agenda has developed its own dynamic with the tendency to exclude environmental movements from the agenda-setting process.

This has led to the constitution of movements as cultural pressure groups. In order to survive, movements must invest in public discourse. They do so by mobilizing frame packages. Thus a market of frame packages which is open to competing frame packers is created. Can they survive the marketplace? Environmental movements will certainly not survive as movements of mass mobilization. The action repertoire will change fundamentally, and with it the relationship between movements and their constituencies. They will survive as a collective actor, taking care of needs and risks that are not covered by the traditional pressure groups, above all by trade unions. Their survival depends on their capacity to keep control of their stakes in public discourse. Survival in this market is contingent upon the successful communication of symbolic packages that resonate with the respective constituency.

Under such conditions protest discourses will continue to play an important role in the development of ecology as a masterframe for a *common-good issue*. Such development can take place in two ways. It may lead to an increasing variety of framing environmentalist positions, with the particular emphasis on economic, political or cultural circumstances. This would see the present dominance of the ecology frame as a temporary phenomenon of actual public discourse, an outcome of fashion cycles. It may also lead to a transformation of public discourse by transforming the masterframe of public discourse in modern societies. The old masterframe of modern society is the industrialist discourse which has dominated the traditional discourse on the natural environment. The industrial master-frame has given a specific meaning to the moral responsibility toward nature and the way in which nature has been conceived both as an empirical reality and as an expressive attitude. It is our proposition that *ecology* provides a new 'masterframe' in advanced modern societies.

The philosophical and intellectual reflection of ecological discourse confers the self-description of something 'new'. I take this claim as a proposition and argue that the discourse which labels itself 'ecological discourse' is a manifestation of a frame change in modern public discourse. This proposition implies that the masterframe of the emerging ecological discourse reorganizes in a 'reflexive' way the structure of the moral, the empirical and the aesthetic framing devices of nature.[72] Its theoretical effects can be seen in the fact that these discourses are described as 'ecological communication' (Luhmann 1989) or 'ecological discourse' (Kitschelt 1984).

The theory of ecological discourse proposed takes environmentalism as a historically and socially specific form of ecological communication that has emerged in the process of European cultural history and reached a peak during the last two decades. Ecological discourse has fostered political ecology and at the same time neutralized the competing deep-ecological and conservationist packages by integrating them. The effect goes even further. While entering public discourse, it has also started to restructure public discourse. These developments have led to the crystallization of a new masterframe capable of mobilizing collective action in advanced modernity. Institutional changes have contributed to channelling these mobilizations. The 'modernization' of identity formations that have so far been considered a romantic backlash or pathological regression, provides another – and perhaps the most important – effect of the ecological masterframe in modern public discourse. The ideological systems and institutional solutions of the nineteenth century are still functioning, but the public discourses centred around these elements never solved the problem of identity construction. Liberalism and socialism failed in this task. Ecology as a political and social world-view could therefore become a way of carrying out this overdue modernization of one of the most consequential aspects of social life.[73] This also means that the age of environmentalism, the collective mobilization for a cause, is over. The age of post-environmentalism begins where ecology is established as a masterframe thus laying the ground for a further development of the cognitive, moral and aesthetic rationality inherent in the culture of modernity.

---

72 Here we enter, through an analysis of environmental discourse, the arena of discussions on the logic of the development of modernity, launched by Habermas and continued by Giddens and others who put emphasis upon the reflexivity built into the development of modernity.

73 This claim is again in line with the recent emphasis on the expressive side of the human existence and its role in the production and reproduction of society. See as the classic Elias (1978, 1982) and for an overview of recent discussions Lash & Friedman (1992).

7

THE POLITICS OF NATURE: A NEW POLITICS?

Post-environmentalism and the emergence of a post-corporatist order

The new phenomenon in the political life of advanced modern society is concerned with the increasing public sensitivity regarding the issue of common goods. To have an ecological consciousness has become part of a general consensus and in some countries has developed into a normative obligation. In attitude surveys, concern for the environment is an item to agree with; the 'environment' is an uncontested issue. Moreover, it is a major resource of meaning in modern societies.

What becomes increasingly an issue is the question of how to deal with an environment that is so highly valued given that it is a common but scarce good. The problem of scarcity gives a political meaning to the environment because common goods invite, as Olson (1965) has shown, free riding. To provide common goods for everybody normative prescriptions are necessary which counteract individual interests. The environment can therefore be defined as a concern for common goods which challenges the idea (and ideal) that the pursuit of individual interests will lead to the realization of the common good.[1] This is to say that in the field of the environment the market model of coordinating individual interests does not work. In order to commit individuals to contribute to the maintenance and enhancement of common goods, constraints have to be imposed upon private actors. A solution to this is a state, regulating and sanctioning individual behaviour. But this solution leads into a paradox: the more the state has to take over such functions, the more it interferes with the idea of the environment as a form of life. The more the environment is to be protected against individual interests, the more it is threatened in its role as a life-world.[2]

This paradox explains why the concern with the environment is an interesting case of understanding how modern societies operate in the

---

1 This is not to say that there has not been such a concern for common goods in old modern society. Concerns for national identity are certainly of this kind, but have not been solved in a modern way. Therefore we see environmentalism as a key to the way these other common good issues might be institutionally regulated.

2 This is the situation of a clash between system and life-world as Habermas (1984, 1987) has analysed it.

advanced stage of their development. The emergence of a multitude of concerns for the environment is tied to a change in the politicization of such concerns. The rise of regulatory agencies within the state is a reaction to the rise of environmental concerns. However, these regulatory agencies can no longer claim to represent the common interest against the particularist interests of civil society. Rather they have to compete with other actors and their concerns for common goods such as the environment. The classic state agencies have to adapt to this situation. Hence the phenomenon of systems of negotiation outside the traditional institutional framework of politics is a key to the institutional transformation that accompanies the rise of nature as a collective concern for a common good.[3]

A further interesting effect is the transformation of corporations towards a form of organization that establishes links to the problem of common goods. Economic organizations no longer stick to conveying the image of a private interest organization, but instead engage in 'public responsibility' discourse. Industrial actors 'embed' their organized collective action in a context in which norms restrict economically possible courses of action. Another effect is the rise of countermovements which promote reactionary discourses on the issues raised by social movements.[4] Concerns mobilize not only protest, but the public. New social movements are no longer the exclusive voice for concerns; countermovements are in the same situation: competition for public attention is growing between them. These effects explain why the media of communication and the symbolic dimension are objectively growing in importance, with repercussions not only on the mobilization of public concerns, but also on regulatory politics.[5]

These developments are linked to the rise of a new field of political competition and a decline of traditional forms of political action. The declining importance of elections (Ginsberg & Shefter 1989) points to a shift in which modern societies regulate themselves through politics. On the contrary, politics is shifting towards a different field with functionally specified links to the state and the field of action defined by state institutions. This does not imply the return to the market and to money as the mechanism of self-regulation. Money is not a sufficient means for regulating common-good issues. But this is not to suggest that market processes no longer play a role. It is their institutional make-up that changes. The type of 'market' which emerges in the environmental field is embedded in a context in which

---

3 This discussion takes up arguments in the recent debate on regulatory politics in a post-welfarist world. See Majone (in press). The general theoretical context is marked by a rather diverse brand of writing for which the label 'new institutionalism' has been used (Ostrom 1990; Shrader-Frechette 1991; Powell & DiMaggio 1991).

4 For the term 'countermovement' see Gale (1986) and Zald & Useem (1987). Good examples are the anti-abortion movement or the movement against evolutionary theories which contradict biblical theories of creation.

5 This is especially obvious for issues such as pollution which have to define purity. See the analysis of policing pollution by Richardson, G. (1982) as an interesting case study.

symbols of trust and reliability, and images of oneself and of others, shape market processes. These are *identity markets* which affect the medium of market relations. Again this changes the logic underlying such processes away from money values and price, and toward symbolic values and their resonance.

Taken together, these developments point to important changes in the way that organizations which deal with the natural environment as a common good are embedded in an institutional framework. This new institutional framework is characterized by the following elements:

1   a cognitive order with the 'ecology frame' as the organizing principle shaping a new type of experience of modernity;
2   a normative order leading to an institutional form beyond the state and market, that is, a self-organizing arrangement of dealing with common-good issues;
3   a public discourse which serves to communicate the ecology frame and to monitor the institutional arrangement by enabling actors to observe each other's performance and by including the public as a third party observer.

The emerging new institutional order is a *post-corporatist order*. The characteristic element of the post-corporatist order is an increasing de-coupling of the self-organization of the emerging institutional order from the state, the emergence of a negotiated order beyond the market and the state, and a new legitimating ideology supporting these arrangements.

In the following, these theoretical premises for an analysis of the institutionalization of environmentalism are discussed. This conceptual framework will serve three purposes:

1   to develop the model of a post-corporatist order in advanced modern societies;
2   to propose a theory of the institutionalization of environmentalism; and
3   to describe the prospects for democratic politics in a post-corporatist order.

Theoretical premises

Institutionalization as the evolution of rule systems

The theory of the 'institutionalization' of environmental protest claims that the open structures of political competition change from a chaotic form to a temporally ordered structure. Structures emerge that allow for coordination and for self-transformation. Order is generated by rule systems that contain within themselves the rules for their change (that is, procedural rules). The emergence of such rules can be explained as the emergent outcome of cumulative rational responses to experiences made in the pursuit of collective action.[6]

Rule systems can be seen as social grammars which fulfil two functions at the same time: (a) the organization of social activities and (b) the structuring of social experience. Following rules in social situations generates an intersubjectivity that is always approximate and never complete. This produces a shared world which is not necessarily consensual, but which works as if it were consensual. Institutions guarantee through such counterfactual assumptions their reproduction. The change of rule systems also follows a dual logic: it is simultaneously chaotic and ordered. Rule systems create order: they set restrictions for social change by including rules for self-transformation into rule systems. However, such rule systems also have to reproduce themselves, that is, survive under the conditions they themselves partially create. This means that evolutionary processes come into play that exert pressure upon rule systems by doing away with ('selecting') one type of rule system and favouring ('retaining') other rule systems. This changes the evolutionary logic of institutional change. The interplay of both processes is still not well understood. This is especially true for the pressure of evolutionary processes on the selection of rule systems (= institutions).[7]

Institutions understood as rule systems are bound to action contexts in which they are anchored. They might be anchored directly in *personality systems* (as 'roles') which is a precarious way of institutionalizing rules. However, the more a society is characterized by 'individualization' the more it becomes dependent upon such individualized 'carriers'. This assumption is characteristic of an important strand of theories of modernity that see this process as the dominating one (Giddens 1990, 1991; Beck 1992). Another strand of arguments is to emphasize *collective actors* (organizations) as carriers of institutional rules. Collective actors differ from individual actors by their organizational make-up, their organizational memory, their organizational identity and their organizational life-world. Such collective actors are central for an institutional perspective, for organizations are no longer understood as stabilizing themselves by their efficiency and through their capacity to realize organizational goals. Instead they stabilize themselves by referring to rules that carry legitimacy and consensus.

When looked at from an organizational perspective institutions do not refer to complete organizations, but are structural elements of organizations. First of all institutional rule systems are *prescriptive rule systems* that correspond in modern societies to general legal rules, the rule of law and its formal rationality which has provided – according to Weber – the basic

---

6 The following types of rule systems are usually distinguished: prescriptive rules, such as norms, laws, etc; descriptive rules, defining properties of things; and evaluative rules, giving a value (good, bad, right, beautiful) to things (Burns & Dietz 1992).

7 But see Burns & Dietz (1992). Earlier formulations can be found in Giesen (1980, 1991) and Eder (1985, 1987).

design of modern institutions, primarily the law and the state.[8] This classical perspective on formal organization[9] certainly covers an important aspect of rule systems; but it covers only a part of it, because legitimacy and consensus can no longer be guaranteed given the declining legitimacy of formal rationality. Prescriptive rule systems are therefore an insufficient tool for understanding institutional forms in complex societies. *Descriptive rule systems* are designed to base the legitimacy of an organization on an empirically rational design, such as a scientific one. The discussion for and against 'technocracy' relates to this way of shaping institutional systems in complex societies.[10] *Evaluative rule systems* base legitimacy on another type of rationality: the cultural rationality of a life-world (with its specific form of practical rationality). Cultural rationality contains formal and scientific rationality as special cases of a cultural myth which serves the function of legitimating a social order. In a famous article Meyer & Rowan (1977) have argued that the reference to formal rationality is a mechanism which conveys the legitimacy of an organization. Furthermore, this does not work because formal rationality is superior but because it is a collectively shared myth creating the legitimacy that is supposed to be inherent in formal rationality.

The emphasis of evaluative over prescriptive rule systems fosters a transition towards an analytic perspective that is different from the classical rationality paradigm. Taking the analytic perspective of cultural theory, social organizations can be conceived as a theatre (Mangham & Overington 1985) in which forms of rationality are staged and enacted through organizational activity which is – from the perspective of the observer – a ritual. Institutionalized myths are even the basic mechanism of organizational growth. This leads to two basic propositions: (a) environments that have institutionalized a greater number of rational myths generate more formal organizations; and (b) organizations that incorporate institutionalized myths are more legitimate. Organizational action must support these

---

8 In my analysis of institutional changes in nineteenth-century Germany (Eder 1985) I relied exclusively upon this dimension. It is sufficient to grasp the normative make-up of institutions and the corresponding functional imperatives of legitimating such institutions (such as the embedding of institutional forms in the rule of law). But this perspective excludes the analysis of the specific way in which such legitimation actually works. For it is not self-evident that the reference to the rule of law is no more than justifying existing rule systems. It has its own dynamics and is itself a special rule system that is relatively independent of the legal forms used for structuring an organizational form.

9 This is the typical way in which political scientists traditionally view institutions. Even when situating institutional analysis in the context of the history of political ideas it sees only the modern state and the rule of law as the solution to the problem of generating a social order which binds the members of a society. However, this solution holds only for modern societies. Irritations start when looking at non-modern institutional systems. This area is left to social anthropology, such as the anthropology of law, of kinship relations, etc. The proposed sociological perspective in institutional analysis aims at overcoming the localism of classical institutional theories.

10 A famous example is the debate between Habermas and Luhmann in the early 1970s. Cf. Habermas & Luhmann (1971).

myths. Organizations must attend to practical activity. The solution to the problem of coordinating these conflicting functions is a loosely coupled state (Meyer & Rowan 1977; Meyer & Scott 1983). The relationship between what organizations really do and what they claim they do is neither completely separate nor unified; they remain loosely supportive of each other. Moreover, this loose coupling becomes more important the more the two functions become functionally differentiated.

Social organizations that no longer use the myth of formal rationality but refer to other forms of rationalizing organizational structures are found to be the type of organizations that have to deal with legitimacy and consensus in organizing collective action. This is the case with social movement organizations that emerged in the course of the last two decades and in which the new social movements grew into a permanent phenomenon in the institutional life of modern societies (Zald & McCarthy 1987). These organizations differ from other organizations (such as economic ones) by the particular 'myths' they use for their legitimation. The emergence of such new organizational 'myths' again has effects upon the traditional myths held by other organizations. What these new 'myths' are and how they shape institutional rule systems ought to be examined more closely.

The proposed analytic perspective also requires a different way of looking at institutional change. The transformation of institutions is not done through intentional action. Institutions are routine adaptive systems in which action (standardized action, trial and error action, bargaining action, etc.) is a means for the evolutionary change of rule systems. Rules are generated by the learning capacities of organizations. Organizations can learn normatively by enhancing action rules and creating legitimacy for them. Or they can learn by reorganizing the cognitive classification of reality, by reframing the world. Organizations are not only carriers of normative rules which challenge other norms and thus raise the question of a better (normative) ground (which is either the law and the state or the rationality of self-interest in the market context); they are also the carrier of a world-view and a discourse which connects these organizations to the society at large. The emergence of new organizational forms (or organized collective actors) forces the environment or organizations to adapt. From the point of view of the institutional system this is a dynamic element in the self-transformation that is inbuilt. This is a new mechanism of institutional learning which is – in line with cognitivistic learning theories[11] – understood as the self-organizing transformation of cognitive structures.

---

11 Here the lead has been given by Piaget (1970). Rule-governed transformation processes have in the meantime been reconstructed not only in children, but also in any form of interaction situation (Miller 1986), organizations (Levitt & March 1988) and institutions (Eder 1985, 1987). The concept of learning thus is opposed to the idea of chaotic changes or functional theories of change. Its relation to evolutionary theories is still an open issue. See Schmid & Wuketits (1987).

From the normative to the cognitive analysis of 'rule regimes'

The analytical distinction between the rule systems that I propose is between prescriptive, descriptive and evaluative rules. Prescriptive, descriptive and evaluative rule systems are related to each other within a historically specific *rule regime*. This becomes the empirical unit of analysis. These rule regimes have traditionally been analysed within the *normative paradigm*.[12] In the normative paradigm prescriptive rules that guide and orient action, that is action rules, define the theoretical point of reference. These have been the focus of the traditional analysis of formal organization: formal rationality defines patterns of action that are considered more rational relative to pre-formal forms of organization. The cognitive side of such rules has simply been taken for granted.[13] The critique of the normative paradigm is formulated in what can be called a *cognitive paradigm*. In the cognitive paradigm rules are seen as mechanisms for classifying and ordering the world. Thus the cognitive paradigm is basically constructionist. It refers to a level of reality that is negotiated before normative action has even started. Thus a 'constructionist' perspective in institutional analysis allows us to take into account a social reality so far excluded from analysis.

The normative paradigm has privileged the prescriptive rule system while assuming a socially neutral form of scientific-technical knowledge and a shared cultural consensus.[14] The traditional theory of norms treats these other rule systems as natural facts. The cognitive paradigm claims that these rule systems are themselves social products and therefore require a theoretical perspective which is capable of grasping them as quasi-natural facts. They require a theory of the social definition and classification of the world, which includes the world of actors, the world of things and the world of artefacts, thus taking into account that normative rule systems presuppose cognitive classifications of the world. To the extent that such cognitive rules are thematized and made the object of competing ways of classifying the social world (its agents and their environment), normative rules are no longer based on safe ground. They become contingent on their controversial cognitive foundation. That the world is no longer taken for granted belongs

---

12 This is the Habermasian programme: to show that rule systems have implicit claims of validity that generate in the ideal situation a consensus between those adhering to such rules. The cognitive aspects are subordinated to this normative structure of communication.

13 Weber struggled with this problem when trying to clarify his notion of formal rationality. He applied it to any modern form of action such as law, science, music, associations, etc. The problem he ran into while extending this notion is that his notion is tied to normative rules which are not basic to some of the areas he referred to. This is obvious when looking at music. But it also applies to ideology and other cultural phenomena, including science.

14 The first point is even characteristic for Habermas, who tries to solve the problem of technical knowledge by defining it in such a way that it remains outside the social realm (technical knowledge as part of instrumental action). For a different, more sociological and cognitivistic perspective see Knorr-Cetina (1981, 1988). The assumption of a shared cultural world is constitutive for Parsonian sociology which means for a major part of sociological analysis of the last two decades. See on this point the discussion in Schmid (1992).

to modernity as much as its rationalism. The more rationalization proceeds, the less the way in which we perceive the world becomes self-evident. Even what we perceive may be contested.

This distinction allows us to go beyond the dominant normative paradigm in institutional analysis and more toward a cognitive paradigm. The latter leads to a different theory of the change of rule regimes. A cognitive analysis of rule regimes provides the necessary grounding of an institutional analysis and at the same time takes seriously the social construction of the world through collective action.[15] Institutions may thus be seen as more than a mere normative force which sanctions or motivates our actions. They can be explained as mechanisms that create the world in which we act. An additional complication is given by the fact that cognitive constructions of the world are already anchored in symbolic representations of the world.[16] There is no social construction of the world that does not use the elements of existing worlds. Thus the reconstruction of rule regimes implies a stripping of symbolic representations from their symbolic packages and an uncovering of rules which structure such symbolic representations. This points to an intimate relationship between cognitive rule regimes and their symbolic embedding. Processes of social construction generated by cognitive rule regimes are embedded in symbolic practices which presuppose normative rules. Thus we never escape the interdependence of the normative and the cognitive levels in institutional analysis. The symbolic dimension provides a possible link between the normative level and the cognitive level by relating the cognitive construction of reality back to social interaction processes in which meaning is attached to the cognitive constructions of reality.[17] Hence the duality of cognitive structure and social process constitutes the central problem of institutional analysis.

A theory of the post-corporatist order

Why create such a complex theoretical framework for analysing the politics of nature? A basic assumption is that environmentalism has forced us to rethink the institutional basis of politics in modern society. This has less to do with the risks that we run in modern societies, as Beck (1992) claims, than with two interrelated factors: the specific cognitive structure of the problem

---

15 Such a theory is implicit in the framing theory I developed above. Framing is – this is the assumption of this complementary theoretical effort – a mechanism of constructing a world within which we apply normative criteria regarding our actions in the world which is already constructed.

16 This analytical aspect has been treated above as symbolic packaging of framing devices which result in frames of social reality.

17 This dimension can be approached through the literature on organizational culture and organizational symbolism. As a good introduction and overview of this field, see Alvesson & Berg (1990).

of nature and the complex social interaction processes between collective actors who emerge in dealing with the problem of nature. The general elements of a cognitive theory of the institutional order of modern societies will be used to construct a specific theory of the institutionalization of social movements. Such a theory will grasp the constitutive role of social movements and collective mobilization for the generation of an institutional order in advanced modern societies. This is the theory of a post-corporatist order. It will focus on the centrality of social movements and describe the modes of their institutionalization: the cognitive and the normative mode.

In social movement research the analysis of collective action has either been caught in an anti-organizational critique or has remained in the traditional paradigm of organizational analysis, the one based on the 'myth of formal rationality' (Meyer & Rowan 1977). The anti-organizational effect produced by the self-understanding of the mobilizers of social movements' campaigns has never been productive in showing the emergent institutional forms that appear in the new social movements. The resource mobilization approach has broken with this anti-organizational image, arguing that movements have become a normal phenomenon in 'organizational society' (Zald & McCarthy 1987). This opens the way for seeing social movements as 'organizations'. So far, however, this idea has restricted itself to the reconstruction of normative rule systems, to rules of action that are 'rationalized' according to criteria of formal rationality, that is, efficient use of existing resources in a given environment. This bias has restricted resource mobilization theory to developing the institutional side of movements' organizations, but it also provides the tools for the analysis of the institutionalization of social movements.

It is in economic theory that the concept of institutions for collective action has been developed (Ostrom 1990). However, the 'new social movements' are institutions for collective action (Eder 1993c) which provide an interesting and critical case for studying the effects of cognitive rule systems on rule regimes. This is because new social movements sustain a cultural orientation which is opposed to the idea of formal rationality. Social movements are oriented toward 'discursivity'. However, this is no more than a catchphrase for a perspective that needs careful analytical treatment. Frame theory is an attempt to add a cognitive and a social dimension to social movement analysis.[18] It not only refers to cognitive constructions of the world, but also to the social processes of giving meaning to a cognitively constructed world.[19]

---

18 Cf. Snow et al. (1986); Snow & Benford (1988, 1992); Johnston (1992); Benford & Hunt (1992). See also the discussion in Chapter 6.

19 An example is the framing of organizational action in the language of organizational takeovers (Hirsch, P.M. 1986) which is characterized by the games frame. Such an analysis refers to symbolic packaging and is a good example of the intersection of cognitive and interactionist levels of analysis. Consciousness-raising in social movements is another example for understanding how culture plays a role in fluid social movement organizations (Hirsch, E.L. 1986, 1990).

Frame theory provides the tools for an institutional analysis which distinguishes between the patterns of perception based on the structural arrangement of signs (classifications) and the process of attributing meaning to these structural arrangements.

To clarify the respective analytical dimensions I define frames as patterns of perception which are like empty cells that can be filled with a variety of meanings.[20] In social movement organizations the processes leading to an organization-specific cognitive order have been described as frame alignment processes. Movement organizations try to create a shared culture among their members by institutionalizing a cognitive order. They develop their own specific ways of looking at reality by defining a movement-specific moral order, scientific knowledge and aesthetic judgement. Such movement-specific frames serve two functions. The social-psychological function is to make sense and legitimate change, reduce strain and stigma experienced by participants. The institutional function is to allow the cultural processing, disseminating and routinizing of innovations, and a building of consensus around them. To bring culture back into the institutional analysis (Friedland & Alford 1991) of movement action means reconstructing the way in which the cognitive constructions of reality are embedded in a society's culture. A movement organization whose cognitive framings do not resonate in a society's culture may construct a social reality, but it does so without relating to the cognitive classifications that underlie the culture of a society. Thus institutionalization means the embedding of an organization in the discourse which a society produces about itself.

The theory of a post-corporatist order is based on the double process of the cognitive and normative institutionalization of social movements into the institutional order of modern society. Social movements enter the discourse of society about itself. This means that social movement organizations become part of a cognitive order which characterizes society as a whole. Such institutionalization precedes the process of institutionalization which coordinates movement organizations with other organized collective actors. This mode of the normative institutionalization of social movements often remains precarious because it is dependent on the permanent affirmation of their anti-institutional sentiment. In most cases, as soon as institutionalization occurs within a movement organization there will be a pressure toward a specific type of institutionalization that minimizes the risk of permanent mobilization.[21] One way in which organized movement action is institutionalized is by being swallowed by traditional political institutions.[22] However, another form of normative institutionalization of which

---

20 The respective analytical categories have been explicated in Chapter 6 in this volume.
21 An excellent discussion of such a process of institutionalizing mobilization is found in Lahusen (1994).
22 The transformation of movement organizations into parties is such a process. This perspective has produced an extensive research, especially in political science. The Green Party literature is the best example (Rüdig 1991).

we should be aware is the *interorganizational field* in which organized social movements interact with other organized collective actors.

Central to the theory of a post-corporatist order is the analytical distinction between a cognitive and normative institutionalization of social movements. In the following I address the cognitive institutionalization engendered by environmentalism and the normative institutionalization engendered by the environmental protest. Post-environmentalism, the historical phase environmental protest is entering today, will be taken as a key to understanding the emerging post-corporatist order in modern society.

Towards post-environmentalism

A new rationality in the post-corporatist order?[23]

The institutionalization of environmentalism refers to the processes of the institutional adaptation and assimilation of the spirit of environmentalism which has been mobilized by environmentalists in the last two decades. This mobilization was fed and inspired by the specific cultural traditions that have produced European modernity. The spirit of environmentalism is – as has been argued above in our 'two-cultures thesis'[24] – the heir of the dual code of modern European culture. By mobilizing for the spirit of environmentalism, the two codings of European cultural traditions – the 'carnivorous' and the 'vegetarian' – are confronted with each other and are forced to find a new *modus vivendi*. My thesis is that this confrontation has led to a *new rationality paradigm* in the institutionalization of environmental politics: the *cultural rationality paradigm*.[25]

This new rationality paradigm combines the two cultural roots of environmentalism.[26] It shows how modern society copes with a dual cultural code that has been politicized by environmentalism and promoted by counterculture traditions. In a situation where counterculture traditions gain importance because of increasing environmental risks, two questions become crucial: first, how do the two modern cultures work in the reproduction of modern societies? And secondly, how do we politically

---

23 In the following I draw heavily, with some further clarifications, on Eder (1994).

24 The first coding of European culture is anchored in Catholic traditions having their roots in the Greco-Christian culture, the second in counterculture traditions having their roots in traditional Jewish culture and Christian fundamentalism. See above Chapter 4.

25 This term has been used to account for risk communication by Krimsky & Plough (1988).

26 This postulate resonates well in recent literature on environmental policy. Hajer (1992) argues for such an approach while criticizing the technocratic self-misunderstanding of the strategy of 'Environmental Performance Review'. See also Hajer (1995) as a general critique of the idea of ecological modernization in European environmental policy since the 1980s. The alternative that he proposes is a discourse-theoretical analysis, which sees facts generated by 'discourse coalitions'. See also Eder (1993b). For parallel attempts cf. Rayner (1991).

solve environmental problems in a society where two incommensurable cultures have arisen and questioned the way in which we perceive nature?

The reconstruction of the dual code underlying European culture has led to the idea of two distinct and even incommensurable cultural traditions underlying present-day environmentalist discourse. *In theoretical terms, the idea of two ways of coding 'nature' is probably the most consequential implication of a cultural analysis of how the relationship of man with nature is transformed into a social and political problem in modern societies.* The notion of a dual coding of nature in ecological discourse has repercussions on institutional politics: environmental politics can no longer work with an objectivist notion of nature. It has to thematize the assumptions that shape the selection and perception of nature in political discourse.

The politics of nature is thus based on contested assumptions. These assumptions imply value judgements which are derived from conflicting cultural definitions of the right and the good. Such a phenomenon has made the politics of nature a widely contested arena of politics. It has become easy to point out the 'ideological character' of this arena and obvious that such a situation is devastating for any concept of *material rationality* (in the Weberian sense, as substantive regulatory rationality). Material rationality no longer makes sense because we know that we do not share a culture in which the 'value' of nature is basically contested. We lack such shared understanding at least in a society that no longer allows for authoritative statements that found rationality on the ideal of objectivity in dealing with nature. What then is to be done?

One proposition that has characterized a large part of the politics of nature is to return to *formal rationality*. In giving up any direct regulation of nature by society, this concept of rationality fosters a return to indirect methods of regulating the relationship of society with nature. Instead of producing direct regulatory means like standards, prohibitions and licences (all of which imply some knowledge concerning the empirical limits for rational standards), indirect means, such as effluent charges or marketable emission permits, are proposed in the search for a political solution to environmental problems.[27] This implies a type of law that distributes rights while abstaining from interfering in individual actions; individual self-interest must decide whether it feels harmed by facts or not. Instead of engaging in a policy dispute over facts, definitions of how much it costs to emit poison into rivers or the air are made collectively binding. Everybody can buy such rights and those concerned are enabled to do more than just complain; they can buy emission rights. However, the main question still remains unanswered: who defines the amount of emission rights? Who controls this 'ecological currency'? There must be somebody who sets the limits for the exploitation of natural resources.

---

27 Similar propositions have been made with respect to the public sphere, e.g. citizenship vouchers which can be given to any movement or organization that people think represents their interest.

Thus the problem of a lack of a collective consensus on what the problems are is avoided by referring to individual self-interest.[28] Instead of prescribing how much pollution human and non-human nature can support, we count on self-interest.[29] Then we run into another problem; for to get the process of environmental self-regulation started we have to limit natural resources. Nature is a scarce good only by definition, and this definition has to be given by some institution. Within the model of formal rationality this is to be done by the *state* as the impartial arbiter in a situation of scarce cultural consensus over the facts at stake in the environmental issue.

The advantage of this solution is that the state does not have to find a true solution to the problem of creating scarcity. It only has to define the scarcity, and within these limits everybody can calculate the factual effects of his or her action. This model of rationality would work, were we able to reduce the cultural context in which the problem of nature is discussed to interest-maximizing individuals and to a state creating the conditions for Pareto-optimal ways of coordinating individual interests. Our historical reconstruction has shown that this is only one half of what the cultural code underlying modern European societies accepts as 'rational'. It is the dominant mode of relating man to nature. This model of rationality is relativized when we acknowledge the existence of more than one culture and even the existence of incommensurable cultures.

The solution I would like to propose is contrary to this notion of the state as a collective actor above 'civil society' in a situation of culturally deep-seated dissensus. It confronts the idea of the state (and the idea of formal rationality that is constitutive for it) with the idea of an institutional procedure that allows an equal distribution of opportunities to communicate about factual knowledge, moral concerns and anxieties about the risks which are present in environmental matters. The rationality that shall account for incommensurable cultures can only be found in a procedure that makes everybody equally responsible for the decisions that are made. Such a procedural solution implies the placement of policy making outside the state in a public ('discursive') context. The simple fact of increased communication over uncertainties (or contradictory certainties) undermines the idea of a state setting limits for self-interested individuals, that is, limits its formal rationality and its variants. The state is just an element of a public context, one of several collective actors in the realm of political communication. Its

---

28 How illusory the idea that objective information might control individual behaviour is, may be 'proven' by the everyday practice of polluting the environment through car driving, etc. Instead of complaining about this, we should be aware that factual information is socially existent not because there is a validity claim of truth to them, as Habermas (1984, 1987) would put it, but because some facts are good for communicating with other people and others not.

29 This solution resembles the arguments of early liberal political and legal theory (this is, in fact, *alteuropäisch!*). Define how much it costs to use political rights (e.g. as years in prison or as number of administrative permissions for collective gatherings), and you will minimize the rationality in politics.

special function then remains to be an arbiter and mediator, a role which the state has taken over in emerging forms of dispute settlement and informal systems of negotiation.

This role of the state becomes apparent the more expert knowledge about environmental matters is debated in public. Knowledge about the environment is increasingly generated by everybody who takes part in public discourse. The increasing communication over environmental facts becomes ever more dependent upon the rationality of this form of communication. The alternative to formal rationality may be called *procedural rationality* (Eder 1986b, 1990a), and this should be sought in conflict-regulating and agenda-setting institutions.[30] Increased communication has, and this is a paradoxical effect, led to a thematization of the cultural assumptions in ecological communication.[31] It has fostered different modes of coordinating interests. One is the model of the accommodation of corporatist interest (in which environmental groups are incorporated in the policy process in a consensual strategy) and the other is a more adversarial model focusing on public enquiry. Both models have been pushed by collective mobilizations for the environmental issue.[32]

The politics of nature is the arena that is most in need of the public sphere where contenders and defenders of nature meet. Politics develops new rituals of political communication by extending its procedures of participation and balancing competing views. Democratic procedures are rituals of communication which presuppose a series of normative assumptions: that everybody can equally participate in them (Eder 1985). In addition, there are additional assumptions which culturally define who has the right to

---

30 An interesting project along these theoretical lines is undertaken by Van den Daele at the Wissenschaftszentrum Berlin. See Van den Daele (1992). Specifically for risk controversies see Rushefsky (1984). A general theoretical model for systems built on procedural rationality is found in Scharpf (1988). The philosophical underpinnings of such a procedural rationality are developed in Shrader-Frechette (1991: 53ff., 77ff.). This latter work explicitly relates the plea for such a rationality with the problems of objectivity and values in risk evaluation. The conclusion drawn is called a 'populist' conception of rationality!

31 This is reflected in recent sociological work on the communication of risks. It shows that not the facts as such but a specific representation of them in communication and by communication is the constitutive element of the process of constructing reality (Johnson & Covello 1987; Rice & Atkin 1989). This insight is politically neutral: everybody can draw upon its implications, the conservative as well as the radical. The central question then becomes a political one. This is what the politics of nature, basically, is about.

32 There is growing literature on this topic. See O'Riordan (1985) among many others. Central to it is the emphasis on participatory elements. This already led to diverse institutionalized forms of dispute settlement and mediation procedures regarding environmental issues. Cf. Wehr (1979) as an early theoretical formulation. An overview of dispute settling from the mid-1970s to the mid-1980s is found in Bingham (1986). See also the report *Improving Dialogue with Communities* (Hance, Chess & Sandman 1988), which describes itself as a *Risk Communication Manual for Government*. This is related to the rise of environmental consulting firms, especially in the United States, but increasingly also in Europe, which specialize in mediating environmental conflicts and resolving environmental disputes. For a re-evaluation of dialogical forms of dispute settling see Eder (1993b).

participate: citizens participate, but who actually counts as a citizen is determined by a cognitive classification that precedes the normative definition of the citizen.[33] Ecological discourse is embedded in these modern rituals of communication, but it discloses additional rules. Our theory proposes that the rule systems underlying ecological communication are rational in a double sense: first, it is rational to engage such rituals of communication in situations of uncertainty. To make decisions in a situation of uncertainty legitimacy is best conveyed by everybody taking part in the decision. However, this proposition does not give a hint about the role that the culture linked with the spirit of environmentalism might play. Any ritual of communication, which includes the new rituals of ecological communication, is embedded in shared cultural assumptions about the world. This leads to the second sense in which the rule systems underlying ecological communication may be seen as rational. Before analysing the normative rules which regulate the institutional game between competing actors in the environmental field (the borders of which are defined by the discursive space of public ecological discourse) the idea of a modern politics of nature first requires the explication of the cognitive presuppositions.

The cognitive institutionalization of environmentalism

The duality of the European cultural traditions which define man's relationship with nature is an interesting case for the institutionalization of a modern social order. The analysis of the cultural roots of modern environmentalism shows that there are conflicting, even incommensurable validity claims over ways of relating man to nature. The culture of environmentalism has not won the battle against the dominant culture, but it has had an important effect. Environmentalism has made it clear that politics does not reside in either one or the other culture, but in the communication of contradictory cultural assumptions about the world. This has led to a reconsideration of the moral values and expressive needs that were excluded in the dominating tradition. Furthermore, it has forced a modification of some of the standards by which the dominant culture has assessed nature in modern societies. The difference between the two cultures not only remains, but has even been fostered by the modern problem of nature. The conflict between competing ways of looking at nature can no longer be resolved by reference to implicit validity claims, as the theory of communicative action (Habermas 1984, 1987) proposes. Communication does not help because it will become never ending, without resolving the conflict between validity claims. Hence the level of validity claims seems to be inadequate to solve the problem of institutionalization. The existence of (at least) two cultural models forces us to look for a

---

33 The social definition of nationality, e. g., is one of the most important symbolic forms defining a citizen.

different level of cultural reality in order to identify the mechanisms that are able to hold together what culture divides.

A theoretical account of the level of cultural analysis beyond the communication of validity claims refers to the cultural presuppositions which are shared collectively without a reference to validity claims: they are, as Mary Douglas (1988) has put it, 'cultural biases'. The two codings of European culture are two such cultural biases which organize collectively-shared perspectives on the world. They define contrary modes of being rational in this culture.

To grasp this difference I propose a distinction between the *justice* perspective and the *purity* perspective. The former excludes what the latter thematizes: a cultural conception of nature that gives to nature a social role beyond being a means for human well-being. From a justice perspective, the instrumentalist tradition of the relation of man to nature can easily find a rational legitimation.[34] Within the purity perspective, this instrumentalism has become illegitimate. This implies that there is a different rationality standard by which to judge the instrumentalist position.

In the cultural conception of nature the 'justice perspective' remains on the level of validity claims. Injustice to nature is a motivation for people to question the basic premises of their relation to nature. It mobilizes animal liberators who see the equal treatment of all beings as the premise of human moral action, a premise characteristic of the utilitarian ethics of animal liberation (Singer 1976). However, the liberation of animals will not challenge man's relation to nature. It will only alleviate some of the consequences that are implied by a culture based on the justice paradigm. For example, it will help to minimize the suffering of animals used for experimental purposes, but it will not change the relationship of man to the animal world. It will not remove man from his moral pedestal. This attitude is paternalism applied to nature, or more precisely, to the animal world. Such a projection can easily be integrated into dominant culture. The relation of man to nature becomes one of a private compensation for the economically instituted use of nature. The use of nature in production will remain unaffected by this pet culture.

The justice perspective adapts the counterculture model of the man–nature relationship to modern culture. As a counterculture tradition, the

---

34 There is one type of moral argumentation that tries to bridge the justice perspective with a non-instrumental view of nature. This has been the utilitarian justification of the relationship between man and nature, an idea that links Bentham to modern environmental economists and has spread, paradoxically, with our greater awareness of the environmental crisis. This utilitarian model of morality can be understood – as it was by Max Weber – as a manifestation of 'material' or 'substantive' rationality. This means applying criteria of justice to a non-instrumental relation with nature. But this utilitarianism has to be based upon anthropo-morphic projections upon the natural world, treating nature like culture. This conflationist view of society and nature ends in ideological discourses on nature – the best examples are the conservationist movements that base their actions upon such conceptions of the world. See Singer (1976, 1979), Salt (1980) and Harwood (1928) as examples.

cultural conception of nature deals with more than rights for nature, namely decency and sentience toward nature. It unveils basic assumptions about society and its cultural order. The 'purity perspective' provides a key for grasping this level of cultural construction of society.[35] The 'purity perspective' codes the difference between nature and culture in a way that is evident in the values attributed to the notion of purity: they are health (referring to bodily and psychic integrity), empathy and life or the complementary notions of sickness, suffering and death.[36] Such values are ones that cannot be divided up to satisfy the needs of as many as possible. Health, bodily integrity and life are holistic values which are indivisible goods. Any form of life that guarantees only a part of them is necessarily incomplete and insufficient.[37]

These values are different from the values underlying the criteria of (distributive) justice; they are values which are constitutive both for the identity of those who discuss and for the discursive context in which discussants relate to each other. There is nothing to distribute because these values relate to goods that are indivisible and non-negotiable. The purity perspective shows us that there are evaluative criteria in the relationship of man to nature which are different from the ones which underlie the perspective of justice. The normative grounds of justice are relative to these cognitive presuppositions. There is certainly a strong affective element in the purity perspective that shapes this relationship, but this is also valid for the justice perspective which acknowledges criteria like sentience and empathy. However, there is more to it than that. Contrasting the justice and the purity perspective forces us to accept the idea that there are not only rights but also (often incommensurable) ideas of a good life which constitute a social order. Philosophically speaking, this implies an argument for the superiority of the good over the just. Such a value hierarchy (which has nothing to do with the traditional value hierarchies based on natural rights) redefines the sources of legitimacy on which an institutional order that responds to the challenge of environmentalism can rely. The spirit of environmentalism forces us to consider a model of rationality different from

---

35 This formulation is derived from the work of Douglas (1966, 1975) who argues that notions of purity belong to elementary cultural structures shaping world-views and forms of social action before they enter the realm of rational and argumentative communication.

36 These remarks need more theoretical elaboration. One only needs to note that sickness, suffering and death are the themes of metaphysics. They are the driving forces of religion-building. Thus the purity–pollution perspective can also be seen as an objectifying way of analysing the religious/metaphysical aspect in the social construction of reality.

37 It is still possible to think of these goods in terms of distributive justice, for example in terms of distributing the scarce number of organs to be transplanted. There is, however, no way of finding a 'good' solution in any such decision. Ultimately, we will be forced to take distributive decisions, but they will no longer be 'just' in an emphatic sense, but only second best solutions.

the one inherited from the 'social question' and institutionalized in the justice model of rationality.[38]

What the purity perspective allows us to see is that before distributing goods social actors have to define what the common good is. Nature as a *common good* is an ideal case for defining what is good for all. Environmentalism has made modern publics sensitive toward a non-instrumental view of an 'unpolluted' nature. In modern ecological discourse this idea has found a short and strict definition: nature is a common good which should not be at the disposition of individual interests. In this formula we decipher the quintessential outcome of a counterculture history: the idea that nature is a good for the whole of society and should be treated as such. Thus the problem of the cognitive basis of a modern institutional order is how to reach a consensus on what is good for all and should be treated as a common good. This raises once more the role of discourse in the construction of a cultural rationality. Since cultural rationality is historically-specific we are left with the idea of minimal procedural requirements for rationality claims when dealing with common goods.

The normative institutionalization of environmentalism

The normative institutionalization of environmentalism refers to the processes of integrating environmentalist collective action, that is, the environmental movement, into an institutional order. The shared cultural concern about nature held by this collective actor has been analysed in the preceding section. This new cognitive context has given rise to new cognitive rule systems shaping modern political discourse. Social movements not only have to organize themselves within the discursive field of modern politics and its cognitive assumptions to find the adequate organizational form, but they also have to reorganize their external relations with other collective actors in political life. The rules governing the interorganizational field of which social movement organizations are a part shape the process of normative institutionalization. The emerging interorganizational field develops traits which transform the modes of political institutionalization that have developed in modern political cultures. A new type of interconnection between civil society (represented by protest actors), the economy (represented by industrial actors, including trade unions) and the political system (represented by modern state agents) emerges. This new order goes beyond corporatism which has developed, to differing degrees, in European democracies in the twentieth century (Schmitter 1977).

---

38 See Van Parijs (1991b) as an interesting attempt to defend this model. He proposes an alternative way of uniting ecological thinking with the traditional liberal emphasis upon the justice perspective by radicalizing the latter (Van Parijs 1992). The justice perspective is linked with the social policy culture of the modern welfare state which is coming to an end, as some theorists of public policy suggest. Cf. Majone (1993).

Table 7.1   *A model of a post-corporatist order*

Institutional location (specific environments)	Market institutions	State institutions	Civil society institutions
basic cultural consensus	profit	justice	good life
carriers (collective actors)	industrial actors	political parties and public administration	NGO's, movement organizations
social units	classes	status groups	moral communities (ecological milieus)
resonances	consumer behaviour	electoral support (voting behaviour)	media resonance
media of communication	money	votes	public discourse
target publics	consumers	voters	opinion holders
institutional myths	rationality	efficiency	discursivity

The rise of environmental movement organizations which deal with common goods creates a strain on the monopoly of the state to provide or guarantee such goods. The provision of common goods becomes a contested issue in policy making. Common goods thus bring the state back in, but not as the key and powerful actor, but as a cooperator in a game. Market-based organizations, the economic corporations, become normatively defined as those who destroy common goods. This makes such organizations an actor in a game they did not want to enter. Thus an institutional system emerges in which normative regulations coordinate actors through rules that are an effect of movement organizations entering this field.

Table 7.1 gives an overview of the dimensions of institutional interorganizational contexts, distinguishing the primary institutional location of collective actors and the specific environments of these actors. The institutional location defines the specific organizational environment within which an organizational actor has to define its action space. This action space and its environment is described in seven dimensions: the concern for specific issues, the specific organizational form of the respective collective actor, the social basis of the organizational actors, the resonances of the respective environments, the media of communication for their respective environments, the target public of the organizational actors and, finally, the institutional myth that is central to an organized actor. The specific logics of the organizational forms of the three collective actors can thus be assessed.

The interorganizational field develops toward a normative order within which institutions for conflict and dispute resolution emerge and whose action ranges from mediation through alternative dispute resolution to 'political dialogues' (Eder 1993b). The normative rules of the game coordinate the conflicting actors in a way that is different from the old models of settling class conflicts.[39] The model proposes that the old corporatist form of handling social cleavages gives way to new post-corporatist forms which engage the three types of actors mentioned above. These new post-corporatist forms focus increasingly on symbolic actions, thus constituting a public discourse which serves as an institutional framework for handling the 'new politics'.

The emerging interorganizational field among these actors changes the rules of the game for the interested *issue publics*. Social movements sensitize the public for the social use of common goods. The modern risk discourses have left a deep imprint on the resonance structure of the public. The environment becomes an issue not only for those who may be mobilized by social movements, but for all. This is where the media come in and take over controversial issues from social movements. It is also where the public enters the institutional system. The public has at its disposal specific means for exerting pressure on organized collective actors: votes, money and public opinion. A complex web of interrelated collective actors emerges which contributes to a reshuffling of the institutional order. To describe this change as normative change provides the image of a chaotic change in which order can be detected only through normative selection. Sorting good and bad norms, according to criteria of efficiency, progress, democracy, individual rights, freedom, and/or equality, allows us to order the chaotic negotiations and renegotiations of normative commitments by participating actors. The emerging post-corporatist order is thus an order in which the normative rules for regulating the environment are institutionalized and at the same time the cognitive presuppositions are constructed reflexively.

The new politics of nature in the post-corporatist order

The 'new politics' is a consequence of the rise of the environmental movement in advanced modern societies. It reflects the social structural changes towards post-industrial society insofar as it is the outgrowth of the new middle classes of post-industrial societies. It has helped to define new social cleavages confronting the life-world of citizens with the power of political and economic actors, thematizing the problem of providing common goods against the interests of those who provide particular goods at the expense of common goods. Finally, it has contributed to the emergence of an institutional framework which tries to civilize these new cleavages through a new form of democratic class struggle.

The paradoxical effect of the emergence and institutionalization of the environmental movement is a simultaneous increase in public discourse and an increasingly loose coupling of decision-making processes and public

---

39 I have called this new normative order a 'new politics of class', pointing to the fact that we still have to do with antagonistic groups of actors (Eder 1993c).

debate. Instead of decrying this phenomenon as a danger to democracy, the neoinstitutionalist perspective enables us to give a different answer. I argue that the problem of the environment in politics will contribute to the solution of the central problem of democracy: how to combine the maximum of liberties for all with the provision of common goods that are endangered by the individualism of a libertarian order.

The neocorporatist and the liberal-pluralist order are the two forms that have shaped the existing institutional order in advanced societies. The alternatives to these orders have been moralized orders and charismatic orders. This cleavage between rational and non-rational orders no longer makes sense. The former two and the latter two, historically, have failed. Given the new problems and issues that relate to the survival of human societies in their natural environments, the historical test will be more demanding: the available options have to face restrictive time constraints. Future consequences have to be taken into account. This mechanism is a first step towards justifying the description of modern societies as reflexive societies. They are not reflexive societies yet, but they have to become reflexive societies. The experience of time constraints creates an objective mechanism to foster ongoing cultural reflexivity and make it a social fact. Reflexive institutions are the characteristics of a post-corporatist order. Their structure and processes are still to be understood and explained. The institutionalization of environmental movements and discourses into modern societies is probably the specific issue field where this general issue will become decisive. This is the general lesson to be learned from the particular case that environmentalism represents as a political phenomenon.

REFERENCES

Abell, P. (1987). *The Syntax of Social Life: The Theory and Method of Comparative Narratives.* Oxford: Oxford University Press.

Alexander, J.C. (1989a). Between progress and apocalypse: social theory and the dream of reason in the twentieth century. In J.C. Alexander & P. Sztompka (Eds.), *Rethinking Progress. Movements, Forces and Ideas at the End of the Twentieth Century* (pp. 15–38). Boston, MA: Unwin Hyman.

Alexander, J.C. (1989b). *Structure and Meaning. Rethinking Classical Sociology.* New York, NY: Columbia University Press.

Alexander, J.C. (1990). Analytic debates: understanding the relative autonomy of culture. In J.C. Alexander & S. Seidman (Eds.), *Culture and Society. Contemporary Debates* (pp. 1–27). Cambridge: Cambridge University Press.

Allan-Michaud, D. (1990). *L'avenir de la société alternative.* Paris: Harmattan.

Alvesson, M., & Berg, P.-O. (1990). *Corporate Culture and Organizational Symbolism. Development, Theoretical Perspectives, Practice and Current Debate.* Berlin/New York: de Gruyter.

Ameta, P.R., & Partridge, S.A. (1989). *The New Vegetarians. Promoting Health and Protecting Life.* New York, NY: Plenum Press.

Amira, K. von. (1891). Thierstrafen und Thierprocesse. *Mitteilungen des Instituts für Österreichische Geschichtsforschung (Innsbruck), 12*, 545–601.

Amy, D.J. (1987). *The Politics of Environmental Mediation.* New York, NY: Columbia University Press.

Anderson, T.L., & Leal, D.R. (1991). *Free Market Environmentalism.* Boulder, CO: Westview Press.

Andrée, R. (1887). *Die Anthropophagie. Eine Ethnographische Studie.* Leipzig: Von Veit & Company.

Archer, M.S. (1988). *Culture and Agency. The Place of Culture in Social Theory.* Cambridge: Cambridge University Press.

Arens, W. (1979). *The Man-Eating Myth. Anthropology & Anthropophagy.* Oxford: Oxford University Press.

Aron, J.P. (1973). *Le mangeur du XIXème siècle.* Paris: Denoel Gonthier.

Ashmore, M. (1989). *The Reflexive Thesis: Writing Sociology of Scientific Knowledge.* Chicago, IL: Chicago University Press.

Attali, J. (1979). *L'ordre cannibale. Vie et mort de la médecine.* Paris: Bernard Grasset.

Attfield, R. (1983a). Christian attitudes to nature. *Journal of the History of Ideas, 44*, 369–386.

Attfield, R. (1983b). *The Ethics of Environmental Concern.* Oxford: Blackwell.

Atwater, T., Salwen, M.B., & Anderson, R.B. (1985). Media agenda-setting with environmental issues. *Journalism Quarterly, 62*, 393–397.

Axelrod, R. (1984). *The Evolution of Cooperation.* New York, NY: Basic Books.

Ayubi, N. (1991). *Political Islam. Religion and Politics in the Arab World.* London: Routledge.

Bachelard, G. (1938). *La formation de l'esprit scientifique. Contribution à une psychanalyse de la connaissance objective.* Paris: Librairie Philosophique J. Vrin.

Bahr, H.-E., Mahlke, H., Mahlke, G., Sölle, D., & Steffensky, F. (1981). *Franziskus in Gorleben. Protest für die Schöpfung.* Frankfurt: Fischer.

Barbour, I. (Ed.). (1973). *Western Man and Environmental Ethics.* Reading: Addison-Wesley.

Barlösius, E. (1987). Riechen und Schmecken – Riechendes und Schmeckendes. Ernährungssoziologische Anmerkungen zum Wandel der sinnlichen Wahrnehmung beim Essen. *Kölner Zeitschrift für Soziologie und Sozialpsychologie, 39*, 367–375.

Barry, B. (1983). Intergenerational justice in energy policy. In D. MacLean & P.G. Brown (Eds.), *Energy and the Future* (pp. 15–30). Totowa, NJ: Rowman & Littlefield.

Basso, E.B. (1972). The Kalapalo dietary system. *Atti del XL Congresso Internazionale Degli Americanisti. Roma-Genova, 3.–10. September 1972*, 629–637.

Bateson, G. (1972). *Steps to an Ecology of the Mind. Collected Essays in Anthropology, Psychiatry, Evolution and Epistemology*. San Francisco, CA: Chandler.

Bauman, Z. (1973). *Culture as Praxis*. London: Routledge & Kegan Paul.

Bauman, Z. (1990). Modernity and ambivalence. *Theory, Culture and Society, 7*, 239–260.

Bauman, Z. (1992). *Modernity and Ambivalence*. Cambridge: Polity Press.

Baumhauer, O.A. (1982). Kulturwandel. Zur Entwicklung des Paradigmas von der Kultur als Kommunikationssystem. Forschungsbericht. *Deutsche Vierteljahresschrift für Literaturwissenschaft und Geistesgeschichte, 56*, 1–167.

Baumol, W.J., & Oates, W.E. (1988 [1975]). *The Theory of Environmental Policy* (rev. ed.). Cambridge: Cambridge University Press.

Beck, U. (1992). *Risk Society. Towards a New Modernity*. London: Sage.

Beck, U. (1993). *Die Erfindung des Politischen*. Frankfurt: Suhrkamp.

Beckford, J.A. (1986). *New Religious Movements and Rapid Social Change*. London: Sage.

Benford, R.D., & Hunt, S.A. (1992). Dramaturgy and social movements: the social construction and communication of power. *Sociological Inquiry, 62*, 36–55.

Bennett, W.L. (1980). The paradox of public discourse: a framework for the analysis of political accounts. *The Journal of Politics, 42*, 792–817.

Berman, M. (1984). *The Reenchantment of the World*. New York, NY: Free Press.

Bingham, G. (1986). *Resolving Environmental Disputes. A Decade of Experience*. Washington, DC: The Conservation Foundation.

Blau, P.M. (1977). *Inequality and Heterogeneity. A Primitive Theory of Social Structure*. New York, NY: The Free Press.

Bloch, E. (1959). *Das Prinzip Hoffnung. 3 Bände*. Frankfurt: Suhrkamp.

Bloch, M. (1974). Symbols, song, dance and features of articulation: is religion an extreme form of traditional authority? *Archives Européennes de Sociologie, 15*, 55–81.

Blumenberg, H. (1973). *Der Prozeß der theoretischen Neugierde. Erweiterte und überarbeitete Neuausgabe von 'Die Legitimität der Neuzeit', dritter Teil*. Frankfurt: Suhrkamp.

Böhme, G., Van den Daele, W., Hohlfeld, R., Krohn, W., Schäfer, W., & Spengler, T. (1978). *Die gesellschaftliche Orientierung des wissenschaftlichen Fortschritts*. Frankfurt: Suhrkamp.

Böhme, G., Van den Daele, W., & Krohn, W. (1972). Alternativen in der Wissenschaft. *Zeitschrift für Soziologie, 1*, 302–316.

Böhme, G., Van den Daele, W., & Krohn, W. (1977). *Experimentelle Philosophie. Ursprünge autonomer Wissenschaftsentwicklung*. Frankfurt: Suhrkamp.

Böhme, H., & Böhme, G. (1983). *Das Andere der Vernunft. Zur Entwicklung von Rationalitätsstrukturen am Beispiel Kants*. Frankfurt: Suhrkamp.

Böhme, R., & Meschkowski, K. (Eds.). (1986). *Die Lust an der Natur. Ein Lesebuch aus Literatur und Wissenschaft*. München: Piper.

Bonß, W. (1990). Zwischen Emanzipation und Entverantwortlichung. Über Chancen und Risiken der Gentechnologie. In K. Grosch, P. Hampe & J. Schmidt (Eds.), *Herstellung der Natur. Stellungnahmen zum Bericht der Enquete-Kommission 'Chancen und Risiken der Gentechnologie'* (pp. 183–206). Frankfurt: Campus.

Bookchin, M. (1980). *Toward an Ecological Society*. Montreal: Black Rose Books.

Bookchin, M. (1982). *The Ecology of Freedom. The Emergence and Dissolution of Hierarchy*. Palo Alto, CA: Stanford University Press.

Boon, J. (1973). Further operations of culture in anthropology: a synthesis of a debate. In L. Schneider & C. Bonjean (Eds.), *The Idea of Culture in the Social Sciences* (pp. 1–32). Cambridge, MA: Harvard University Press.

Borneman, E. (1975). *Das Patriarchat. Ursprung und Zukunft unseres Gesellschaftssystems*. Frankfurt: Fischer.

Bosselmann, K. (1986). Eigene Rechte für die Natur? Ansätze einer ökologischen Rechtsauffassung. *Kritische Justiz, 19*, 1–22.

Bourdieu, P. (1980). *Le sens pratique*. Paris: Minuit.

Bourdieu, P. (1984a). *Homo Academicus*. Paris: Minuit.

Bourdieu, P. (1984b). *The Distinction. A Social Critique of the Judgment of Taste*. Cambridge, MA: Harvard University Press.

Bourdieu, P. (1985). The social space and the genesis of groups. *Theory and Society, 14*, 723–744.

Brady, I. (1982). The myth-eating man. Review of W. Arens, The Man-Eating Myth: Anthropology and Anthropophagy. *American Anthropologist, 84*, 595–611.

Bramwell, A. (1989). *Ecology and History: The Greening of the West Since 1880*. New Haven, CT: Yale University Press.

Brand, K.-W. (1990). Cyclical aspects of new social movements: waves of cultural criticism and mobilization cycles of new middle-class radicalism. In R.J. Dalton & M. Kuechler (Eds.), *Challenging the Political Order. New Social and Political Movements in Western Democracies* (pp. 23–42). Cambridge: Polity Press.

Brand, K.-W. (1993). Strukturveränderungen des Umweltdiskurses in Deutschland. *Forschungsjournal Neue Soziale Bewegungen, 6*, 16–24.

Brinkmann, R. (1978). Romantik als Herausforderung. Zu ihrer wissenschaftsgeschichtlichen Rezeption. In R. Brinkmann (Ed.), *Romantik in Deutschland* (pp. 7–37). Stuttgart: Metzler.

Brosius, H.-B., & Kepplinger, H.M. (1990). The agenda-setting function of television news. Static and dynamic views. *Communication Research, 17*, 183–211.

Brown, G., & Yule, G. (1983). *Discourse Analysis*. Cambridge: Cambridge University Press.

Brüggemeier, F.-J., & Rommelspacher, Th. (1987). *Besiegte Natur. Geschichte der Umwelt im 19. und 20. Jahrhundert*. München: Beck.

Brunschwig, H. (1975). *Gesellschaft und Romantik in Preußen im 18. Jahrhundert. Die Krise des preußischen Staates am Ende des 18. Jahrhunderts und die Entstehung*. Frankfurt: Ullstein.

Burke, P. (1974). *Tradition and Innovation in Renaissance Italy*. London: Fontana/Collins.

Burns, T.R., & Dietz, T. (1992). Cultural evolution: social rule systems, selection and human agency. *International Sociology, 7*, 259–283.

Callicott, J.B. (1992). Animal liberation: a triangular affair. In E.C. Hargrove (Ed.), *The Animal Rights/Environmental Ethics Debate* (pp. 37–69). Albany, NY: State University of New York Press.

Capra, F. (1985). *Wendezeit – Bausteine für ein neues Weltbild* (2nd ed.). Bern: Scherz.

Carroll, M.P. (1977). One more time: Leviticus revisited. *Archives Européennes de Sociologie, 18*, 339–346.

Centre for the Study of Environmental Change. (1991). *The Emerging Ethical Mood on Environmental Issues in Britain. With an Annex A: The Historical Context of Ethical Choice – Dr Paul Morris, and Annex B: Environmentalism and Contemporary Moral Discourse – Mr Bronislaw Szerszynski* (Report to the World Wide Fund for Nature (UK)). Lancaster: Lancaster University, Fylde College, Centre for the Study of Environmental Change.

Chagnon, N.A. (1968). *Yanomamö: The Fierce People*. New York, NY: Holt, Rinehart & Winston.

Chagnon, N.A. (1974). *Studying the Yanomamö*. New York, NY: Holt, Rinehart & Winston.

Cheal, D. (1990). Social construction of consumption. *International Sociology, 5*, 299–318.

Cicourel, A.V. (1980). Three models of discourse analysis: the role of social structure. *Discourse Processes, 3*, 101–132.

Claessens, D., & Claessens, K. (1979). *Kapitalismus als Kultur. Entstehung und Grundlagen der bürgerlichen Gesellschaft*. Frankfurt: Suhrkamp.

Clark, S.L.R. (1977). *The Moral Status of Animals*. Oxford: Clarendon Press.

Clastres, P. (1972). *Chronique des Indiens Guayaki. Ce que savent les Aché, chasseurs nomades du Paraguay* (2nd ed.). Paris: Plon.

Coleman, J.S. (1990). *Foundations of Social Theory*. Cambridge, MA: Belknap Press.

Conrad, J. (1983). Gesellschaft und Risikoforschung – Ein Interpretationsversuch. In J. Conrad (Ed.), *Gesellschaft, Technik und Risikopolitik* (pp. 217–247). Berlin/Heidelberg/ New York: Springer.

Conrad, J. (1987). *Risiko und Ritual* (discussion papers IIUG dp 87–14). Berlin: Wissenschaftszentrum Berlin für Sozialforschung.

Cook, F.L., Taylor, T.R., Goetz, E.G., Gordon, M.T., Protess, D., Leff, D.R., & Molotch, H.L. (1983). Media and agenda setting: effects on the public, interest group leaders, policy makers, and policy. *Public Opinion Quarterly, 47*, 16–35.

Corsaro, W.A. (1981). Communicative processes in studies of social organization: sociological approaches to discourse analysis. *Text, 1*, 5–63.

Dalton, R.J. (1994). *The Green Rainbow. Environmental Groups in Western Europe*. New Haven, CT: Yale University Press.

Dalton, R.J., & Küchler, M. (Eds.). (1990). *Challenging the Political Order. New Social and Political Movements in Western Democracies*. Cambridge: Polity Press.

Davies, D. (1977). An interpretation of sacrifice in Leviticus. *Zeitschrift für alttestamentliche Wissenschaft, 89*, 387–398.

Davies, D. (1981). *Human Sacrifice – in History and Today*. New York, NY: William Morrow and Company.

De Roose, F., & van Parijs, P. (1991). *La pensée écologiste. Essai d'inventaire à l'usage de ceux qui la pratiquent comme de ceux qui la craignent*. Bruxelles: De Boeck Université.

Deléage, J.-P. (1991). *Histoire de l'écologie. Une science de l'homme et de la nature*. Paris: La Découverte.

Deléage, J.-P. (1992). Ecologie: les nouvelles exigences théoriques. *Ecologie Politique, 1*, 1–12.

Detienne, M. (1979). Pratiques culinaires et esprit de sacrifice. In M. Detienne & J.P. Vernant (Eds.), *La cuisine du sacrifice en pays grec* (pp. 7–35). Paris: Gallimard.

Detienne, M., & Svenbro, J. (1979). Les loups au festin ou la cité impossible. In M. Detienne & J.P. Vernant (Eds.), *La cuisine du sacrifice en pays grec* (pp. 215–237). Paris: Gallimard.

Detienne, M., & Vernant, J.-P. (Eds.) (1979). *La cuisine du sacrifice en pays grec*. Paris: Gallimard.

Diamond, A.S. (1974). *In Search of the Primitive. A Critique of Civilization*. New Brunswick, NJ: Transaction.

Diener, P., & Robkin, E.E. (1978). Ecology, evolution, and the search for cultural origins: the question of Islamic pig prohibition. *Current Anthropology, 19*, 493–540.

Dietz, T., & Burns, T.R. (1992). Human agency and the evolutionary dynamics of culture. *Acta Sociologica, 35*, 187–200.

Dijksterhuis, J. (1956). *Die Mechanisierung des Weltbildes*. Göttingen/Heidelberg: Springer.

DiMaggio, P.J. (1988). Classification in art. *American Sociological Review, 52*, 440–455.

Dobson, A., & Lucardie, P. (Eds.). (1993). *The Politics of Nature. Explorations in Green Political Theory*. London: Routledge.

Dole, G. (1961). Endocannibalism among the Amahuaca Indians. *Transactions of the New York Academy of the Sciences, 24*, 567–573.

Donati, P.R. (1992). Political Discourse Analysis. In M. Diani & R. Eyerman (Eds.), *Studying Collective Action* (pp. 136–167). London: Sage.

Donati, P.R. (1995). Mobilitazione delle risorse e trasformazione organizzativa: il caso dell' ecologia politica in Italia. *Quaderni di Scienza Politica, 11*, 167–199.

Donati, P.R. (1996). Building a unified movement: resource mobilization, media work and organizational transformation in the Italian Environmentalist Movement. *Research in Social Movements, Conflict and Change, 19*.

Dornstreich, M.D., & Morren, G.E.B. (1974). Does New Guinea cannibalism have a nutritional value? *Human Ecology, 2*, 1–12.

Douglas, M. (1966). *Purity and Danger. An Analysis of Concepts of Pollution and Taboo*. London: Routledge & Kegan Paul.

Douglas, M. (1973). *Natural Symbols. Explorations in Cosmology*. Harmondsworth: Penguin.

Douglas, M. (1975). *Implicit Meanings. Essays in Anthropology*. London: Routledge & Kegan Paul.

Douglas, D. (1984). Standard social uses of food: introduction. In M. Douglas (Ed.), *Food in the Social Order. Studies of Food and Festivities in Three American Communities*. New York, NY: Russell Sage Foundation.

Douglas, M. (1986a). *How Institutions Think*. Syracuse, NY: Syracuse University Press.

Douglas, M. (1986b). *Risk Acceptability According to the Social Sciences*. London: Routledge & Kegan Paul.

Douglas, M. (1988). A typology of cultures. In M. Haller, H.J. Hoffmann-Nowottny & W. Zapf (Eds.), *Kultur und Gesellschaft. Verhandlungen des 24. Deutschen Soziologentags, des 11. Österreichischen Soziologentags und des 8. Kongresses der Schweizerischen Gesellschaft für Soziologie in Zürich 1988* (pp. 85–97). Frankfurt: Campus.

Douglas, M., & Isherwood, B. (1980). *The World of Goods: Towards an Anthropology of Consumption*. Harmondsworth: Penguin.

Douglas, M., & Wildavsky, A. (1982). *Risk and Culture: An Essay on the Selection of Technical and Environmental Dangers*. Berkeley, CA: University of California Press.

Dower, N. (Ed.). (1989). *Ethics and Environmental Responsibility*. Aldershot: Avebury.

Drechsel, P. (1984). Vorschläge zur Konstruktion einer Kulturtheorie, und was man unter einer Kulturinterpretation verstehen könnte . In E.W. Müller, R. König, K.P. Koepping & P. Drechsel (Eds.), *Ethnologie als Sozialwissenschaft. Sonderheft 26 der Kölner Zeitschrift für Soziologie und Sozialpsychologie* (pp. 44–84). Opladen: Westdeutscher Verlag.

Dreitzel, H.P. (1976). Sur la signification politique de la culture. In N. Birnbaum, H.P. Dreitzel, S. Moscovici, R. Sennett, R. Supek & A. Touraine (Eds.), *Au-dela de la crise* (pp. 87–136). Paris: Seuil.

Dreitzel, H.P. (1981). The socialization of nature: Western attitudes towards body and emotions. In P. Heelas & A. Lock (Eds.), *Indigenous Psychologies. The Anthropology of the Self* (pp. 205–223). London: Academic Press.

Dumont, L. (1967). *Homo Hierarchicus*. Paris: Gallimard.

Dumont, L. (1970). Religion, politics and society in the individualistic universe. *Proceedings of the Royal Anthropological Institutions of Great Britain and Ireland 1970*, 31–41.

Dumont, L. (1977). *Homo Aequalis, I. Genèse et épanouissement de l'idéologie économique*. Paris: Gallimard.

Durkheim, E. (1968 [1912]). *Les formes élémentaires de la vie réligieuse: le système totémique en Australie*. Paris: Presses Universitaires de France.

Durkheim, E., & Mauss, M. (1963). *Primitive Classifications*. Chicago, IL: The University of Chicago Press.

Edelstein, W., & Nunner-Winkler, G. (Eds.). (1986). *Zur Bestimmung der Moral. Philosophische und sozialwissenschaftliche Beiträge zur Moralforschung*. Frankfurt: Suhrkamp.

Eder, K. (1976). *Die Entstehung staatlich organisierter Gesellschaften. Ein Beitrag zu einer Theorie sozialer Evolution*. Frankfurt: Suhrkamp.

Eder, K. (1985). *Geschichte als Lernprozeß? Zur Pathogenese politischer Modernität in Deutschland*. Frankfurt: Suhrkamp.

Eder, K. (1986a). Der permanente Gesellschaftsvertrag. Zur Kritik der ökonomischen Theorie des Sozialen. In L. Kern & H.P. Müller (Eds.), *Gerechtigkeit, Diskurs oder Markt? Die neuen Ansätze in der Vertragstheorie* (pp. 67–81). Opladen: Westdeutscher Verlag.

Eder, K. (1986b). Prozedurale Legitimität. Moderne Rechtsentwicklung jenseits von formaler Rationalisierung. *Zeitschrift für Rechtssoziologie, 7*, 1–30.

Eder, K. (1986c). Soziale Bewegung und kulturelle Evolution. Überlegungen zur Rolle der neuen sozialen Bewegungen in der kulturellen Evolution der Moderne. In J. Berger (Ed.), *Die Moderne – Kontinuitäten und Zäsuren. Sonderband 4 der Sozialen Welt* (pp. 335–357). Göttingen: Schwartz.

Eder, K. (1987). Learning and the evolution of social systems. An epigenetic perspective. In M. Schmid & F.M. Wuketits (Eds.), *Evolutionary Theory in Social Science* (pp. 101–125). Dordrecht/Boston: Reidel.

Eder, K. (1988). *Die Vergesellschaftung der Natur. Studien zur sozialen Evolution der praktischen Vernunft*. Frankfurt: Suhrkamp.

Eder, K. (1990a). Prozedurales Recht und Prozeduralisierung des Rechts. Einige begriffliche Klärungen. In D. Grimm (Ed.), *Wachsende Staatsaufgaben – sinkende Steuerungsfähigkeit des Rechts* (pp. 155–186). Baden-Baden: Nomos.

Eder, K. (1990b). The cultural code of modernity and the problem of nature: a critique of the naturalistic notion of progress. In J. Alexander & P. Sztompka (Eds.), *Rethinking Progress: Movements, Forces and Ideas at the End of the Twentieth Century* (pp. 67–87). London/New York: Unwin Hyman.

Eder, K. (1992a). Contradictions and social evolution. A theory of the social evolution of modernity. In H. Haferkamp & N.J. Smelser (Eds.), *Social Change and Modernity* (pp. 320–349). Berkeley, CA: University of California Press.

Eder, K. (1992b). Framing and communicating environmental problems. Public discourse and the dynamics of environmental consciousness in Europe. Outline of a research project. Florence: Unpublished manuscript, European University Institute.

Eder, K. (1992c). Il paradosso della cultura. Oltre una teoria consensualista della cultura. *Fenomenologia e Società, 15* (2) (*Errata corrige Bibliografia 15* (3)), 17–39.

Eder, K. (1993a). La communication écologique et la culture environnementaliste. In D. Bourg (Ed.), *La nature en politique ou l'enjeu philosophique de l'écologie* (pp. 121–137). Paris: L'Harmattan/Association Descartes.

Eder, K., & Brand, K.-W. (1993b). *Reflexive Institutionen? Eine Untersuchung zur Herausbildung eines neuen Typus institutioneller Regelungen im Umweltbereich* (Projektvorschlag (DFG-Projektnummer Ed 25/7)). München: Münchner Projektgruppe für Sozialforschung.

Eder, K. (1993c). *The New Politics of Class. Social Movements and Cultural Dynamics in Advanced Societies*. London: Sage.

Eder, K. (1994). Rationality in environmental discourse: A cultural approach. In W. Rüdig (Ed.), *Green Politics. Volume Three* (pp. 9–37). Edinburgh: University of Edinburgh Press.

Eisenstadt, S.N., & Roniger, L. (1984). *Patrons, Clients and Friends*. Cambridge: Cambridge University Press.

Elias, N. (1978). *The Civilising Process. Vol. I: The History of Manners*. Oxford: Blackwell.

Elias, N. (1982). *The Civilising Process. Vol. II: State Formation and Civilisation (US: Power and Civility)*. Oxford: Blackwell.

Elkington, J., & Burke, T. (1989). *The Green Capitalists: How to Make Money and Protect the Environment*. London: Victor Gollancz.

Elster, J. (1989). *The Cement of Society. A Study of Social Order*. New York, NY: Cambridge University Press.

Elster, J. (1991). Rationality and social norms. *Archives Européennes de Sociologie, 32*, 109–129.

Engels, F. (1951). *Dialektik der Natur*. Berlin: Dietz Verlag.

Erbring, L., Goldenberg, E.N., & Miller, A.H. (1980). Front-page news and real-world cues: a new look at agenda-setting by the media. *American Journal of Political Science, 24*, 16–49.

Erdheim, M. (1973). *Prestige und Kulturwandel. Eine Studie zum Verhältnis subjektiver und objektiver Faktoren des kulturellen Wandels zur Klassengesellschaft bei den Azteken*. Frankfurt: Focus.

Erdheim, M. (1982). *Die gesellschaftliche Produktion von Unbewußtheit. Eine Einführung in den ethnopsychoanalytischen Prozeß*. Frankfurt: Suhrkamp.

Evans, E.P. (1906). *The Criminal Prosecution and Capital Punishment of Animals*. London: Heinemann.

Evans-Pritchard, E.E. (1937). *Witchcraft, Oracles and Magic Among the Azande*. Oxford: Clarendon Press.

Eyerman, R., & Jamison, A. (1991). *Social Movements: A Cognitive Approach*. Cambridge: Polity Press.

Fairclough, N. (1989). *Language and Power*. London: Longman.

Fairclough, N. (1992). *Discourse and Social Change*. Cambridge: Polity Press.

Ferber, C. von. (1980). Ernährungsgewohnheiten: Zur Soziologie der Ernährung. *Zeitschrift für Soziologie, 9*, 221–235.

Fides, N. (1991). *Meat: A Natural Symbol*. London: Routledge.

Fischer, K., & Schot, J. (Eds.). (1993). *Environmental Strategies of Industry*. Washington, DC: Island Press.

Fisher, W.R. (1984). Narration as a human communication paradigm: the case of public moral argument. *Communication Monographs, 51*, 1–22.

Forde, D. (Ed.). (1970). *African Worlds. Studies in the Cosmological Ideas and Social Values of African Peoples* (7th ed.). London: Oxford University Press.

Foucault, M. (1966). *Les mots et les choses*. Paris: Gallimard.

Friedland, R., & Alford, R. (1991). Bringing society back in: symbols, practices, and institutional contradictions. In W.W. Powell & P. DiMaggio (Eds.), *The New Institutionalism in Organizational Analysis* (pp. 232–263). Chicago, IL: University of Chicago Press.

Friedman, J. (1974). Marxism, structuralism and vulgar materialism. *Man, 9*, 444–469.

Friedman, J. (1992). Narcissism, roots and postmodernity: the constitution of selfhood in the global crisis. In S. Lash & J. Friedman (Eds.), *Modernity and Identity* (pp. 331–366). Oxford: Blackwell.

Gale, R.P. (1986). Social movements and the state: the environmental movement, countermovement, and government agencies. *Sociological Perspectives, 29*, 202–240.

Gamson, W.A. (1992). *Talking Politics*. Cambridge: Cambridge University Press.

Gamson, W.A., & Modigliani, A. (1987). The changing culture of affirmative action. In R.D. Braungart & M.M. Braungart (Eds.), *Research in Political Sociology* (Vol. 3, pp. 137–177). Greenwich, CT: JAI Press.

Gamson, W.A., & Modigliani, A. (1989). Media discourse and public opinion on nuclear power: a constructionist approach. *American Journal of Sociology, 95*, 1–38.

Garn, S.M., & Block, W.D. (1970). The limited nutritional value of cannibalism. *American Anthropologist, 72*, 106.

Gebauer, G., & Wulf, C. (1992). *Mimesis. Kultur, Kunst, Gesellschaft*. Reinbek: Rowohlt.

Gehlen, A. (1960). *Sozialpsychologie*. Reinbek: Rowohlt.

Giddens, A. (1984). *The Constitution of Society. Outline of the Theory of Structuration*. Berkeley, CA: University of California Press.

Giddens, A. (1990). *The Consequences of Modernity*. Cambridge: Cambridge University Press.

Giddens, A. (1991). *Modernity and Self-Identity. Self and Society in the Late Modern Age*. Cambridge: Polity Press.

Giedion, S. (1948). *Mechanization Takes Command*. Oxford: Oxford University Press.

Giesen, B. (1980). *Makrosoziologie. Eine evolutionstheoretische Einführung*. Hamburg: Hoffmann und Campe.

Giesen, B. (1991). Code, process and situation in cultural selection. *Cultural Dynamic, 4*, 172–185.

Giesen, B., & Lau, C. (1981). Zur Anwendung darwinistischer Erklärungsstrategien in der Soziologie. *Kölner Zeitschrift für Soziologie und Sozialpsychologie, 33*, 229–256.

Ginsberg, B., & Shefter, M. (1989). *Politics by Other Means. The Declining Importance of Elections in America*. New York, NY: Basic Books.

Ginsberg, M. (1956). *Essays in Sociology and Social Philosophy III*. Melbourne/London/Toronto: Heinemann.

Girard, R. (1972). *La violence et le sacré*. Paris: Bernard Grasset.

Godelier, M. (1973). *Horizon, trajets marxistes en anthropologie*. Paris: Maspero.

Godelier, M. (1991). Mythe et histoire. *Annales. Economies, Sociétés, Civilisations*, 541–558.

Goody, J. (1977). *The Domestication of the Savage Mind*. Cambridge: Cambridge University Press.

Goody, J. (1982). *Cooking, Cuisine and Class. A Study in Comparative Sociology*. Cambridge: Cambridge University Press.

Gouldner, A.W., & Peterson, R.A. (1962). *Notes on Technology and the Moral Order*. Indianapolis, IN: Bobbs-Merrill.

Graf, V. (1986). Die Vegetarier. *Der Alltag. Sensationsblatt des Gewöhnlichen. Schwerpunkt: Tiere, 3*, 46–51.

Granovetter, M.S. (1985). Economic action and social structure: the problem of embeddedness. *American Journal of Sociology, 91*, 481–510.

Green, A.R.W. (1975). *The Role of Human Sacrifice in the Ancient Near East*. American Schools of Oriental Research, Dissertation Series 1.

Grefe, C., Heller, P., Herbst, M., & Pater, S. (1985). *Brot des Siegers – Das Hackfleisch-Imperium*. Frankfurt: Lamuv.

Grignon, C., & Grignon, C. (1980). Styles d'alimentation et goûts populaires. *Revue française de sociologie, 21*, 531–569.

Gusfield, J.R. (1981a). Social movements and social change: perspectives of linearity and fluidity. In L. Kriesberg (Ed.), *Research in Social Movements, Conflict and Change* (Vol. 4, pp. 317–339). Greenwich, CT: JAI Press.

Gusfield, J.R. (1981b). *The Culture of Public Problems: Drinking-Driving and the Symbolic Order*. Chicago, IL: University of Chicago Press.

Habermas, J. (1968a). Arbeit und Interaktion. In (*idem*), *Technik und Wissenschaft als 'Ideologie'* (pp. 9–47). Frankfurt: Suhrkamp.

Habermas, J. (1968b). *Erkenntnis und Interesse*. Frankfurt: Suhrkamp.

Habermas, J. (1968c). Technik und Wissenschaft als 'Ideologie'. In (*idem*), *Technik und Wissenschaft als 'Ideologie'* (pp. 48–103). Frankfurt: Suhrkamp.

Habermas, J. (1979). *Communication and the Evolution of Society*. London: Heinemann.

Habermas, J. (1984). *The Theory of Communicative Action: Reason and the Rationalization of Society. Volume I*. Boston, MA: Beacon Press.

Habermas, J. (1987). *The Theory of Communicative Action: Lifeworld and System. A Critique of Functionalist Reason. Volume II*. Boston, MA: Beacon Press.

Habermas, J. (1989). *The Structural Transformation of the Public Sphere: an Inquiry into a Category of Bourgeois Society*. Cambridge, MA: MIT Press.

Habermas, J. (1992). *Faktizität und Geltung. Beiträge zur Diskurstheorie des Rechts und des demokratischen Rechtsstaats*. Frankfurt: Suhrkamp.

Habermas, J., & Luhmann, N. (1971). *Theorie der Gesellschaft oder Sozialtechnologie – Was leistet die Systemforschung?* Frankfurt: Suhrkamp.

Hajer, M.A. (1992). The politics of environmental performance review: choices in design. In E. Lykke (Ed.), *Achieving Environmental Goals. The Concept and Practice of Environmental Performance Review*. London: Belhaven Press.

Hajer, M.A. (1995) *The Politics of Environmental Discourse: A Study of the Acid Rain Controversy in Great Britain and the Netherlands*. Oxford: Clarendon.

Hance, B.J., Chess, C., & Sandman, P.M. (1988). *Improving Dialogue with Communities: A Risk Communication Manual for Government. Environmental Communication Research Program, New Jersey Agricultural Experiment Station*. New Brunswick, NJ: Rutgers University.

Hansen, A. (1991). The media and the social construction of the environment. *Media, Culture and Society, 13*, 443–458.

Hansen, A. (1993a). Greenpeace and press coverage of environmental issues. In A. Hansen (Ed.), *The Mass Media and Environmental Issues* (pp. 150–178). Leicester: Leicester University Press.

Hansen, A. (Ed.) (1993b). *The Mass Media and Environmental Issues*. Leicester: Leicester University Press.

Hardt, S. (1987). *Tod und Eros beim Essen. Mit einem Vorwort von Hartmut Böhme*. Frankfurt: Suhrkamp.

Hargrove, E.C. (1989). *Foundations of Environmental Ethics*. Englewood Cliffs, NJ: Prentice-Hall.

Harner, M. (1977a). The ecological basis for Aztec sacrifice. *American Ethnologist, 4*, 117–135.

Harner, M. (1977b). The enigma of Aztec sacrifice. *Natural History, 76*, 47–51.

Harris, M. (1968). *The Rise of Anthropological Theory. A History of Culture*. New York, NY: Crowell.

Harris, M. (1977). *Cows, Pigs, Wars, and Witches. The Riddles of Culture*. London: Fontana.

Harris, M. (1978). *Cannibals and Kings. The Origins of Cultures*. New York, NY: Random House.

Harris, M. (1979). *Cultural Materialism: The Struggle for a Science of Culture*. New York, NY: Random House.

Hart, H.L.A. (1980). Death and utility. *New York Review of Books. May 15, 1980*, 25–32.

Harwood, D. (1928). *Love of Animals, and How it Developed in Great Britain*. New York, NY: Columbia University Library.

Hays, S.P. (1958). *Conservation and the Gospel of Efficiency: the Progressive Conservation Movement, 1890–1920*. Cambridge, MA: Harvard University Press.

Hays, S.P. (1987). *Beauty, Health and Permanence. Environmental Politics in the United States 1955–1985*. Cambridge: Cambridge University Press.

Heinsohn, G. (1979). Theorie des Tötungsverbotes und des Monotheismus bei den Israeliten sowie der Genese, Durchsetzung und Rolle der christlichen Familienmoral. In B. Wassermann & J. Müller (Eds.), *L'invitation au voyage – Festschrift für Alfred Sohn-Rethel zum 80. Geburtstag*. Bremen: Wassmann.

Heinsohn, G., Knieper, R., & Steiger, O. (1979). *Menschenproduktion. Allgemeine Bevölkerungstheorie der Neuzeit*. Frankfurt: Suhrkamp.

Heinsohn, G., & Steiger, O. (1985). *Die Vernichtung der weisen Frauen. Beiträge zu Theorie und Geschichte von Bevölkerung und Kindheit*. Herbstein: März.

Heinsohn, G., & Steiger, O. (1987). Warum mußte das Speculum zweimal erfunden werden? – Eine Replik. *Kritische Justiz, 20*, 200–207.

Heise, D., Levski, G., & Wardwell, J. (1976). Further notes on technology and the moral order. *Social Forces, 55*, 316–337.

Hepp, C. (1987). *Avantgarde – Moderne Kunst, Kulturkritik und Reformbewegungen nach der Jahrhundertwende*. München: Deutscher Taschenbuch Verlag.

Herpin, N. (1980). Comportements alimentaires et contraintes sur les emplois du temps. *Revue française de sociologie, 21*, 599–628.

Hess, H. (1987). *Rauchen. Geschichte, Geschäfte, Gefahren*. Frankfurt: Campus.

Hill, J.N. (1977a). Systems theory and the explanation of change. In J.N. Hill (Ed.), *Explanation of Prehistoric Change* (pp. 59–104). Albuquerque, NM: University of New Mexico Press.

Hill, J.N. (Ed.). (1977b). *Explanation of Prehistoric Change*. Albuquerque, NM: University of New Mexico Press.

Hirsch, E.L. (1986). The creation of political solidarity in social movement organizations. *Sociological Quarterly, 27*, 373–387.

Hirsch, E.L. (1990). Sacrifice for the cause: group processes, recruitment, and commitment in a student social movement. *American Sociological Review, 55*, 243–254.

Hirsch, P.M. (1986). From ambushes to golden parachutes: corporate takeovers as an instance of cultural framing and institutional integration. *American Journal of Sociology, 91*, 800–837.

Hobsbawm, E.J. (1952). The machine breakers. *Past and Present, 1*, 57–70.

Hobsbawm, E.J. (1972). *Primitive Rebels: Studies of Archaic Forms of Social Movements in the XIXth and XXth Centuries* (2nd ed.). Manchester: Manchester University Press.

Hobsbawm, E.J. (1981). *Bandits* (rev. ed.). New York, NY: Pantheon.

Honneth, A. (1982). Work and instrumental action. *New German Critique, 26*, 31–54.

Horton, R. (1967). African traditional thought and Western science. *Africa, 37*, 50–71, 155–187.

Hubert, H., & Mauss, M. (1968a). Essai sur la nature et la fonction du sacrifice. In V. Karady (Ed.), *Marcel Mauss. Oeuvres 1. Les fonctions sociales du sacré: I* (pp. 193–354). Paris: Minuit.

Hubert, H., & Mauss, M. (1968b). L'introduction à l'analyse de quelques phénomènes religieux (1906). In V. Karady (Ed.), *Marcel Mauss. Oeuvres 1. Les fonctions sociales du sacré: I* (pp. 3–106). Paris: Minuit.

Hund, W.D. (1978). Probleme einer materialistischen Theorie der Kultur. In W.D. Hund & D. Kramer (Eds.), *Beiträge zur materialistischen Kulturtheorie* (pp. 45–101). Köln: Pahl-Rugenstein.

Ishige, N. (1977). Roasting dog (or a substitute) in an earth oven: an unusual method of preparation from Ponape. In J. Kuper (Ed.), *The Anthropologists' Cookbook* (pp. 203–205). London: Routledge & Kegan Paul.

Jamison, A., Eyerman, R., & Cramer, J. (1990). *The Making of the New Environmental Consciousness. A Comparative Study of Environmental Movements in Sweden, Denmark and the Netherlands*. Edinburgh: Edinburgh University Press.

Japp, K.P. (1987). Risiken der Technisierung und die neuen sozialen Bewegungen. In G. Bechmann (Ed.), *Risiko und Gesellschaft*. Opladen: Westdeutscher Verlag.

Jerouschek, G. (1986). Hexenprozesse als staatsterroristische Bevölkerungs politik. *Kritische Justiz, 19*, 443–458.

Johnson, B.B., & Covello, V.T. (Eds.). (1987). *The Social and Cultural Construction of Risk. Essays on Risk Selection and Perception*. Dordrecht: Reidel.

Johnston, H. (1992). *'Fightin' Words': Discourse, Frames and the Cultural Analysis of Social Movements*. San Diego, CA: Unpublished manuscript, UCSD.

Jonas, H. (1984). *The Imperative of Responsibility. In Search of an Ethics for the Technological Age*. Chicago, IL: University of Chicago Press.

Kamper, D., & Wulf, C. (Eds.). (1982). *Die Wiederkehr des Körpers*. Frankfurt: Suhrkamp.

Kamper, D., & Wulf, C. (Eds.). (1984). *Das Schwinden der Sinne*. Frankfurt: Suhrkamp.

Kandel, R.F., & Pelto, G.H. (1980). The health food movement. Social revitalization or alternative maintenance system? In N.W. Jerome, R.F. Kandel & G.H. Pelto (Eds.), *Nutritional Anthropology. Contemporary Approaches to Diet and Culture* (pp. 327–363). Pleasantville, NY: Redgrave Publishing Company.

Karsten, R. (1926). *The Civilization of the South American Indians*. London: Kegan Paul.

Katalyse e.V. (1986). *Das Ernährungsbuch*. Köln: Kiepenheuer & Witsch.

Kippenberg, H.-G. (Ed.). (1977). *Seminar: Die Entstehung der antiken Klassengesellschaft*. Frankfurt: Suhrkamp.

Kippenberg, H.-G., & Luchesi, B. (Eds.). (1978). *Magie. Die sozialwissenschaftliche Kontroverse über das Verstehen fremden Denkens*. Frankfurt: Suhrkamp.

Kirk, G.S. (1970). *Myth. Its Meaning and Functions in Ancient and Other Cultures*. Berkeley/Los Angeles, CA: University of California Press.

Kitschelt, H. (1984). *Der ökologische Diskurs. Eine Analyse von Gesellschaftskonzeptionen in der Energiedebatte*. Frankfurt: Campus.

Knorr-Cetina, K. (1981). *The Manufacture of Knowledge*. Oxford/New York, NY: Pergamon.

Knorr-Cetina, K. (1988). The micro-social order: towards a reconception. In N.G. Fielding (Ed.), *Actions and Structure: Research Methods and Social Theory* (pp. 21–53). London: Sage.

König, M.E.P. (1973). *Am Anfang der Kultur. Die Zeichensprache des frühen Menschen*. Frankfurt: Ullstein.

König, R. (1973). *Handbuch der empirischen Sozialforschung. 12 Bände (1973–1978)*. Stuttgart: Enke.

Krabbe, W.R. (1974). *Gesellschaftsveränderung durch Lebensreform. Strukturmerkmale einer sozialreformerischen Bewegung im Deutschland der Industrialisierungsepoche*. Göttingen: Vandenhoeck & Ruprecht.

Krimsky, S., & Plough, A. (1988). *Environmental Hazards. Communicating Risks as a Social Process*. Dover, MA: Auburn House.

Küchler, M. (1990) Ökologie statt Ökonomie: Wählerpräferenzen im Wandel? In M. Kaase & H.D. Klingemann (Eds.), *Wahlen und Wähler. Analysen aus Anlaß der Bundestagswahl 1987 (Schriften des Zentralinstituts für sozialwissenschaftliche Forschung der Freien Universität Berlin Band 60)* (pp. 419–444). Opladen: Westdeutscher Verlag.

Kuper, J. (Ed.). (1977). *The Anthropologists' Cookbook*. London: Routledge & Kegan Paul.

Lahusen, C. (1994). The praxis of political mobilization. A sociological inquiry into public campaigns of social movement organizations. Unpublished doctoral dissertation, European University Institute, Florence.

Lanternari, V. (1960). *Religiöse Freiheits- und Heilsbewegungen unterdrückter Völker*. Neuwied/Berlin: Luchterhand.

Lanternari, V. (1976). Nativistic and socio-religious movements: a reconsideration. *Comparative Studies in Society and History, 18*, 483–503.

Lash, S., & Friedman, J. (Eds.). (1992). *Modernity and Identity*. Oxford: Blackwell.

Laum, B. (1924). *Heiliges Geld. Eine historische Untersuchung über den sakralen Ursprung des Geldes*. Tübingen: Mohr.

Leach, E. (1964). Anthropological aspects of language: animal categories and verbal abuse. In E.H. Lenneberg (Ed.), *New Directions in the Study of Language* (pp. 23–64). Cambridge, MA: MIT Press.

Leach, E. (1976). *Culture and Communication: The Logic by which Symbols are Connected*. Cambridge: Cambridge University Press.

Leder, K.B. (1986). *Todesstrafe. Ursprung, Geschichte, Opfer*. München: DTV.

Legros, D. (1977). Chance, necessity, and mode of production: a Marxist critique of cultural evolutionism. *American Anthropologist, 79*, 26–41.

Leiris, M. (1930). L'oeil de l'ethnographe. *Documents, 2*, 404–414.

Leiris, M. (1950). L'Ethnographe devant le colonialisme. *Les Temps Modernes, 6*, 357–374.

Lepenies, W. (1977). Das Ende der Naturgeschichte und der Beginn der Moderne. Verzeitlichung und Enthistorisierung in der Wissenschaftsgeschichte des 18. und 19. Jahrhunderts. In R. Koselleck (Ed.), *Studien zum Beginn der modernen Welt* (pp. 317–351). Stuttgart: Klett.

Lepenies, W. (1978). *Das Ende der Naturgeschichte. Wandel kultureller Selbstverständlichkeiten in den Wissenschaften des 18. und 19. Jahrhunderts*. Frankfurt: Suhrkamp.

Lévi-Strauss, C. (1955). *Tristes tropiques*. Paris: Plon.

Lévi-Strauss, C. (1962). *La pensée sauvage*. Paris: Plon.

Lévi-Strauss, C. (1963). *Structural Anthropology*. New York, NY: Basic Books.

Lévi-Strauss, C. (1964a). Le triangle culinaire. *L'Arc, 62*, 19–29.

Lévi-Strauss, C. (1964b). *Mythologiques I: Le cru et le cuit*. Paris: Plon.

Lévi-Strauss, C. (1964c). *Totemism*. London: Merlin Press.

Lévi-Strauss, C. (1967). *Les structures élémentaires de la parenté* (2nd ed.). Paris/Den Haag: Mouton.

Lévi-Strauss, C. (1968a). *Mythologiques III: L'origine des manières de table*. Paris: Plon.

Lévi-Strauss, C. (1968b). *Tristes tropiques* (2nd ed.). Paris: Plon.

Lévi-Strauss, C. (1973). *Anthropologie structurale deux*. Paris: Plon.

Levitt, B., & March, J.G. (1988). Organizational learning. *Annual Review of Sociology, 14*, 319–340.

Liberatore, A. (1991). Problems of transnational policymaking: environmental policy in the European Community. *European Journal of Political Research, 19*, 281–305.

Lindenberg, S. (1983). The new political economy: its potential and limitations for the social sciences in general and for sociology in particular. In W. Sodeur (Ed.), *Ökonomische Erklärungen sozialen Verhaltens* (pp. 7–66). Duisburg: Verlag der Sozialwissenschaftlichen Kooperative.

Lindenberg, S. (1986). How sociological theory lost its central issue and what can be done about it. In S. Lindenberg, J.S. Coleman & S. Nowak (Eds.), *Approaches to Social Theory* (pp. 19–24). New York, NY: Russell Sage Foundation.

Linse, U. (1983a). *Barfüßige Propheten. Erlöser der zwanziger Jahre*. München: Siedler.

Linse, U. (Ed.). (1983b). *Zurück, o Mensch, zur Mutter Erde. Landkommunen in Deutschland 1890–1933*. München: Deutscher Taschenbuch Verlag.

Loeb, E.M. (1974). *The Blood Sacrifice Complex* (1923). Millwood, NY: Kraus Reprint.

Loisy, A. (1920). *Essai historique sur le sacrifice*. Paris: Emile Nourry.

Lorenzen, P. (1960). *Die Entstehung der exakten Wissenschaften*. Berlin: Springer.

Lovelock, J. (1989). *The Ages of Gaia. A Biography of Our Living Earth*. Oxford: Oxford University Press.

Lowe, P.D. (1990). Environmental management in West European countries: social movement, ecological problems and institutional problems. In J. De Bardeleben (Ed.), *Environmental Problems in Europe, East and West*. New York, NY: Oxford University Press.

Lowe, P.D., & Rüdig, W. (1986). Review article: political ecology and the social sciences – the state of the art. *British Journal of Sociology, 16*, 513–550.

Luhmann, N. (1978). Geschichte als Prozeß und die Theorie soziokultureller Evolution. In K.G. Faber & Ch. Meier (Eds.), *Historische Prozesse* (pp. 413–440). München: Deutscher Taschenbuch Verlag.

Luhmann, N. (1980). *Gesellschaftsstruktur und Semantik. Studien zur Wissenssoziologie der modernen Gesellschaft (1. Band)*. Frankfurt: Suhrkamp.

Luhmann, N. (1981). *Gesellschaftsstruktur und Semantik. Studien zur Wissenssoziologie der modernen Gesellschaft (2. Band)*. Frankfurt: Suhrkamp.

Luhmann, N. (1984). *Soziale Systeme. Grundriß einer allgemeinen Theorie*. Frankfurt: Suhrkamp.

Luhmann, N. (1985a). Die Autopoiesis des Bewußtseins. *Soziale Welt, 36*, 402–446.
Luhmann, N. (Ed.). (1985b). *Soziale Differenzierung. Zur Geschichte einer Idee*. Opladen: Westdeutscher Verlag.
Luhmann, N. (1989). *Ecological Communication*. Chicago, IL: University of Chicago Press.
Luhmann, N. (1990). *Essays on Self-Reference*. New York, NY: Columbia University Press.
Luke, T.W. (1988). The dreams of deep ecology. *Telos, 76*, 65–92.
MacIntyre, A. (1985). *After Virtue. A Study in Moral Theory* (1st ed. 1981) (2nd ed.). London: Duckworth.
MacIntyre, A. (1988). *Whose Justice? Which Rationality?* London: Duckworth.
Maier, A. (1938). *Die Mechanisierung des Weltbildes im 17. Jahrhundert*. Leipzig: Meiner.
Maier, A. (1955). *Metaphysische Hintergründe der spätscholastischen Naturphilosophie*. Rome: Ed. di storia e letteratura.
Majone, G. (1993). Wann ist Policy-Deliberation wichtig? In A. Héritier (Ed.), *Policy-Analyse. Kritik und Neuorientierung* (pp. 97–115). Opladen: Westdeutscher Verlag (in English:When does policy deliberation matter? Florence: Unpublished manuscript, European University Institute, 1993).
Majone, G. (1994). The rise of the regulatory state in Europe. *West European Politics, 17*, 77–101.
Majone, G. (in press). Ideas, interests and policy change. In H. Richter (Ed.), *A Sceptical Child of the Enlightenment: Studies in the Thought of C.E. Lindblom*. Boulder, CO: Westview Press.
Malinowski, B. (1948). *Magic, Science and Religion and Other Essays*. New York, NY: Free Press (reprinted 1984 by Greenwood Press).
Malinowski, B. (1994 [1944]). *A Scientific Theory of Culture and Other Essays*. Chapel Hill, NC: University of North Carolina Press.
Mangham, I., & Overington, M.A. (1985). *Organization as Theatre. A Social Psychology of Dramatic Appearances*. New York, NY: Wiley & Sons.
Mann, M. (1986). *The Sources of Social Power. A History of Power from the Beginning to A.D. 1760 (Vol. I)*. Cambridge, MA: Harvard University Press.
Marcuse, H. (1964). *One-Dimensional Man*. Boston, MA: Beacon.
Marcuse, H. (1968a). Über den affirmativen Charakter der Kultur. In (*idem*), *Kultur und Gesellschaft. Band 1*. Frankfurt: Suhrkamp.
Marcuse, H. (1968b). Über die philosophischen Grundlagen des wirtschaftswissenschaftlichen Arbeitsbegriffs. In (*idem*), *Kultur und Gesellschaft. Band 2* (pp. 7–48). Frankfurt: Suhrkamp.
Maren-Griesebach, M. (1982). *Philosophie der Grünen*. München/Wien: Schwarzenberg.
Marshack, A. (1972). *The Roots of Civilization*. New York, NY: McGraw-Hill.
Marx, K. (1953a). *Grundrisse der Kritik der Politischen Ökonomie (Rohentwurf) 1857–1858*. Berlin: Dietz Verlag.
Marx, K. (1953b). Ökonomisch-philosophische Manuskripte (1844). *Marx Engels Werke, Ergänzungsband 1*. Berlin (DDR): Dietz Verlag.
Mason, S.F. (1962). *A History of the Sciences* (2nd ed.). New York, NY: Colliers Books.
McCombs, M.E. (1981). The agenda-setting approach. In D.D. Nimmo & K.R. Sanders (Eds.), *Handbook of Political Communication* (pp. 121–140). Beverly Hills, CA: Sage.
McCombs, M.E., & Shaw, D.L. (1972). The agenda-setting function of mass media. *Public Opinion Quarterly, 36*, 176–187.
McCombs, M.E., & Shaw, D.L. (1977a). Agenda-setting and the political process. In D.L. Shaw & M.E. McCombs (Eds.), *The Emergence of American Political Issues: The Agenda-Setting Function of the Press* (pp. 149–156). St. Paul, MN: West Publishing Company.
McCombs, M.E., & Shaw, D.L. (1977b). The agenda-setting function of the press. In D.L. Shaw & M.E. McCombs (Eds.), *The Emergence of American Political Issues: The Agenda-Setting Function of the Press* (pp. 1–18). St. Paul, MN: West Publishing Company.
McCracken, G. (1988). *Culture and Consumption. New Approaches to the Symbolic Character of Consumer Goods and Activities*. Bloomington, IN: Indiana University Press.

McKibben, B. (1990). *The End of Nature*. London: Viking.

Medick, H. (1977). Die protoindustrielle Familienwirtschaft. In P. Kriedtke, H. Medick & J. Schlumbohm (Eds.), *Industrialisierung vor der Industrialisierung. Gewerbliche Warenproduktion auf dem Land* (pp. 90–154). Göttingen: Vandenhoeck & Ruprecht.

Mennell, S. (1985). *All Manners of Food: Eating and Taste in England and France from the Middle Ages to the Present*. Oxford: Blackwell.

Mennell, S. (1987). On the civilizing of appetite. *Theory, Culture and Society, 4*, 373–403.

Mennell, S. (1990). Decivilising processes: theoretical significance and some lines of research. *International Sociology, 5*, 205–224.

Merchant, C. (1980). *Death of Nature: Women, Ecology and the Scientific Revolution*. London: Harper & Row.

Meyer, J.W., & Rowan, B. (1977). Institutionalized organizations: formal structure as myth and ceremony. *American Journal of Sociology, 83*, 340–363.

Meyer, J.W., & Scott, W.R. (1983). *Organizational Environments. Ritual and Rationality*. Beverly Hills, CA: Sage.

Milbrath, L.W. (1984). *Environmentalists. Vanguard for a New Society*. Albany, NY: State University of New York Press.

Miller, D. (1987). *Material Culture and Mass Consumption*. Oxford: Blackwell.

Miller, M. (1986). *Kollektive Lernprozesse. Studien zur Grundlegung einer soziologischen Lerntheorie*. Frankfurt: Suhrkamp.

Miller, M. (1987). Culture and collective argumentation. *Argumentation, 1*, 127–154.

Mintz, S.W. (1985). *Sweetness and Power. The Place of Sugar in Modern History*. New York, NY: Viking.

Moore-Lappé, F. (1978). *Die Öko-Diät. Wie man mit wenig Fleisch gut ißt und die Natur schont*. Frankfurt: Fischer.

Moscovici, S. (1968). *L'histoire humaine de la nature*. Paris: Flammarion.

Moscovici, S. (1972). *La société contre nature*. Paris: Union Générale d'Editions.

Moscovici, S. (1976). Le réenchantement du monde. In N. Birnbaum, H.P. Dreitzel, S. Moscovici, R. Sennett, R. Supek & A. Touraine (Eds.), *Au-dela de la crise* (pp. 137–176). Paris: Seuil.

Moscovici, S. (1979). *Hommes domestiques et hommes sauvages* (2nd ed.). Paris: Christian Bourgois.

Moscovici, S. (1990). Questions for the twenty-first century. *Theory, Culture and Society, 7*, 1–19.

Müller, K.E. (Ed.). (1983). *Menschenbilder früher Gesellschaften*. Frankfurt: Campus.

Nash, R.F. (1982). *Wilderness and the American Mind* (3rd ed.). New Haven, CT: Yale University Press.

Nash, R.F. (1989). *The Rights of Nature: A History of Environmental Ethics*. Madison, WI: University of Wisconsin Press.

Needham, J. (1972). *The Grand Titration. Science and Society in East and West*. London: Allen & Unwin.

Nicholson, M. (1970). *The Environmental Revolution*. London/New York: Hodder & Stoughton and McGraw-Hill.

Nicholson, M. (1987). *The New Environmental Age*. Cambridge: Cambridge University Press.

Nitschke, A. (1967). *Naturerkenntnis und politisches Handeln im Mittelalter. Körper – Bewegung – Raum*. Stuttgart: Klett.

Nöcker, R. (1983). *Körner und Keime. Der Sprossengarten im Zimmer* (6th ed.). München: Heyne.

Noth, M. (1965). *Leviticus: A Commentary*. London: SCM Press.

Nothdurft, W., & Spranz-Fogasy, T. (1986). Der kulturelle Kontext von Schlichtung. Zum Stand der Schlichtungs-Forschung in der Rechts-Anthropologie. *Zeitschrift für Rechtssoziologie, 7*, 31–52.

Nunner-Winkler, G. (1986). Ein Plädoyer für einen eingeschränkten Universalismus. In W. Edelstein & G. Nunner-Winkler (Eds.), *Zur Bestimmung der Moral. Philosophische und sozialwissenschaftliche Beiträge zur Moralforschung* (pp. 126–144). Frankfurt: Suhrkamp.

O'Riordan, T. (1985). Approaches to regulation. In H. Otway & M. Peltu (Eds.), *Regulating Industrial Risks. Science, hazards and public protection* (pp. 20–39). London: Butterworths.

O'Riordan, T., & Wynne, B. (1987). Regulating environmental risks: a comparative perspective. In P.R. Kleindorfer & H.C. Kunreuther (Eds.), *Insuring and Managing Hazardous Risks: From Seveso to Bhopal and Beyond* (pp. 389–410). Berlin: Springer.

Offe, C. (1983). Arbeit als soziologische Schlüsselkategorie? In J. Matthes (Ed.), *Krise der Arbeitsgesellschaft?* (pp. 38–65). Frankfurt: Campus.

Olson, M. (1965). *The Logic of Collective Action. Public Goods and the Theory of Groups.* Cambridge, MA: Harvard University Press.

Opp, K.-D. (1983). *Die Entstehung sozialer Normen. Ein Integrationsversuch soziologischer, sozialpsychologischer und ökonomischer Erklärungen.* Tübingen: Mohr.

Oppitz, M. (1975). *Notwendige Beziehungen. Abriß der strukturalen Anthropologie.* Frankfurt: Suhrkamp.

Ortiz, A. (1971). *The Tewa World. Space, Time, Being and Becoming in a Pueblo Society* (2nd ed.). Chicago, IL: University of Chicago Press.

Ostrom, E. (1990). *Governing the Commons. The Evolution of Institutions for Collective Action.* New York, NY: Cambridge University Press.

Parsons, T. (1971). *The System of Modern Societies.* Englewood Cliffs, NJ: Prentice Hall.

Passmore, J. (1974). *Man's Responsibility for Nature. Ecological Problems and Western Traditions.* London: Duckworth.

Passmore, J. (1975). The treatment of animals. *Journal of the History of Ideas, 36,* 196–218.

Pearce, D., Markandya, A., & Barbier, E.B. (1989). *Blueprint for a Green Economy: A Report for the UK Department of the Environment.* London: Earthscan.

Pepper, D. (1984). *The Roots of Modern Environmentalism.* London: Croom Helm.

Piaget, J. (1950a). *Introduction à l'Epistémologie Génétique. Tome I: La Pensée Mathématique.* Paris: Presses Universitaires de France.

Piaget, J. (1950b). *Introduction à l'Epistémologie Génétique. Tome II: La Pensée Physique.* Paris: Presses Universitaires de France.

Piaget, J. (1950c). *Introduction à l'Epistémologie Génétique. Tome III: La Pensée Biologique, la Pensée Psychologique et la Pensée Sociologique.* Paris: Presses Universitaires de France.

Piaget, J. (1970). *Genetic Epistemology.* New York, NY: Columbia University Press.

Porritt, J. (1984). *Seeing Green: The Politics of Ecology Explained.* Oxford: Basil Blackwell.

Porritt, J., & Winner, D. (1988). *The Coming of the Greens.* London: Fontana.

Potter, J. (1989). What is reflexive about discourse analysis: the case of reading readings. In S. Woolgar (Ed.), *Knowledge and Reflexivity. New Frontiers in the Sociology of Knowledge.* London: Sage.

Potter, J., & Wetherell, M. (1987). *Discourse and Social Psychology. Beyond Attitudes and Behaviour.* London: Sage.

Powell, W.W., & DiMaggio, P.J. (Eds.). (1991). *The New Institutionalism in Organizational Analysis.* Chicago, IL: University of Chicago Press.

Prigogine, I., & Stengers, I. (1979). *La nouvelle alliance: metamorphose de la science.* Paris: Gallimard.

Queiroz, M.I. de. (1968). *Réforme et révolution dans les sociétés traditionelles. Histoire et ethnologie des mouvements messianiques.* Paris: Anthropos.

Rammert, W. (1983). *Die soziale Dynamik der technischen Entwicklung.* Opladen: Westdeutscher Verlag.

Rappaport, R.A. (1979). *Ecology, Meaning, and Religion.* Richmond, CA: North Atlantic Books.

Raschke, J. (1985). *Soziale Bewegungen. Ein historisch-systematischer Grundriß.* Frankfurt: Campus.

Raub, W., & Voss, T. (1986). Die Sozialstruktur der Kooperation rationaler Egoisten. *Zeitschrift für Soziologie, 15,* 309–323.

Rayner, S. (1991). A cultural perspective on the structure and implementation of global environmental agreements. *Evaluation Review, 15,* 75–102.

Redclift, M. (1990). Economic models and environmental values: a discourse on theory. In

R.K. Turner (Ed.), *Sustainable Environmental Management. Principles and Practice* (pp. 51–66). London/Boulder, CO: Belhaven Press/Westview Press.

Reese, S.D. (1991). Setting the media's agenda: a power balance perspective. In J.A. Anderson (Ed.), *Communication Yearbook* (Vol. 14, pp. 309–340). Newbury Park, CA: Sage.

Rensch, B. (1973). *Gedächtnis, Begriffsbildung und Planhandlungen bei Tieren*. Berlin/Hamburg: Paul Parey.

Revel, J.-F. (1982). *Culture and Cuisine. A Journey through the History of Food*. Garden City, NY: Doubleday & Company.

Ribeiro, D. (1971). *Der zivilisatorische Prozeß*. Frankfurt: Suhrkamp.

Rice, R.E., & Atkin, C.K. (Eds.). (1989). *Public Communication Campaigns* (2nd ed.). Newbury Park, CA: Sage.

Richardson, G. (1982). *Policing Pollution: A Study of Regulation and Enforcement*. Oxford: Clarendon Press.

Richardson, J.J. (Ed.). (1982). *Policy Styles in Western Europe*. London: Allen & Unwin.

Riehl, W.H. (1976). *Die bürgerliche Gesellschaft. Herausgegeben und eingeleitet von Peter Steinbach*. Frankfurt/Berlin/Wien: Ullstein.

Rittvo, H. (1989). *The Animal Estate. The English and Other Creatures in the Victorian Age*. Cambridge, MA: Harvard University Press.

Rödel, U. (1983). Die Grünen und das Prinzip der Basisdemokratie. In W. Schäfer (Ed.), *Neue soziale Bewegungen: Konservativer Aufbruch in buntem Gewand* (pp. 97–106). Frankfurt: Fischer.

Rogers, E.M., & Dearing, J.W. (1988). Agenda-setting research: Where has it been, where it is going? In J. Anderson (Ed.), *Communication Yearbook 11* (pp. 555–593). Newbury Park, CA: Sage.

Romer, A.S. (1970). *Entwicklungsgeschichte der Tiere (Band I und II)*. Lausanne: Editions Rencontre.

Roper, M.K. (1969). A survey of evidence for intrahuman killing in the Pleistocene. *Man, 10*, 427–459.

Rorty, R. (1979). *Philosophy and the Mirror of Nature*. Princeton, NJ: Princeton University Press.

Roniger, L. (1983). Modern patron-client relations and historical clientelism. Some clues from Ancient Republican Rome. *Archives Européennes de Sociologie, 24*, 64–95.

Ross, E.B. (1978). Food taboos, diet, and hunting strategy: the adaption to animals in Amazon cultural ecology. *Current Anthropology, 19*, 1–36.

Rothschild, E. (1980, 22 May – 4 June). Hangchow retrouvé. *London Review of Books*, pp. 3–5.

Rüdig, W. (1990). *Anti-Nuclear Movements: A World Survey of Opposition to Nuclear Energy*. London: Longman.

Rüdig, W. (1991). *The Green Wave: A Comparative Analysis of Ecological Parties*. Cambridge: Polity Press.

Rusche, G., & Kirchheimer, O. (1981). *Sozialstruktur und Strafvollzug. Vermehrt um einen Anhang mit zwei Aufsätzen von Georg Rusche und um ein Nachwort von Heinz Steinert*. Frankfurt: Europäische Verlagsanstalt.

Rushefsky, M. (1984). Institutional mechanisms for resolving risk controversies. In S.G. Hadden (Ed.), *Risk Analysis, Institutions, and Public Policy* (pp. 133–149). Port Washington, NY: Associated Faculty Press.

Rust, A. (1974). *Urreligiöses Verhalten und Opferbrauchtum des eiszeitlichen Homo Sapiens*. Neumünster: Wachholtz.

Sahlins, M. (1963). On the sociology of primitive exchange. In M. Banton (Ed.), *The Relevance of Models for Social Anthropology* (pp. 139–236). London: Tavistock.

Sahlins, M. (1972). *Stone Age Economics*. London: Tavistock.

Sahlins, M. (1976). *Culture and Practical Reason*. Chicago, IL: University of Chicago Press.

Sahlins, M. (1978). Culture as protein and profit. *New York Review of Books*, 23 November, pp. 45–52.

Sahlins, M. (1979). Cannibalism: An Exchange. *New York Review of Books,* 22 March, pp. 45–47.

Sahlins, M. (1981). *Historical Metaphors and Mythical Realities. Structure in the Early History of the Sandwich Islands Kingdom.* Ann Arbor, MI: University of Michigan Press.

Sahlins, M.D., & Service, E.R. (1960). *Evolution and Culture.* Ann Arbor, MI: University of Michigan Press.

Salt, H.S. (1980). *Animals' Rights Considered in Relation to Social Progress.* (Rev. ed. with preface by Peter Singer (Original 1892).). Clarks Summit, Pennsylvania: Society for Animal Rights.

Salvatore, A. (1994). The making (and unmaking) of political Islam. Florence: European University Institute, unpublished doctoral dissertation.

Sanders, W.T., & Price, B.J. (1962). *Mesoamerica. The Evolution of a Civilization.* New York, NY: Random House.

Schäfer, W. (1985). *Die unvertraute Moderne: Historische Umrisse einer anderen Natur- und Sozialgeschichte.* Frankfurt: Fischer.

Scharpf, F.W. (1988). Verhandlungssysteme, Verteilungskonflikte und Pathologien der politischen Steuerung. In M.G. Schmidt (Ed.), *Staatstätigkeit – international und historisch vergleichende Analysen. Sonderheft 19 der Politischen Vierteljahresschrift* (pp. 61–87). Opladen: Westdeutscher Verlag.

Schimank, U. (1983). *Neoromantischer Protest im Spätkapitalismus: Der Widerstand gegen die Stadt- und Landschaftsverödung.* Bielefeld: AJZ-Verlag.

Schivelbusch, W. (1980). *Das Paradies, der Geschmack und die Vernunft. Eine Geschichte der Genußmittel.* München: Hanser.

Schluchter, W. (1979). The paradoxes of rationalization. In G. Roth & W. Schluchter (Eds.), *Max Weber's Vision of History* (pp. 11–64). Berkeley/Los Angeles, CA: University of California Press.

Schluchter, W. (1981). *The Rise of Western Rationalism: Max Weber's Developmental History.* Berkeley/Los Angeles, CA: University of California Press.

Schmid, M. (1982). Habermas' theory of social evolution. In J.B. Thompson & D. Held (Eds.), *Habermas: Critical Debates* (pp. 162–180). London: Macmillan.

Schmid, M. (1992). The place of culture in the theory of social action. A critique of the theory of culture of Talcott Parsons. In R. Münch & N.J. Smelser (Eds.), *Theory of Culture* (pp. 88–120). Berkeley, CA: University of California Press.

Schmid, M., & Wuketits, F.M. (1987). *Evolutionary Theory in Social Science.* Dordrecht/ Boston, MA: Reidel.

Schmidt, A. (1971). *Der Begriff der Natur in der Lehre von Marx* (2nd ed.). Frankfurt: EVA.

Schmitter, P.C. (1977). Modes of interest mediation and models of societal change in Western Europe. *Comparative Political Studies, 10,* 7–21.

Schneider, L., & Bonjean, C. (Eds.). (1980). *The Idea of Culture in the Social Sciences.* Cambridge, MA: Harvard University Press.

Schütt, H.-P. (Ed.). (1990a). *Die Vernunft der Tiere.* Frankfurt: Kneip.

Schütt, H.-P. (1990b). Einleitung. In H.P. Schütt (Ed.), *Die Vernunft der Tiere* (pp. IX–XL). Frankfurt: Kneip.

Schwarz, R. (1978). *Bewußte Ernährung. Übersicht über Wege zu einer gesunden Ernährung und Versuch einer Synthese* (5th ed.). Oldenburg/Hunt: Edition Wandlungen.

Séjourné, L. (1971). *Altamerikanische Kulturen. Fischer Weltgeschichte Band 21.* Frankfurt: Fischer.

Service, E.R. (1962). *Primitive Social Organization. An Evolutionary Perspective.* New York, NY: Random House.

Service, E.R. (1975). *Origins of the State and Civilization. The Process of Cultural Evolution.* New York, NY: Norton.

Sessions, G. (1987). The deep ecology movement: a review. *Environmental Ethics, 8,* 105–125.

Shankman, P. (1969). Le rôti et le bouilli: Lévi-Strauss' theory of cannibalism. *American Anthropologist, 71,* 54–69.

Shewder, R.A. (1984). Anthropology's romantic rebellion against the enlightenment, or there's more to thinking than reason and evidence. In R.A. Shewder & R.A. LeVine (Eds.), *Culture Theory. Essays on Mind, Self, and Emotion* (pp. 27–66). Cambridge: Cambridge University Press.

Shrader-Frechette, K.S. (1991). *Risk and Rationality. Philosophical Foundations for Populist Reforms.* Berkeley, CA: University of California Press.

Simmel, G. (1957). Soziologie der Mahlzeit. In G. Simmel (Ed.), *Brücke und Tür* (pp. 243–250). Stuttgart: Koehler.

Singer, P. (1976). *Animal Liberation. A New Ethics for our Treatment of Animals.* Cambridge: Cambridge University Press.

Singer, P. (1979). *Practical Ethics.* Cambridge: Cambridge University Press.

Smelser, N.J. (1985). Evaluating the model of structural differentiation in relation to educational change in the nineteenth century. In J. Alexander (Ed.), *Neofunctionalism* (pp. 113–130). Beverly Hills, CA: Sage.

Snow, D.A., & Benford, R.D. (1988). Ideology, frame resonance, and participant mobilization. In B. Klandermans, H. Kriesi & S. Tarrow (Eds.), *From Structure to Action: Comparing Social Movement Research Across Cultures* (Vol. 1, International Social Movement Research, pp. 197–217). Greenwich, CT: JAI Press.

Snow, D.A., & Benford, R.D. (1992). Master frames and cycles of protest. In A.D. Morris & C.M. Clurgh Mueller (Eds.), *Frontiers in Social Movement Theory* (pp. 133–155). New Haven, CT: Yale University Press.

Snow, D.A., Rochford, E.B., Worden, S.K., & Benford, R.D. (1986). Frame alignment processes, micromobilization and movements participation. *American Sociological Review, 51*, 464–481.

Soler, J. (1979). The dietary prohibitions of the Hebrews. *New York Review of Books,* 14 June, pp. 24–30.

Spee, F. v. (1982). *Cautio Criminalis oder Rechtliches Bedenken wegen der Hexenprozesse (Nachdruck der Übersetzung von 1939).* München: Deutscher Taschenbuch Verlag.

Sprandel, R. (1972). *Mentalitäten und Systeme. Neue Zugänge zur mittelalterlichen Geschichte.* Stuttgart: Union.

Sprondel, W. (1986). Kulturelle Modernisierung durch antimodernistischen Protest. Der lebensreformerische Vegetarismus. In F. Neidhardt, M.R. Lepsius & J. Weiß (Eds.), *Kultur und Gesellschaft. Sonderheft der KZfSS* (Vol. 27, pp. 314–330). Opladen: Westdeutscher Verlag.

Statham, P. (1992). Political pressure or cultural communication? An analysis of the significance of environmental action in public discourse: a methodological technique for qualitative data collection. Florence: Unpublished manuscript, European University Institute.

Statham, P. (1995). Pressing matters: public communication and environmental organisations in contemporary societies – the British case. Unpublished doctoral thesis. Florence: European University Institute.

Stone, C. (1987). *Earth and Other Ethics. The Case for Moral Pluralism.* New York, NY: Harper & Row.

Stürmer, M. (1979). *Herbst des alten Handwerks. Zur Sozialgeschichte des 18. Jahrhunderts.* München: Deutscher Taschenbuch Verlag.

Swidler, A. (1986). Culture in action: symbols and strategies. *American Sociological Review, 51*, 273–286.

Tambiah, S.J. (1969). Animals are good to think and good to prohibit. *Ethnology, 8*, 423–459.

Terdiman, R. (1985). *Discourse/Counter-Discourse. The Theory and Practice of Symbolic Resistance in Nineteenth-Century France.* Ithaca, NY: Cornell University Press.

Teuteberg, H.J. (Ed.). (1992). *European Food History: A Research Review.* Leicester: Leicester University Press.

Teuteberg, H.J., & Wiegelmann, G. (1972). *Der Wandel der Nahrungsgewohnheiten unter dem Einfluß der Industrialisierung.* Göttingen: Vandenhoeck & Ruprecht.

Thomas, B. (1986). *Vollkorn bietet mehr.* Bad Homburg: Diaita-Verlag.

Thomas, K. (1973). *Religion and the Decline of Magic. Studies in Popular Beliefs in Sixteenth- and Seventeenth-Century England.* Harmondsworth: Penguin.

Thomas, K. (1983). *Man and the Natural World. A History of the Modern Sensibility*. New York, NY: Pantheon Books.

Thomasius, C. (1986). *Vom Laster der Zauberei. Über die Hexenprozesse (De Crimine Magiae Processus Inquisitorii contra Sagas) (Nachdruck der Übersetzung von 1967)*. München: Deutscher Taschenbuch Verlag.

Thompson, E.P. (1971). The moral economy of the English crowd in the eighteenth century. *Past and Present, 50*, 76–136.

Thompson, M. (1984). Among the energy tribes: a cultural framework for the analysis and design of energy policy. *Policy Sciences, 17*, 321–339.

Thompson, M. (1991). Plural rationalities: The rudiments of a practical science of the inchoate. In J.A. Hansen (Ed.), *Environmental Concerns. An Inter-disciplinary Exercise* (pp. 243–256). London/New York: Elsevier Applied Science.

Thompson, M., Ellis, R., & Wildavsky, A. (1990). *Cultural Theory, or, Why All that is Permanent is Bias*. Boulder, CO: Westview Press.

Toulmin, S. (1972). *Human Understanding*. Princeton, NJ: Princeton University Press.

Touraine, A. (1973). *Production de la société*. Paris: Seuil.

Touraine, A. (1978). *La voix et le regard*. Paris: Seuil.

Trepl, L. (1987). *Geschichte der Ökologie. Vom 17. Jahrhundert bis zur Gegenwart*. Frankfurt: Athenäum.

Turner, V. (1977). Sacrifice as a quintessential process. *History of Religions, 16*, 189–215.

Van Baal, J. (1971). *Symbols for Communication. An Introduction to the Anthropological Study of Religion*. Assen: Van Gorcum.

Van den Daele, W. (1987). Der Traum von der 'alternativen' Wissenschaft. *Zeitschrift für Soziologie, 16*, 403–418.

Van den Daele, W. (1992). Scientific evidence and the regulation of technical risks: twenty years of demythologizing the experts. In N. Stehr & R.V. Ericson (Eds.), *The Culture and Power of Knowledge. Inquiries into Contemporary Societies* (pp. 323–340). Berlin: de Gruyter.

Van den Daele, W. (1993). Hintergründe der Wahrnehmung von Risiken der Gentechnik: Naturkonzepte und Risikosemantik. In Bayrische Rück (Ed.), *Risiko ist ein Konstrukt* (pp. 169–189). München.

Van den Daele, W. (1994). Technikfolgenabschätzung als politisches Experiment. Diskursives Verfahren für Technikfolgenabschätzung des Anbaus von Kulturpflanzen mit gentechnisch erzeugter Herbizidresistenz. In G. Bechmann & Th. Petermann (Eds.), *Interdisziplinäre Technikfolgenabschätzung. Genese, Folgen, Diskurs* (pp. 111–146). Frankfurt: Campus.

Van Dijk, T.A. (1985). Structure of news in the press. In T. van Dijk (Ed.), *Discourse and Communication. New Approaches to the Analysis of Mass Media Discourse and Communication* (pp. 69–93). Berlin: de Gruyter.

Van Dijk, T.A. (1988). *News as Discourse*. Hillsdale, NJ: Lawrence Erlbaum Associates.

Van Parijs, P. (1991a). Epilogue: les deux écologismes. In F. de Roose & P. van Parijs (Eds.), *La pensée écologiste. Essai d'inventaire à l'usage de ceux qui la pratiquent comme ceux qui la craignent* (pp. 135–155). Bruxelles: De Boeck Université.

Van Parijs, P. (1991b). *Qu'est-ce qu'une société juste?* Paris: Seuil.

Van Parijs, P. (Ed.). (1992). *Arguing for Basic Income: Ethical Foundations for Radical Reform*. London: Verso.

Veblen, T. (1953 [1899]). *The Theory of the Leisure Class. An Economic Study of Institutions*. New York, NY: The New American Library.

Vernant, J.-P. (1962). *Les origines de la pensée grecque*. Paris: Presses Universitaires de France.

Vernant, J.-P. (1971). *Mythe et pensée chez les Grecs. Etudes de psychologie historique (Vols 1–2)*. Paris: Maspero.

Vernant, J.-P. (1979). A la table des hommes. Mythe de fondation du sacrifice chez Hésiode. In M. Detienne & J.P. Vernant (Eds.), *La cuisine du sacrifice en pays grec* (pp. 37–132). Paris: Gallimard.

Wagley, C. (1977). *Welcome of Tears. The Tapirapé Indians of Central Brazil*. New York, NY: Oxford University Press.

Walens, S. (1981). *Feasting with Cannibals. An Essay on Kwakiutl Cosmology*. Princeton, NJ: Princeton University Press.

Wehr, P. (1979). Environmental peace-making: problem, theory, and method. In L. Kriesberg (Ed.), *Research in Social Movements, Conflict and Change* (pp. 63–82). Greenwich, CT: JAI Press.

Weiß, J. (1986). Wiederverzauberung der Welt? Bemerkungen zur Wiederkehr der Romantik in der gegenwärtigen Kulturkritik. In F. Neidhardt, R.M. Lepsius & J. Weiß (Eds.), *Kultur und Gesellschaft. Sonderheft 27 der Kölner Zeitschrift für Soziologie und Sozialpsychologie* (pp. 286–301). Opladen: Westdeutscher Verlag.

Weizsäcker, C.F. v. (1971). *Die Einheit der Natur. Studien*. München: Beck.

Wetherell, M., & Potter, J. (1988). Discourse analysis and the identification of interpretative repertoires. In C. Anataki (Ed.), *Analysing Everyday Explanation. A Casebook of Methods* (pp. 168–183). London: Sage.

White, L. (1967). The roots of our ecological crisis. *Science*, 1203–1207.

White, L. (1973). On Christian arrogance toward nature. In R. Detweiler, J.N. Sutherland & M.S. Werthmann (Eds.), *Environmental Decay in its Historical Context* (pp. 19–27). Glenview: Scott, Foresman & Co.

Wiesenthal, H. (1993). *Realism in Green Politics. Social Movements and Ecological Reform in Germany*. Manchester: Manchester University Press.

Williams, R. (1982). *Dream Worlds. Mass Consumption in Late Nineteenth-Century France*. Berkeley, CA: University of California Press.

Williams, R. (1983). Culture. In D. McClellan (Ed.), *Marx: The First Hundred Years*. New York, NY: St Martin's Press.

Willis, R.G. (1984). Strukturale Analyse von Mythen und oraler Literatur. In E.W. Müller, R. König, K.P. Koepping & P. Drechsel (Eds.), *Ethnologie als Sozialwissenschaft. Sonderheft 26 der Kölner Zeitschrift für Soziologie und Sozialpsychologie* (pp. 141–157). Opladen: Westdeutscher Verlag.

Wittfogel, K.A. (1932). Die natürlichen Ursachen der Wirtschaftsgeschichte. *Archiv für Sozialwissenschaft und Sozialpolitik, 67*, 466–492/711–773.

Woolgar, S. (Ed.). (1988). *Knowledge and Reflexivity. New Frontiers in the Sociology of Knowledge*. London: Sage.

Worster, D. (1987). *Nature's Economy. A History of Ecological Ideas*. Cambridge: Cambridge University Press.

Wulf, H.A. (1987). *'Maschinenstürmer sind wir keine'. Technischer Fortschritt und sozial-demokratische Arbeiterbewegung*. Frankfurt: Campus.

Wuthnow, R. (1987). *Meaning and Moral Order: Explorations in Cultural Analysis*. Berkeley, CA: University of California Press.

Wynne, B. (1988a) *Risk Management and Hazardous Waste: Implementation and the Dialectics of Credibility*. London: Springer.

Wynne, B. (1988b). Technology as cultural process. In E. Baark & U. Svedin (Eds.), *Man, Nature & Technology. Essays on the Role of Ideological Perceptions* (pp. 80–104). London: Macmillan.

Wynne, B. (1991). Sheepfarming after Chernobyl: a case study in communicating scientific information. In H. Bradby (Ed.), *Dirty Words: Writings on the History and Culture of Pollution* (pp. 139–160). London: Earthscan.

Young, J. (1990). *Post Environmentalism*. London: Belhaven Press.

Zald, M.N., & McCarthy, J.D. (Eds.). (1987). *Social Movements in an Organizational Society*. New Brunswick/Oxford: Transaction Books.

Zald, M.N., & Useem, B. (1987). Movement and countermovement interaction: mobilization, tactics, and state involvement. In M.N. Zald & J.D. McCarthy (Eds.), *Social Movements in an Organizational Society* (pp. 247–272). New Brunswick/Oxford: Transaction Books.

Zerries, O. (1983). Yanoama. In K.E. Müller (Ed.), *Menschenbilder früher Gesellschaften. Ethnologische Studien zum Verhältnis von Mensch und Natur* (pp. 143–177). Frankfurt: Campus.

INDEX